Unforgettable!

The items featured on the cover are a capsule of LA sports history. Can you identify them? (For those who can't, please turn to page 224.)

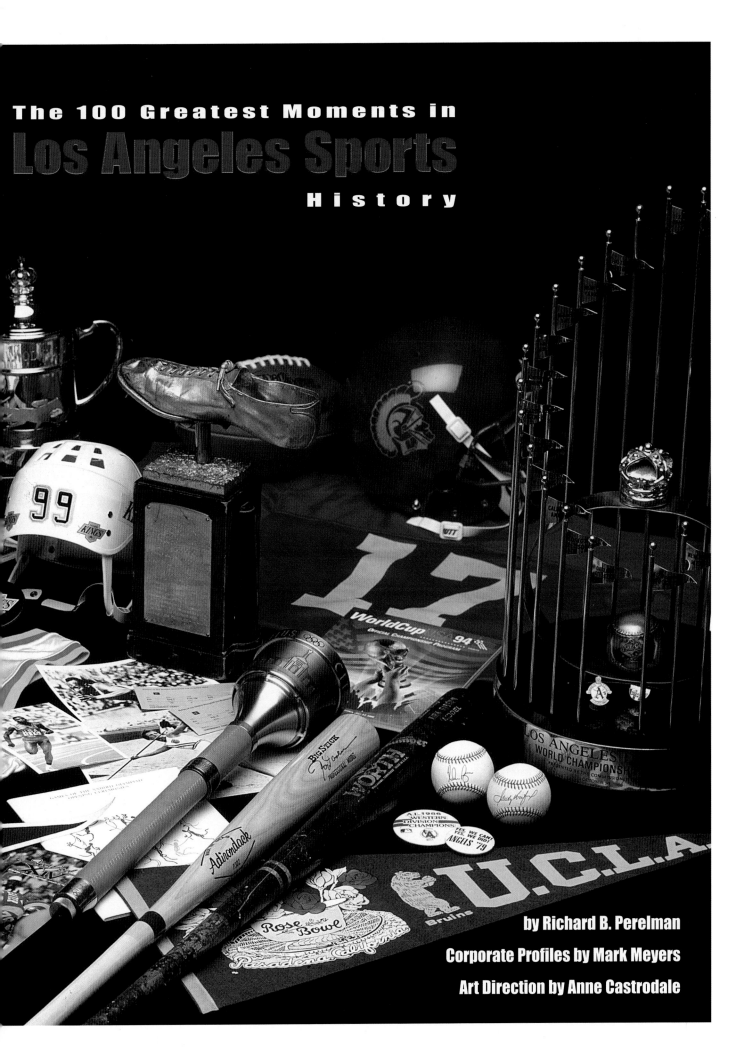

The 100 Greatest Moments in
Los Angeles Sports
History

by Richard B. Perelman

Corporate Profiles by Mark Meyers

Art Direction by Anne Castrodale

Towery Publishing, Inc. in cooperation with the Los Angeles Sports Council,
with a special thanks to the Los Angeles Times.

Library of Congress Cataloging-in-Publication Data

Perelman, Richard B., 1956-
    Unforgettable! : the 100 greatest moments in Los Angeles sports
history / by Richard B. Perelman ; corporate profiles by Mark Meyers
; art direction by Anne Castrodale.
        p.   cm.
    "Produced in cooperation with the Los Angeles Sports Council."
    Includes index.
    ISBN 1-881096-21-1
    1. Sports—California—Los Angeles—History.   I. Meyers, Mark,
1962-   . II. Title.
GV584.5.L7P47 1995
796'.09794'94--dc20   95-36666
                                                                        CIP

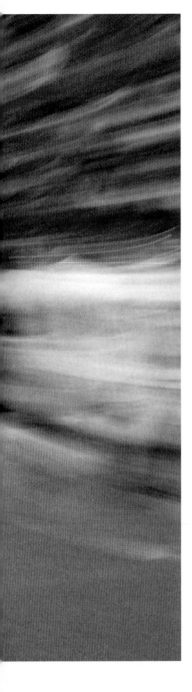

Contents

Towery Publishing, Inc., 1835 Union Avenue, Memphis, TN 38104

Publisher: J. Robert Towery
Executive Publisher: Jenny McDowell
National Sales Manager: Stephen Hung
Project Directors: Bruce Cuddy, Wilma Jean Dallam, Thom Singer, Michele Sylvestro
Research: Perelman, Pioneer & Company

Executive Editor: David Dawson
Senior Editor: Michael C. James
Associate Editor/Profile Director: Lynn Conlee
Associate Editors: Mary Jane Adams, Lori Bond, Carlisle Hacker, Jason Vest

Creative Director: Brian Groppe
Profile Designer: Lee Swets
Sports Logos Designer: Michael Forsythe
Production Assistants: Diana Eppes, Brenda Pattat
Technical Director: William H. Towery

A letter from the Los Angeles Sports Council

This is a book about sports and athletes, but it also is a book about Southern California.

As this book amply demonstrates, no city in the world can match the greater Los Angeles area for the breadth and depth of its rich sports tradition. It is a tradition that includes two Olympic Games, the finals of the FIFA World Cup, and countless national championships and major events in virtually every sport, except those requiring snow, of course.

In the public's imagination, sports have always seemed intertwined with the L.A. lifestyle. This may in part have to do with our great climate, but there is more to it than that. The most important benefit of sports is the sense of community identity it provides.

In Southern California, a sense of community can be hard to come by. Los Angeles-area residents don't share a common urban environment. Some of us live near the beach, some in the mountains, and some in the desert. Los Angeles County alone contains 83 incorporated cities—and that's in addition to Los Angeles itself.

What cuts through this geographic clutter and provides a regional sense of community is sports. When we host a major event or when one of our teams is on a winning streak, we feel a sense of pride, participation, and shared experience with our neighbors that otherwise does not occur in Southern California. In a significant way, such events help us to become a closer and a better community.

The popularity of sports also has to do with the fascination all of us have in watching individuals who are among the best in the world at what they do. As sports fans, we all are insatiably curious to see how a top athlete will perform when a championship or big game is on the line.

Most of us go to work in the morning without knowing whether the day ahead of us will be important or memorable later on. However, top athletes regularly encounter situations that are known ahead of time to be important to themselves, their teams, or their fans. When these situations arise, they know that at any moment their performance, watched by millions, can put them in the record book as either a hero or a goat. It is a kind of pressure that is difficult for most of us to imagine.

In these pages, you will find 100 stories of people who faced that pressure and responded unforgettably.

David Simon

David Simon, President
Los Angeles Sports Council

Introduction

This is a book devoted to excitement, exhilaration, and outright joy. It celebrates just a few of the brilliant moments in sports that have taken place in the greater Los Angeles area, or that have been achieved by individuals and teams that came from the area or in some way represented it.

The specific moments and their placement within the top 100 were determined by a process which took almost one year to complete. The Los Angeles Sports Council asked its membership, the area's sportswriters and sportscasters, and the more than 5,000 members of the Los Angeles Athletic Club to select, by open ballot, the greatest moments in the area's history, ranked from 1 to 25. A special veterans committee was created to consider events that took place prior to 1958 and that may not have been fully considered by the main block of (younger) voters. Each moment nominated on a ballot received points according to its placement on that ballot: the top-ranked moment received 25 points, while each ballot's last-ranked moment received only one point.

To be considered, moments had to have taken place in the greater Los Angeles area (Los Angeles, Orange, Ventura, Riverside, and San Bernardino counties) or had to involve a person or team from the area.

The results were fascinating. The top 60 moments were clearly distinguished from the others nominated and are presented here in essentially the order of their point standings. Some nominations of specific moments were combined for the purposes of our poll; for example, the phenomenon of "Fernando-mania" and 1981 World Series championship seemed to us to be too interconnected to be split into separate moments, so the point totals for these two nominations were combined to produce the final ranking.

The remaining 40 moments were much harder to finalize. More than 170 nominations for these last 40 slots were received, not to mention those submitted by the veterans committee. In the course of a thoroughly enjoyable but exhausting meeting of more than five hours, a special task force resolved the last 40 moments to be included and their order.

With the exception of the momentous move of the Dodgers from Brooklyn to Los Angeles in 1958—truly a turning point in the history of sports in Los Angeles—we declined to include the many moves of franchises to the area, or the birth of new teams. Certainly, the attraction and importance of the area bears noting as team after team moved to Southern California or was born as an expansion franchise. We note here the best-known of the many teams that have made the Los Angeles area their home:

    1946 Rams move from Cleveland to Los Angeles;
    1958 Dodgers move from Brooklyn to Los Angeles;
    1960 Lakers move from Minneapolis to Los Angeles;
    1961 Angels begin play as an American League expansion team;
    1967 Kings begin play as a National Hockey League expansion team;
    1982 Raiders move from Oakland to Los Angeles;
    1984 Clippers move from San Diego to Los Angeles;
    1993 Mighty Ducks begin play as a National Hockey League expansion team.

The same is true for the opening of major arenas and stadiums in the area. As the interest and importance of sports has increased, so has the demand for better, more modern places to play and watch:

    1923 Opening of the Los Angeles Memorial Coliseum and the Rose Bowl in Pasadena;
    1924 Opening of the Olympic Auditorium;
    1934 Opening of Santa Anita Park;
    1938 Opening of Hollywood Park;
    1959 Opening of the Los Angeles Memorial Sports Arena;
    1962 Opening of Dodger Stadium;
    1962 Opening of the Long Beach Arena;
    1965 Opening of UCLA's Pauley Pavilion;
    1966 Opening of Anaheim Stadium;
    1967 Opening of The Forum in Inglewood;
    1969 Opening of UCLA's Drake Stadium;
    1993 Opening of the Anaheim Arena, better known as the Arrowhead Pond in Anaheim;
    1994 Opening of the Pyramid in Long Beach.

Even now, new stadiums are under consideration as the push for better and more pleasant surroundings continues for both spectator and competitor.

But the impact of the people, the teams, and the places they play pales against the thrills generated by their efforts. The final list of the 100 greatest moments includes 16 different sports plus two Olympic Games in which many sports were contested. The favorite sport in the poll was football, with 25 of the 100 moments, plus an additional 40 nominations. Baseball was next with 18 moments and 24 nominations, followed by basketball with 15 moments and 18 nominations, track and field with 13 moments and 10 nominations, and horse racing with four moments and nine additional nominations.

This kind of work could not have been assembled without the continuous, courteous, and outstanding help of dozens of individuals who contributed time, energy, books, clippings, pictures, memorabilia, or simply personal opinions. I would like to specifically thank the following individuals whose efforts made this book possible:

Tom Seeberg of the California Angels; George Long, Tim Long, and Dennis Hammond of Long Photography; Duke Llewellyn of the Los Angeles Athletic Club; Tommy Hawkins and John Olguin of the Los Angeles Dodgers; Nick Salata of the Los Angeles Kings; Raymond Ridder of the Los Angeles Lakers; Jane Goldstein of Santa Anita Park; Jack French and Jocelyn Engel of the Tournament of Roses Association; Marc Dellins and Terry O'Donnell of UCLA; Tim Tessalone of USC; Bill Peck; and many others whom I have certainly omitted in error.

A special thanks is additionally due to Wayne Wilson and Michael Salmon of the Paul Ziffren Sports Resource Center at the Amateur Athletic Foundation of Los Angeles. Without this invaluable, virtually all-in-one resource, the research for this book would have been practically insurmountable. This facility and its dedicated staff are recommended without qualification to anyone interested in sports research.

The leadership of the Los Angeles Sports Council and Towery Publishing, Inc. have my thanks for their faith in me and our Perelman, Pioneer & Co. team, which conducted the voting and assembled the research and photography. Specifically, I would like to acknowledge the assistance, encouragement, and help of Sports Council Chairman John Argue and President David Simon, and Towery Publishing President Bob Towery, as well as David Dawson, Brian Groppe, and Anne Castrodale of the Towery Publishing team. In addition, I would be remiss if I did not express thanks to the Los Angeles Times for providing important materials and for their help in marketing and distributing this book.

I would also like to thank those who have worked most closely with me in making this project happen, especially Pat Harris, Karel Kreshek, Kristi Manning, and Ted Whalen of Perelman, Pioneer & Co., and longtime friends including Dwain Esper, Bud Furillo, Mark Meyers, Mort Tenner, and Jack Tobin.

Finally, I hope that the reader will enjoy our work and the rankings, even if he or she does not always agree with the outcome. We will consider our effort a marvelous success if you have even half as much fun reading and rejoicing over these great moments in sports as we had researching, writing, and reliving them ourselves.

Richard B. Perelman
Los Angeles, California
April 1995

The 100 Greatest Moments in Los Angeles Sports History

1   **World Series: Los Angeles Dodgers 5, Oakland Athletics 4**
October 15, 1988

2   **Olympic Games: After Los Angeles, the Games Will Never Be the Same**
July 28, 1984

3   **College Football: Trojans Roll Seven Second-Half Sevens to Bomb Irish, 55-24**
November 30, 1974

4   **College Basketball: Coach John Wooden Says Farewell after His 10th NCAA Title, a 92-85 Victory over Kentucky**
March 31, 1975

5   **College Football: The Battle for Number 1: USC 21, UCLA 20**
November 18, 1967

6   **NBA Finals: Johnson Is Truly Magic as Lakers Win Title**
May 16, 1980

7   **Baseball: Koufax's Fourth No-Hitter Is Perfect**
September 9, 1965

8   **Olympic Games: Los Angeles Becomes a New Star in the Olympic Movement**
July 30, 1932

9   **Super Bowl XVIII: Allen, Raiders Scalp Redskins, 38-9**
January 22, 1984

10   **Baseball: Dodgers Beat Giants in First Los Angeles Home Game, 6-5**
April 18, 1958

11   **NBA Finals: Lakers Down Celtics to End 25 years of Frustration**
June 9, 1985

12   **Ice Hockey: Kings Finally Wear Conference Crown**
May 29, 1993

13   **NBA Finals: Riley Stands behind Guarantee as Lakers Win Again**
June 22, 1988

14   **World Series: Dodgers Win World Title over ChiSox, 4-2**
October 8, 1959

15   **NBA Finals: Lakers Hoist First Championship Banner against Knicks**
May 7, 1972

16   **World Series: Dodgers Sweep Aside Yanks in Four Straight**
October 6, 1963

17   **Baseball: Hershiser Breaks Drysdale's Major-League Scoreless Innings Mark**
September 28, 1988

18   **Basketball: Lakers Streak to 33rd Straight Win**
January 7, 1972

19   **World Series: Fernando-maniac Dodgers Win over Yankees**
October 28, 1981

20   **NFL Championship: Rams Return the Favor to Cleveland, 24-17**
December 23, 1951

21   **XV FIFA World Cup: USA 2, Colombia 1**
June 22, 1994

22   **College Basketball: Bruins Streak past Irish for 61st Straight Win**
January 27, 1973

23   **Super Bowl XIV: Rams Take Steelers to the Limit**
January 20, 1980

24   **Olympic Track and Field: King Carl Crowned in Los Angeles**
August 11, 1984

25   **Ice Hockey: Gretzky Traded to the Kings**
August 9, 1988

26   **Rose Bowl: Bruins Twice as Nice against Michigan State**
January 1, 1966

27   **Baseball: Drysdale Sets Major-League Mark of 58 Scoreless Innings**
June 8, 1968

28   **Baseball: Nolan's Fourth No-No Knots Him with Koufax**
June 1, 1975

29   **Baseball: Campanella's Night Lights Up Los Angeles**
May 7, 1959

30   **Ice Hockey: Gretzky Becomes the Greatest One**
October 15, 1989

31   **College Football: Big Bad Bruins Bash Troy, 34-0, to Win National Title**
November 20, 1954

32   **College Football: Davis! Davis! Davis! Davis! Davis! Davis!**
December 2, 1972

33   **Baseball: Wills Becomes the Top Thief in Major-League History**
September 23, 1962

34   **Rose Bowl: USC's Longest Quarter Ends . . . in Victory!**
January 1, 1963

35   **College Football: Beban Bombs Bruins into Rose Bowl, 20-16**
November 20, 1965

36   **Rose Bowl: USC 7, Duke 3**
January 2, 1939

37   **Baseball: Miracle Finish Lifts Angels**
October 11, 1986

38   **College Basketball Final: Walton's Near-perfect 44 Defeats Memphis State**
March 26, 1973

39   **Baseball: Jackie Robinson Breaks Baseball's Color Barrier**
April 15, 1947

40   **College Football Championship: Troy's Baker Kicks Irish National Title Hopes, 16-14**
November 21, 1931

41   **Olympic Track and Field: Bruin Generations Face Off in Tokyo**
September 6, 1960

42   **Rose Bowl: USC 18, Ohio State 17**
January 1, 1975

43   **Super Bowl I: McGee Puts the Hammer on Kansas City, 35-10**
January 15, 1967

44   **World Series: Welch Juices Jackson to Save Dodger Win**
October 11, 1978

45   **NBA Finals: West's Ultimate Clutch Shot**
April 29, 1970

46   **Golf: Hogan Lives It Up on the Riviera**
January 5, 1948

47   **College Basketball: Alcindor Sees Bruins Humiliate Houston, 101-69 in NCAA Semi**
March 22, 1968

48   **Ice Hockey: The Miracle on Manchester**
April 10, 1982

1

World Series:
Los Angeles Dodgers 5, Oakland Athletics 4
October 15, 1988

"I don't believe what I just saw!"

CBS radio announcer Jack Buck spoke for baseball fans around the world when he summed up Kirk Gibson's one-on, two-out pinch-hit home run off baseball's best relief pitcher, Dennis Eckersley, to win the first game of the 1988 World Series.

Buck had reason to disbelieve the outcome. The A's had taken a 4-to-2 lead in the second inning when José Canseco—leader of one of the most fearsome offensive machines baseball had ever produced—belted a grand-slam home run off Dodger pitcher Tim Belcher. With ace right-hander Dave Stewart on the mound, things looked good for Oakland manager Tony LaRussa. After all, the A's had won 104 games during the regular season, and the team had swept the Boston Red Sox—four games to none—to breeze to the American League pennant.

The Dodgers had more trouble winning the Western Division with a 94-67 record. Kirk Gibson—the fiery, former Detroit Tigers outfielder who was acquired during the off-season as a free agent—provided the Dodgers with the offensive firepower and leadership to complement a solid pitching staff led by Cy Young Award winner Orel Hershiser (23-8), Tim Leary (17-11), and Belcher (12-6). It took the Dodgers seven dramatic games in the National League Championship Series to win the pennant from the New York Mets, with Hershiser pitching a shutout to win the decisive match, 6-0.

After Canseco's grand slam, the game settled down a bit. Los Angeles pitchers Tim Leary and Brian Holton kept the A's in check, while the Dodgers tried to scratch their ex-teammate Stewart for runs. Playing without Gibson, who was suffering from severe ligament damage in his left knee, the Dodgers got one run back in the sixth inning when Mike Marshall singled and eventually scored on a Mike Scioscia single. But by the time Dodger reliever Alejandro Peña took over in the eighth inning, time was running out for the Dodgers, who trailed 4-3.

Peña and Stewart each pitched scoreless eighth innings, and Peña got the A's out in the top of the ninth as well. To close out the Dodgers, LaRussa brought in the right-hander Eckersley, who had saved all four Oakland victories in the American League Championship Series and who had 45 saves for the season.

Leading off for the Dodgers in the bottom of the ninth was Scioscia, who popped out. Third baseman Jeff Hamilton then struck out, bringing up shortstop Alfredo Griffin. But Dodgers manager Tommy Lasorda substituted for him with former A's outfielder Mike Davis. The left-handed Davis worked Eckersley for a walk and brought up Peña's spot in the order.

Having already used pinch hitters Danny Heep, Tracy Woodson, José Gonzalez, and Davis, Lasorda finally turned to Gibson, who could only hobble to the plate.

A left-handed batter, former-Tiger Gibson was well familiar with Eckersley from his eight seasons in Detroit. While Davis stole second, Gibson and Eckersley battled to a 3-2 count, with Gibson fouling off four pitches. The next delivery was a slider tailing toward the outside part of the plate, which Gibson managed to get around and smash toward the outfield, where it flew over the eight-foot wall and into the right field stands.

Eckersley's head went down as Davis danced and Gibson staggered around the bases and 55,983 fans cheered deliriously. Gibson, the National League's Most Valuable Player in 1988, would not play again during the Series, but it didn't matter. His home run started the Dodgers on the way to another World Championship and a 4-1 Series triumph.

To this day, there are millions of baseball fans who agree with Jack Buck. They saw, but they still can't believe it.

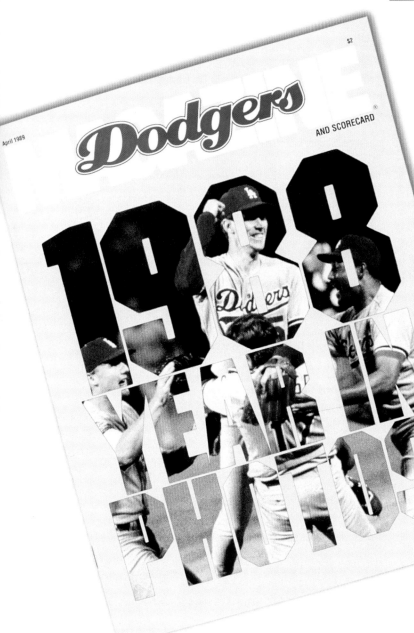

April 1989

Dodgers AND SCORECARD®

$2

1988 YEAR IN REVIEW

Kirk Gibson is congratulated by Coach Joe Amalfitano after hitting a dramatic game-winning home run in Game 1 of the 1988 World Series against the Oakland A's.

Seat 15 | DODGER STADIUM
GAME 7 $40.00
RESERVED
1988 WORLD SERIES

Row A | Aisle 7

1988 World Series

Dodgers

vs.
AMERICAN LEAGUE CHAMPIONS

RAIN CHECK
subject to the conditions set forth on back hereof

DO NOT DETACH THIS COUPON

PETER V. UEBERROTH
Commissioner of Baseball

GAME 7

DODGER STADIUM
GAME 7 $40.00
RESERVED
1988 WORLD SERIES
Seat 15 | Row A | Aisle 7

Clockwise from top left: U.S. diver Greg Louganis celebrates one of his two gold medals; Los Angeles Mayor Tom Bradley waves the Olympic flag at the Opening Ceremonies; Antonio McKay anchors the winning U.S. 4x400-meter relay team; and a goalie sees some action in a game of water polo at Pepperdine University.

Olympic Games:
After Los Angeles, the Games Will Never Be the Same
July 28, 1984

It was the Summer Olympic Games nobody wanted. In the aftermath of the terrorism in Munich in 1972, the ruinous financial overruns in Montreal in 1976, and the uncertainty over the upcoming games in Moscow in 1980, only Los Angeles was willing to bid for the Games of the XXIII Olympiad in 1984.

However, even though the situation was different, L.A. was the heir apparent to host the 1984 Summer Olympics, having finished third in a three-city derby for the 1976 Games and second to Moscow for the 1980 honors. Despite the fact that the city government would not guarantee the Games' finances, causing intense resistance from many of the members of the International Olympic Committee, the IOC finally granted the Games to Los Angeles—with the United States Olympic Committee as financial guarantor—on October 7, 1978.

Six months later, the Los Angeles Olympic Organizing Committee (LAOOC) had been formed under the chairmanship of noted attorney Paul Ziffren and President Peter Ueberroth, a little-known travel services executive. What transpired next was just short of miraculous.

Having been handed a $300,000 debt piled up by the Southern California Committee for the Olympic Games (SCCOG), Ueberroth and his board of directors arranged for a quick auction of U.S. television rights to the Games. Ueberroth and noted television and film producer David L. Wolper finally convinced ABC to submit a winning bid of $225 million, which greatly exceeded the previous record of $85 million bid by NBC for the 1980 Games.

In addition, Ueberroth and his top marketing adviser, Joel Rubenstein, upped the ante by limiting the number of sponsorships available and requiring a minimum commitment of $4 million in cash and/or goods and services. As a result, sponsorship and merchandising programs generated an unheard-of total of $122.5 million.

The organization of the Games moved forward under the primary direction of Executive Vice President/General Manager Harry L. Usher. A national, 82-day relay run of the Olympic torch in 33 states, covering 9,375 miles, brought enthusiasm for the Games to a fever pitch all across the country and especially in Southern California. When the Games finally came and Wolper's magical opening ceremonies began at 4:37 p.m. on July 28, a record 140 nations had come to participate. A total of 7,078 athletes, 9,150 journalists and technicians, and some 33,000 volunteers were joined by 5.72 million spectators in a 16-day festival that produced dozens of memorable moments, including Carl Lewis' four-gold-medal performance in track and field (see Moment 24), Mary Lou Retton's spine-tingling victory in the women's gymnastics all-around (see Moment 58), and Joan Benoit's courageous win in the first Olympic women's marathon (see Moment 89).

Unfortunately, 19 National Olympic Committees, including the Soviet Union, Czechoslovakia, the German Democratic Republic, Hungary, Poland, and Cuba, decided not to participate, primarily in retribution for the U.S.-led boycott of the Moscow Games four years earlier.

The results of the Los Angeles Games were nonetheless spectacular. Thirteen world records and 90 Olympic records were set or equaled during the competition. One final record was the financial success of the organizers, who finished with a surplus of $235 million, far surpassing all expectations. Sixty percent of those funds were later distributed to the U.S. Olympic Committee and its national governing bodies, while 40 percent was retained in Southern California to benefit athletic programs for youth through the Amateur Athletic Foundation of Los Angeles.

In his after-the-Games book, *Making It Happen*, Ken Reich of the *Los Angeles Times* wrote, "By any standard, the Los Angeles Olympic Games were a fabulous success. The people of Los Angeles, who frequently are terribly blasé—sated as they are with big events of all kinds—took the Games to heart." As it had in 1932 (see Moment 8), Los Angeles said "yes" when it was oh-so-fashionable to say "no way."

Like its predecessor, the Olympic Games 52 years before, the revolutionary organizing effort in Los Angeles has changed the way the Olympic movement works forever. The Games will never be the same.

**College Football:
Trojans Roll Seven Second-Half Sevens to
Bomb Irish, 55-24**

November 30, 1974

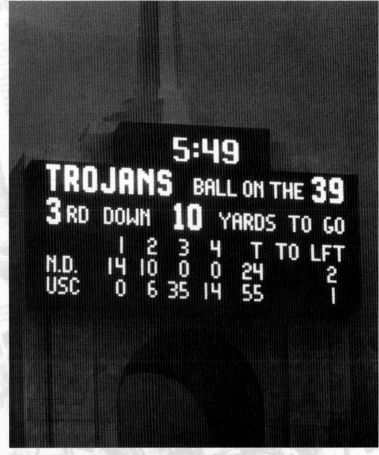

Left: Anthony Davis danced in the Coliseum end zone 10 times during his career against Notre Dame but never more jubilantly than in 1974.

As the teams trotted off the field at halftime, the scoreboard showed that a very good (9-1) Notre Dame team had clearly overmatched a very good (8-1-1) USC team, 24-6. Irish fullback Wayne Bullock scored first on a two-yard run with only 5:40 played in the first quarter, followed quickly by Pete Demmerle's catch of a 29-yard touchdown pass from Notre Dame quarterback Tom Clements.

Already up 14-0, the Irish continued to march as the second quarter opened, moving easily through the Trojan defense on short runs and passes by Clements. When Mark McLane ran the final nine yards through the Trojan defense with only 53 seconds to play, the Irish enjoyed a 24-0 lead.

Even USC's quick drive to a touchdown, with Pat Haden passing to Anthony Davis for eight yards, was marred by Notre Dame's block of Chris Limahelu's point-after try. Then the half ended.

"At halftime, we reminded them of the 1964 game," noted USC coach John McKay (see Moment 49). "We needed something to happen, and after that we thought we could score on them about anytime."

With his typical dry humor, McKay also outlined what could make the difference right out of the locker room. "They had kicked to A.D. [Anthony Davis] earlier in the game and during halftime we discussed that there was no NCAA rule against us blocking on kickoffs."

Notre Dame did kick off to Davis to start the half. After catching it two yards deep, he picked up a sensational block from Ricky Bell and steamed down the left sideline for a touchdown. The Trojan celebration was wild. And, though USC missed the two-point conversion, their momentum was not deterred.

Notre Dame was pinned deep on the ensuing kickoff and USC held them to three downs and a punt. Well-positioned on the Irish 38-yard line, Haden completed a 31-yard second-down pass to J.K. McKay. On the next play, Davis burst over from six yards and a touchdown. With the conversion, the Trojans had fought back to 24-19 in just over two minutes.

Then the roof started to cave in on the Irish. Demmerle fumbled three plays later and USC started at the Notre Dame 31. Haden's consecutive passes to Shelton Diggs and McKay put the ball on the four-yard line, and Davis romped in from there. He also scored on a two-point conversion and USC led—led!—27-24 with 8:37 still left to play in the quarter.

Notre Dame gave up the ball without a first down on its third straight series of the second half, and a punt to USC's Marvin Cobb was returned 56 yards to the Irish 19. It took only three more plays for Haden to hit McKay for an 18-yard touchdown and a 34-24 Trojan lead. The Coliseum crowd of 83,552 was cheering too hard to feel stunned.

Notre Dame finally mounted a drive on the next series, taking nine plays to reach the USC 35. However, Clements' next pass was intercepted by Charles Phillips and returned to midfield. Five plays gained only six yards, but then Haden arched a bomb to McKay at the one, and when he skipped across the goal line, USC had a 41-24 lead. The third quarter was amazingly over—but the Trojans were not finished yet.

Eric Penick fumbled on Notre Dame's first play from scrimmage in the fourth quarter and Kevin Bruce recovered. Haden had no problem shredding the Irish secondary again to find Diggs for a 16-yard touchdown and a 48-24 lead.

There was still 14:43 to play in the game, so Clements started moving the Irish with vigor from his own 20 to his own 49 in four plays. But his fifth play was an errant pass that Phillips intercepted and returned 58 yards for a touchdown—USC 55, Notre Dame 24. The Trojans had scored seven touchdowns in the first 16:44 of the second half.

Clements played only one more series; Vince Evans replaced Haden as quarterback and the game eventually ground to an end. Haden summed it up best: "If someone with a crystal ball had told me beforehand what was going to happen, I would have said, 'Put that guy away.' It was pure fantasy."

College Basketball:
Coach John Wooden Says Farewell after His
10th NCAA Title, a 92-85 Victory over Kentucky
March 31, 1975

He won with big teams that were thought to be unbeatable. He won with small teams that were not supposed to be contenders. But the Wizard of Westwood, better known as UCLA Coach John Wooden, won like no one ever has, right on to the very end.

During the 1975 NCAA tournament, after a heart-stopping 75-74 overtime win over Louisville—against former UCLA player and Assistant Coach Denny Crum in the NCAA semifinals—Wooden quietly told his players that after 27 seasons, he would retire following the championship game against Kentucky.

The focus and pressure was then even more intense for his players who carried with them the legacy of Hazzard, Goodrich, Alcindor, Wicks, Rowe, Walton, Wilkes, and the rest of the stars who helped create the brilliant Bruin basketball tradition. UCLA started senior all-American Dave Meyers and sophomore Marques Johnson at forwards, sophomore semifinal hero Richard Washington at center, and senior Pete Trgovich and junior Andre McCarter at guards.

In front of a packed house of 15,151 at the San Diego International Sports Arena, the Bruins worked hard to gain a 43-40 lead at halftime. But in the second half, Joe Hall's Kentucky team was physical and tough and cut a 74-67 UCLA lead to 76-75 with 6:23 to play. Then, Wildcat star Kevin Grevey clashed with Meyers on a jumper that resulted in a charging foul against Meyers. "I was upset on the call because I felt he went under me as I got off the shot," Meyers said. In protest of the call, Meyers banged the floor and was called for a technical foul.

Grevey was then entitled to shoot a one-and-one, as well as the technical shot, and the Wildcats were also awarded the ball. But Grevey, who finished the game with 34 points, missed the one-and-one shot and missed the technical—his only missed free throws of the game in 10 tries—and then reserve James Lee was called for an offensive foul. The Bruins weathered the challenge, and thanks to balanced scoring from Washington (28 points), Meyers (24), Trgovich (16), and Ralph Drollinger (10)—who was the only reserve to play in the game for UCLA—the Bruins edged Kentucky, 92-85, for their 10th NCAA title in 12 seasons.

"They were not expected to win the championship," said Wooden later of his final team, "but they played as if they did not know how to lose. They showed tremendous courage and determination."

More importantly, UCLA's 1975 championship win over Kentucky served as a fitting farewell to the man known throughout the world of basketball as "Coach."

The end of an era: The national champion Bruins celebrate a 10th title in 12 years after John Wooden's final game as UCLA coach, with (left to right) Bruin Trainer Ducky Drake, Assistant Coach Frank Arnold, Wooden, and Assistant Coach Gary Cunningham in the front row.

All eyes are on USC's O.J. Simpson [32] as he cuts back toward the middle of the field on the way to his game-winning, 64-yard touchdown (above). Left, Bruin quarterback Gary Beban shares his disappointment over the 21-20 loss with ABC's Bill Fleming.

College Football:
The Battle for Number 1: USC 21, UCLA 20
November 18, 1967

The rivalry between USC and UCLA has turned and burned in dozens of sports over more than a half century. But it never shone more brightly than on the Coliseum turf in November, 1967, when the two teams squared off before 90,772 spectators to decide the city championship, the conference title, the West's Rose Bowl representative, the Heisman Trophy winner, and amazingly, a shot at the national championship.

The Bruins were led by quarterback Gary Beban and had a 7-0-1 record, having tied Oregon State, 16-16. USC was riding on the talents of junior tailback O.J. Simpson, whose sprinter's speed had helped conquer every foe except Oregon State, which beat USC, 3-0. UCLA was ranked first in the nation, USC (8-1) was ranked fourth.

The first quarter was a tight struggle with little offensive movement on either side. But Beban engineered a 47-yard drive capped by sophomore tailback Greg Jones' race through the left tackle spot for a 12-yard touchdown and a 7-0 lead. At the end of the quarter, a promising Bruin series was stopped when Beban's pass to Jones in the left flat was intercepted by Trojan defensive back Pat Cashman, who dashed down the sideline for a 55-yard touchdown that tied the game as the quarter ended.

UCLA continued to generate most of the offense in the second quarter, but only USC scored. A first down reverse by USC flanker Earl McCullouch gained 52 yards to the UCLA 28. Four plays later, Simpson bounced off several tacklers and twisted into the end zone from 13 yards away. The subsequent Bruin drive covered 55 yards but ended in frustration as Zenon Andrusyshyn's soccer-style, 32-yard field goal try was blocked by USC's 6-8 Bill Hayhoe. Going into halftime, USC led 14-7.

The second half continued the pattern of tight defense as the teams tugged at each other. Beban, already playing with extremely sore ribs, was attacked savagely by USC's defensive line, and he even had to leave the game midway through the third quarter. But that was after he'd thrown a 53-yard touchdown pass to George Farmer on UCLA's second play of the half to tie the game at 14. UCLA missed a chance to take the lead late in the quarter when Andrusyshyn's field goal try from the 37 was blocked, again by Hayhoe.

As the fourth quarter began, Beban (back in the game but still sore) took the initiative. Starting on his own 35, he completed passes to Rich Spindler, Dave Nuttall, and Jones to reach the USC 28. After two runs, Beban found Nuttall again over the middle at the four, and the split end romped into the end zone for a 20-14 Bruin lead. The point-after-touchdown try by Andrusyshyn went wide.

Now Simpson, who had gained only 30 yards in the first half, went to work. He returned the kickoff 34 yards, gained three yards on first down, and then took the handoff from quarterback Toby Page on third and eight from his 36. Although the play—an audible called at the line by Page—was designed to go to the left, Simpson cut back, picked up a critical block by USC end Ron Drake, and raced across the field for 64 yards and a touchdown to tie the game. Rikki Aldridge's point-after was good and USC led, 21-20.

The resilient Bruins took the ball and moved immediately from their own 14 to the USC 49 in two plays. But that was as close to the goal line as they would get for the rest of the game. The Trojan defense mounted a fierce charge at Beban that yielded four sacks and a loss of 43 yards in the final three UCLA series. In the last 10:38, the Bruins managed only three first downs, while USC protected the ball and managed four first downs, enough to run down the clock. At the end, Beban endured one last sack by Jim Gunn, Tim Rossovich, and Willard Scott to end the battle at the Bruin 28.

In the end, Simpson had run for 177 yards for the Trojans. UCLA's Beban completed 16 of 24 passes for 301 yards, but had been hit for 80 yards in rushing losses (-59 net). Although UCLA had outgained USC, 344-305, the Trojans won the city and conference titles, the Rose Bowl berth, and, with a win over Indiana on January 1, the national championship.

The Bruins had to settle for Beban's victory in the Heisman Trophy balloting, but under the rules of the day, they were ineligible for any other bowl game. UCLA coach Tommy Prothro was gracious and correct afterward when he said, "They were a little better."

NBA Finals:
Johnson Is Truly Magic as Lakers Win Title
May 16, 1980

As a Michigan State sophomore, Earvin "Magic" Johnson led the Spartans to the NCAA championship, defeating Larry Bird and Indiana State in the final.

As a Michigan State junior, er . . . that is, Los Angeles Lakers rookie, Johnson had his team in the finals again, but this was a best-of-seven games series against Julius Erving and the Philadelphia 76ers.

The brilliant rookie had teamed with brilliant players, including the NBA's Most Valuable Player, Kareem Abdul-Jabbar; forwards Jamaal Wilkes and Jim Chones; guard Norm Nixon; and reserves Michael Cooper and Spencer Haywood, to win the Western Conference with the league's best record of 60-22. Johnson was the first rookie to start in the NBA All-Star game in 11 years, and after an 18.0 points-per-game, 7.7 rebounds-per-game, and 7.3 assists-per-game rookie record, he had helped lead the Lakers into the NBA finals for the 15th time.

The Billy Cunningham-coached 76ers won 59 games during the regular season and featured the spectacular play of Erving and the equally unbelievable antics of center Darryl "Chocolate Thunder" Dawkins, plus forwards Caldwell Jones and Bobby Jones, as well as playmaking guard Maurice Cheeks.

The teams split the first four games before the Lakers took game five at the Forum, 108-103. Abdul-Jabbar led the way with 40 points, but suffered a severely sprained left ankle and didn't even make the trip to Philadelphia for game six. He had to watch at home.

But the Lakers revamped their lineup, with coach Paul Westhead starting Wilkes and Chones at forward, Nixon and Cooper at guard, and Johnson . . . Johnson? . . . at center.

It was hard to fathom, but the 18,276 faithful at The Spectrum watched the Lakers take a 32-29 lead at the end of the quarter. The game was tied at the half, 60-60, but the Lakers were not going away.

In the third quarter, Johnson, Chones, Wilkes, and reserve forward Mark Landesberger charged the boards, and their strong rebounding led to a 33-23 edge at the end of the quarter and a 10-point lead (93-83) going into the fourth period. But the Sixers, despite being outhustled and outrebounded, got back to within 103-101 with 5:16 left. Then Magic took over.

Despite his size disadvantage at 6-9, the 20-year-old Johnson scored 11 of his team's next 20 points on an assortment of hooks, jumpers, and layups to race away from the Sixers, who could only answer with six points. The Lakers won going away, 123-107.

Johnson's leadership and belief in his own ability and that of his team made the difference. While Erving had 27 points for Philadelphia, he was outplayed by Wilkes, who had 37 on 16-of-30 field goals, plus 10 rebounds.

Landesberger had 10 rebounds and five points, Chones contributed 10 more rebounds and 11 points, and Cooper added 16 points and six assists. The Lakers outrebounded Philadelphia 17-7 on the offensive end and had a 52-36 edge for the game.

But Johnson was the centerpiece. Playing center for the first time since high school, he shot 15-of-23 from the field, was 14 of 14 from the free throw line, collected 15 rebounds, and had seven assists in 47 minutes en route to winning the Most Valuable Player award for the series.

Johnson was jubilant during the postgame celebration, but remembered how the Lakers had come so far. Looking into the television cameras, it was as if he were talking one-on-one to the injured Lakers captain: "Big fella, we did it for you," he said. "Kareem is the one who got us this far," he explained. "And he was with us (in spirit) tonight."

The 76ers agreed. "The Lakers played like they could feel him in spirit," Caldwell Jones explained. "They played with the intensity you need to be a champion."

Scott Ostler, writing in the *Los Angeles Times*, summed it up perfectly: "When they erect a statue of Magic Johnson in some prominent location in L.A., as they surely will soon, chiseled on the pedestal will be Magic's favorite saying: 'It's winnin' time.'"

It surely was.

Danny Goodman
Concessions
Dodger Stadium

Side 1   33⅓ RPM

Last Inning Sandy Koufax
Perfect Game
Actual Reproduction as
narrated by Vince Scully

Sandy Koufax (right) celebrates with his teammates after he pitches his perfect game at Dodger Stadium. It was the fourth no-hitter of his outstanding career.

7
Baseball:
Koufax's Fourth No-Hitter Is Perfect
September 9, 1965

Sandy Koufax was the finest left-handed pitcher—or any kind of pitcher for that matter—in baseball in the 1960s. His combination of speed and control made him the dominant force behind the Dodgers' winning pennant drives in 1963, 1965, and 1966.

He had pitched no-hit, no-run games in 1962, 1963, and 1964. And in 1965 the Dodgers, who were trailing the San Francisco Giants in the pennant race by a half-game, entered a night game at Dodger Stadium against the Chicago Cubs with Koufax (21-7 for the season) lined up to pitch against Bob Hendley (2-2). A Thursday night crowd of 29,139 showed up to watch.

Koufax and Hendley dueled methodically. Neither side mounted a rally or got a hit through four innings. The closest Chicago got was a line drive by rookie left fielder Byron Browne that was caught by Dodger center fielder Willie Davis.

In typical style, the Dodgers manufactured an unearned run in the fifth. Lou Johnson drew a leadoff walk, was sacrificed to second by Ron Fairly, stole third, and came home when catcher Chris Krug made an error on the throw, sailing it into left field. One run, no hits, one error.

Hendley finally gave up a hit to Johnson, a bloop double in the seventh, but Koufax was unyielding. By the eighth, the fans were screaming on every play; Frank Finch, writing in the *Los Angeles Times*, noted that the "tension in the last two innings was almost unbearable." But Sandy whipped a called third strike by All-Star third baseman Ron Santo, struck out All-Star first baseman Ernie Banks, and whiffed Browne.

By the top of the ninth, both teams, the fans, and a radio audience hanging on Vin Scully's every word were coming apart as Krug came to the plate. Koufax—on his way to a major league record of 382 strikeouts in a single season—struck him out swinging for his 12th "K" of the night. Then Joe Amalfitano pinch-hit for shortstop Don Kessinger and also struck out, on three pitches!

Finally, the veteran Harvey Kuenn was sent up to pinch-hit for Hendley. An outstanding hitter, who was at the end of his career but with a lifetime batting average of .303, Kuenn worked the count to two balls and two strikes, but then swung and missed a Koufax fastball to become the 14th and final Cub strikeout victim of the night. The Dodgers won the game 1-0.

Koufax became the first pitcher ever to throw four no-hitters, and lost in the excitement was the one-hit, one-walk performance of Hendley.

"I think the stuff I had tonight was the best I've had all season," Koufax told the *Los Angeles Times* after the game. "I had a real good fastball, and that sort of helps your curve."

He also knew he had been in a battle. "It's a shame Hendley had to get beaten that way," Koufax noted. "But I'm glad we got that run or we might have been here all night."

Jim Healy, the incomparable Los Angeles-area sportscaster who mixed news and views with sound effects and sound bites for nearly 40 years, may have said it best. "Sandy Koufax was the only pitcher I ever saw who I expected to throw a shutout every time he pitched." On that one night in 1965, he was much, much better than that.

Chicago CUBS
vs. Los Angeles DODGERS

EXECUTIVE BOX 1
No. 1
THIRD BASE SIDE
No.

THU.
SEP. 9 1965
8:00 P.M.

DODGER STADIUM —— LOS ANGELES

ADMIT ONE

COMPLIMENTARY

Olympic Games:
Los Angeles Becomes a New Star in the Olympic Movement
July 30, 1932

On a clear and marvelous day, a capacity crowd of 105,000 watched as Charles Curtis, vice president of the United States, declared the Games of the X Olympiad officially open.

In front of him were 1,328 competitors from 37 nations, who would compete in boxing, cycling, equestrian events, fencing, field hockey, the modern pentathlon, rowing, shooting, swimming, track and field, weight lifting, wrestling, and even in fine arts competitions. It was hard to imagine that this day had finally come.

The Los Angeles cause had been advanced by William May Garland, a noted civic leader, who had first approached the International Olympic Committee (IOC) during the 1920 Games in Antwerp. His presentation was so well received that Garland was later made an IOC member. Still, the candidacy of Los Angeles foundered due to the long distances between America and the European nations that provided most of the competitors.

After the 1924 and 1928 Games were awarded in Antwerp, Garland's impressive presentation—and IOC founder Baron Pierre de Coubertin's desire to hold the Games in the "New World" often—led to the choice of Los Angeles to have the 1932 Games by acclamation at the 1923 IOC Session in Rome.

Garland and his team of organizers then set out to make the most of their opportunity. The giant Memorial Coliseum, the city's monument to those who gave their lives in World War I, was already hosting USC football games and track-and-field competitions. New facilities sprang up to host boxing (the Olympic Auditorium) and swimming (the Los Angeles Swim Stadium adjacent to the Coliseum).

And an entirely new concept, the Olympic Village, was born. Set in the Baldwin Hills area, the Village was occupied solely by men. Row upon row of Mexican ranch-house-style cottages provided the living quarters, with each nation assigned its own dining room and

hef. Meetings with the public were handled in the giant administration house at the entrance. Evening entertainment was offered in an open-air theater that seated 2,000, offering live theater and movies of the previous day's competitions. The female competitors were housed separately, but with similar facilities, in the Chapman Park hotel in the Wilshire district. All of this at a modest charge of $2 per person per day.

But the Games came as the Depression had spread worldwide. Great doubt that the Games would even be held shadowed the event virtually until it began. As the athletes arrived from nation after nation, however, Southern California was gripped in an Olympic frenzy, the likes of which would not be seen again for 52 years (see Moment 2).

The streets were decorated, the autograph seekers were out in force, and new heroes dominated the sports pages for two weeks in late July and early August.

The competition was hot. The highlights included the sprinting of double gold medalist Eddie Tolan (USA) in the 100 and 200 meters, and the setting of a new world record (46.2 seconds) by Bill Carr to defeat Ben Eastman in the 400 meters. Britain's Thomas Hampson ran the 800 meters in a world record 1:49.8, while the crowd screamed at Finland's Lauri Lehtinen as he passed Ralph Hill (USA) on the inside to win the 5,000 meters. The crowd's calls for Lehtinen's disqualification for interference turned to applause when Bill Henry, the Games technical director, took the microphone and admonished the more than 80,000 in attendance, "Remember, please, these people are our guests."

The crowd's favorite was clearly the brilliant Texas schoolgirl Mildred "Babe" Didriksen, who won gold medals in the 80-meter hurdles and javelin (with new world records), as well as a silver medal in the high jump (see Moment 60). She was denied victory only when her technique was judged improper upon clearing the same height

as winner Jean Shiley. New world records were set in each of the six women's track-and-field events.

And there was more. The Japanese thrilled the capacity crowds at the Swim Stadium with victories in five of the six men's swimming events. The only non-Japanese winner was Clarence "Buster" Crabbe, who won the 400-meter freestyle; in later years he became better known as a film star for his portrayal of Flash Gordon. American women won four of five swimming events, while American men and women swept the springboard and platform diving events.

The rowing program provided the climax of the Games as the American eights from the University of California fought off three other crews to win the final by at most a foot.

The mass of new records, the magnificent weather, and the large and enthusiastic crowds led to the inevitable sadness about the end of the Games on August 14. Again, more than 100,000 attended the ceremonies at the Coliseum and watched as the Olympic flag was lowered to the somber melody of "Taps," and the flame atop the Coliseum peristyle was extinguished.

The Games were over, but the legacy had begun. In the depths of the Depression, the Games were not only a symbol of the growing importance of Los Angeles, but of its business acumen as well. A profit of more than $1 million was generated, and the technical mastery of the organizers—in particular Garland, Zack Farmer, Gwynn Wilson, and Bill Henry—was hailed as the best of its time. De Coubertin said, "The important thing in the Olympic Games is not winning, but taking part." In 1932, Los Angeles had done both.

Super Bowl XVIII:
Allen, Raiders Scalp Redskins, 38-9
January 22, 1984

As the 14-4 Los Angeles Raiders and the 16-2 Washington Redskins faced off before a capacity crowd of 72,920 at Tampa Stadium, everyone expected a close finish, much like the 37-35 Redskins win at RFK Stadium when the teams had met in early October.

But on the 13th play from scrimmage, Derrick Jensen blocked Jeff Hayes' fourth-down punt from the Redskins' 30. By the time Jensen finally captured the rolling ball, he was in the Washington end zone, and the Raiders had a 6-0 lead. Chris Bahr's conversion made it 7-0, Los Angeles, after 4:52 had come off the clock.

A punting duel ensued well into the second quarter, and the Raiders took possession on their own 35 with 10:48 to go in the half. All three previous Los Angeles series had started with successful runs, but this time quarterback Jim Plunkett looked to the speedy Cliff Branch and his perfect route to split the double coverage for a 50-yard gainer to the Washington 15. One play later, Branch took advantage of a play-action fake by Plunkett to get open for a 12-yard touchdown. Bahr's kick made it 14-0.

The Redskins stormed back, reaching the Raiders' seven, but Mark Moseley had to kick a 24-yard field goal with 3:05 to play.

Plunkett was ready when the Raiders took over on their own 20. Marcus Allen's runs of 11 and 7 yards, coupled with Plunkett's razor-sharp passing got the Raiders to the Washington 37, but a holding penalty stalled the drive, and Ray Guy had to punt. Washington took over on its 12 with 12 seconds to play in the half.

Instead of simply running out the clock, Redskins coach Joe Gibbs then called for a screen pass, which had been a big play all year. From a triple right formation, the play was designed to go to the left to running back Joe Washington. But the lob pass into the flat was intercepted by linebacker Jack Squirek, who rumbled into the end zone for his first touchdown since his high school days. With Bahr's conversion, it was 21-3, Raiders, at halftime.

The Redskins came out with fire in their eyes to start the second half and scored on their first possession. Fullback John Riggins, the star of the previous year's Super Bowl, bowled over from the one, and the defending champions were within 21-9 as Moseley's conversion try was blocked.

But the Raiders were unimpressed. On the very next series, a Plunkett pass for Malcolm Barnwell was incomplete, but Washington was penalized 38 yards for interference by rookie cornerback Darrell Green. From the Washington 30, it took only six plays before Marcus Allen darted up the middle for five yards and scored a touchdown with 7:06 to play in the quarter. Los Angeles 28, Washington 9.

The battle raged back and forth, and the Redskins looked to get back in the game again after recovering a Branch fumble at the Raiders' 35 as the third quarter wound down. On fourth and one at the 26, Riggins blasted over left tackle, but linebacker Rod Martin stood him up and stopped him for no gain. Raiders' ball, at their own 26, with 12 seconds to go in the quarter.

Now Allen ended the Redskins' hopes. As the quarter ended, he swept left, cut into the middle, and raced back toward the left sideline for a 74-yard touchdown. With Bahr's conversion, the third quarter ended: Los Angeles 35, Washington 9.

Allen knew the play was supposed to sweep left, but he saw an opening and darted through. "It was the best run I've had in the NFL," he said. "I didn't think of what to do on the run; I just let instinct take over."

The game ended at 38-9, as the Raiders' defense corralled the high-octane offense of Joe Theismann, Riggins, and company. Los Angeles gained 385 yards in all, with Plunkett completing 16 of 25 passes for 172 yards.

Allen's 20 carries netted 191 yards and set a Super Bowl record; he was honored as the game's Most Valuable Player. It was coach Tom Flores' second Super Bowl win, the first coming three years earlier when his Oakland Raiders defeated Philadelphia, 27-10.

Flores was the quarterback on the first Al Davis-coached Raiders team, and his leadership continued to demonstrate the Raiders' enduring "Commitment to Excellence."

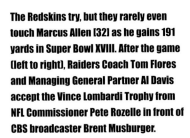

The Redskins try, but they rarely even touch Marcus Allen [32] as he gains 191 yards in Super Bowl XVIII. After the game (left to right), Raiders Coach Tom Flores and Managing General Partner Al Davis accept the Vince Lombardi Trophy from NFL Commissioner Pete Rozelle in front of CBS broadcaster Brent Musburger.

10

Baseball:
Dodgers Beat Giants in First Los Angeles Home Game, 6-5
April 18, 1958

A napkin. That's the reason the Dodgers came west to Los Angeles.

In October 1956, after concluding a promising set of talks with Washington Senators Owner Calvin Griffith about moving his club to Los Angeles, County Supervisor Kenneth Hahn went to New York to see the latest edition of the Subway Series as the Yankees battled the Brooklyn Dodgers. He was accompanied by columnist Vincent X. Flaherty of the *Los Angeles Herald-Examiner*, who had pushed relentlessly for a major-league team in Los Angeles for five years.

Griffith was interested. He agreed to continue the talks in Los Angeles and would come to the West Coast by train (a four-day trip) soon. But during the game, Hahn received a note on a napkin from Dodgers Owner Walter O'Malley. The message: Don't sign with Griffith; let's talk about moving the Dodgers west.

On October 12, while on the way to a series of exhibitions in Japan, O'Malley met Hahn at the Statler Hotel (now the Los Angeles Downtown Hilton and Towers) and told him that he would relocate the Dodgers to Los Angeles for the 1958 season. He also said he would deny it if the news was leaked. Hahn recalled later that O'Malley said faithful Brooklyn fans "would murder me" if they knew the team would be leaving.

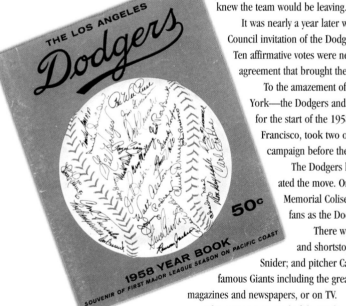

It was nearly a year later when a quiet lobbying effort to obtain the needed City Council invitation of the Dodgers to Los Angeles exploded into a public debate. Ten affirmative votes were needed, and the Council voted 10-4 to approve the agreement that brought the Dodgers westward.

To the amazement of baseball fans everywhere—and especially in New York—the Dodgers and the New York Giants both moved to the West Coast for the start of the 1958 season. The Giants, now relocated to San Francisco, took two of three games from the Dodgers to start the 1958 campaign before the action moved to Los Angeles.

The Dodgers home opener demonstrated why O'Malley had initiated the move. On Friday afternoon, April 18, the Los Angeles Memorial Coliseum was filled with a major-league record of 78,672 fans as the Dodgers took the field.

There were the Boys of Summer: first baseman Gil Hodges and shortstop Pee Wee Reese; outfielders Carl Furillo and Duke Snider; and pitcher Carl Erskine on the mound. Opposing them were the famous Giants including the great Willie Mays, who had heretofore been seen only in magazines and newspapers, or on TV.

The game was typical of the Dodgers-Giants rivalry. Los Angeles used two hits each from Snider, Charlie Neal, and rookie Dick Gray (including a home run) to pile up a 6-4 lead heading into the ninth inning.

Then Giant rookie Jim Davenport doubled off the short left-field screen and appeared to close the gap to 6-5 when Willie Kirkland ripped a triple to center. But Gray noticed that Davenport missed the bag, appealed the play, and Davenport was called out. Kirkland then scored on Mays' infield single, but the run only got the Giants to 6-5 before Clem Labine retired the last two batters to preserve the first of many Dodger wins in Los Angeles.

THE DODGERS'
WALTER O'MALLEY

NBA Finals:
Lakers Down Celtics to End 25 Years of Frustration
June 9, 1985

The parquet floor of the Boston Garden was the scene of so many Celtics' heroics. Above it, there hung the many NBA championship banners from the rafters. Eight of them told of victories by the Celtics over the Lakers in NBA Championship series spread over 25 years.

In 1985, though, things looked different. This time, the Lakers led in games, 3-2, as the sixth game started. After winning 36 of the last 42 regular-season games and breezing through two play-off series, Boston humiliated the Lakers in the opening game, 148-114. But determination, plus 30 points from center Kareem Abdul-Jabbar, 22 from reserve guard Michael Cooper, and 13 assists by Magic Johnson, led to a stunning 109-102 victory to even the series. The teams split the next two games in Los Angeles before the Lakers sprinted to a 64-51 halftime advantage in game five at the Forum and cruised to a 120-111 win to take a 3-2 edge. Abdul-Jabbar led all scorers with 36, and he, James Worthy (42), and Johnson (32) combined for 95 points, 21 rebounds, 25 assists, and 4 blocked shots.

The Celtics' plan for game six was simple: get the ball to Larry Bird. Despite nagging injuries to his right elbow and index finger, he was fearless in shooting from the field. Teammate Kevin McHale was equally danger-ous in the low post and, at game's end, led all scorers with 32 points.

But the Lakers were equally tenacious, and after a 55-55 tie at halftime, the Los Angeles defense—and Abdul-Jabbar—went into action. Boston scored only 18 points in the third quarter, while the Lakers scored 27 en route to an 82-73 lead that they never relinquished. Bird scored 28 points, but hit only 12 of 29 from the field, including an 0-2 performance from behind the three-point line. Guard Dennis Johnson was only 3 of 15; center Robert Parrish, 5 of 14; and guard Danny Ainge converted just 3 of 16. Decades of basketball statistics show that defense wins championships: the Celtics shot just 38.5 per-cent from the field, while the Lakers made 51.1 percent of their 84 field goal attempts.

Abdul-Jabbar was everywhere. Moving easily in the low post, he spun and skyhooked his way to 13-of-21 shooting and totaled 29 points—18 in the second half. Worthy was equally impressive, hitting 11 of his 15 field goals and scoring 28 points, while Johnson had 10 rebounds and 14 assists to accompany 14 points.

At the end, the Lakers stunned a disbelieving, sellout crowd of 14,890 with a 111-100 victory that gave them their fourth NBA title overall and their third in the past six years. It also made up for an embarrassing seven-game loss to the Celtics in the NBA Finals a year before. "I was aware of the past," Abdul-Jabbar said after the final game, "but that wasn't what motivated me. The thing that motivated me was last year. When I retire—and it won't be long now—I can look back on this with great feeling. We beat Boston in Boston."

Lakers Coach Pat Riley, flush with the same satisfaction his players felt in finally beating Boston in a championship series, smiled and said, "When we get our championship rings, we're going to have a diamond set on a parquet floor."

Johnson (32), Worthy (42), and the Lakers get revenge for a particularly galling defeat the year before by beating Boston for the 1985 NBA title.

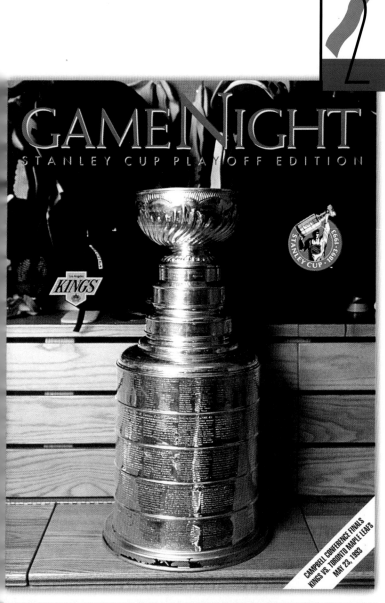

Ice Hockey:
Kings Finally Wear Conference Crown
May 29, 1993

It was exhilarating, exhausting, and ultimately unbelievable. The Kings—so often disappointed in the Stanley Cup play-offs—finally won the right to play for hockey's ultimate prize with a heart-pounding, 5-4 win over the Toronto Maple Leafs at Maple Leaf Gardens.

The road was difficult for the Kings, who finished only third in the Smythe Division that season, to reach even the Campbell Conference finals, a feat they had never before achieved. But under new Coach Barry Melrose, their punishing offensive intensity buried the second-place Calgary Flames four games to two, as well as division champion Vancouver, also 4-2, despite having won only two of the nine regular-season games against the Canucks.

Now Melrose's Kings, the improbable new darlings of the Los Angeles sports scene, lined up against Toronto, who had beaten L.A. twice and tied them once in four meetings that season. They split the first four games, then battled each other through two frantic, nerve-racking overtime contests. Facing elimination at home in game six, Wayne Gretzky scored with 1:41 played in overtime to even the series with a 5-4 win.

Toronto's Doug Gilmour and Wendel Clark were both in the top five in league play-off scoring for the season, but Gretzky—the greatest point producer ever to play hockey (see Moment 30)—showed that this would be his night, opening the scoring with a beautiful short-handed goal at 9:48 in the first period. Nearly eight minutes later, Gretzky's pass set up Tomas Sandstrom's eighth play-off goal for a 2-0 Kings lead.

But Clark and Glenn Anderson scored in the first eight minutes of the second period to even the game, before Gretzky broke loose for a 25-foot slap shot from the right side for a 3-2 lead at the end of the second period.

A third straight overtime game looked likely as the third period opened as Clark slammed home his 10th play-off goal for a 3-3 tie with only 1:25 played in the period. The Kings managed just one shot on Toronto goaltender Felix Potvin through the first 16 minutes of the period, but a sudden opportunity presented itself when Alexei Zhitnik's attempt skipped past two Maple Leaf defenders and a sliding Potvin onto the stick of Tony Granato, who scored for a 4-3 Kings lead with just 3:51 to play in the game.

Disaster struck again almost immediately for Toronto: 37 seconds later, Gretzky's wraparound pass from behind the goal bounced off the skate of Toronto defenseman Dave Ellett and into the net for a 5-3 Kings lead and screams of anxiety from the 15,720 who had stuffed themselves into Maple Leaf Gardens. The final three minutes saw Ellett's fourth goal of the play-offs, Toronto's last-ditch effort using an extra attacker in the place of goaltender Potvin and heart-in-your-throat pressure on the Kings' goal until L.A.'s Marty McSorley finally cleared the puck out of his zone with just five seconds to play.

"The greatest player in the world beat us tonight," said Toronto General Manager Cliff Fletcher afterward. He meant Gretzky, of course, who had three goals and an assist but was oblivious to the pressure.

"This isn't pressure," The Great One told Lisa Dillman of the *Los Angeles Times*. "It's fun to play in a game like this." Kings Owner Bruce McNall wasn't as sure: "I'm a basket case," he said afterward. "Wayne kept saying, 'Relax, don't worry about it.'"

That the Kings went on to lose to Montreal in their first-ever Stanley Cup championship series, four games to one, was disappointing but remains overshadowed by the excitement of their achievement, including making hockey fans out of millions of warm-weather Angelenos. That feat will forever remain a monument to Gretzky, the king of the Kings.

A strong defense by Tony Granato (22) and Marty McSorley (33) in front of goalie Kelly Hrudey (right) helps lead the Kings to their first Stanley Cup final, over Toronto.

NBA Finals:
Riley Stands behind Guarantee as
Lakers Win Again
June 22, 1988

Long after it was over, *The National Sports Review* said simply, "In the long annals of outrageous boasts, this one was definitely seeded in the top five."

"This one" was Lakers Coach Pat Riley's guarantee that his team would repeat as NBA champions in 1988 after stomping their way to the championship in 1987.

That 1987 championship was enough to make anyone predict a dynasty. The Lakers steamed through the regular season with a brilliant 65-17 record, easily the best in the league. They swept through the play-offs, crumpling Denver by three games to none; Golden State, four games to one; and Seattle, in four straight. In the finals, even the hated Boston Celtics were no match, losing in six games. Magic Johnson's memorable "junior, junior, junior skyhook" sent Boston down 107-106 in the pivotal game five in the Boston Garden as he swooped through the middle and delivered the game winner from 10 feet with 7 seconds to play.

In clinching the title at the Forum, Kareem Abdul-Jabbar came up with a season-high 32 points; James Worthy added 22; Johnson had 16 (along with 19 assists); and center Mychal Thompson added 15 points.

The new season brought the pressure of trying to repeat, something no team had done since Bill Russell's Celtics pulled it off in 1968-69. But the Lakers appeared equal to the challenge. They had Abdul-Jabbar, Johnson, Worthy, A.C. Green, and Byron Scott for starters and top reserves in Thompson, Kurt Rambis, and Michael Cooper. They again raced to the best record in the league at 62-20 and started well in the play-offs, sweeping San Antonio in three games in the first round.

But the Western Conference semifinals against Utah was another story. The Jazz battled the Lakers to a 3-3 tie, and Scott's 29 points and Johnson's 16 assists and nine rebounds were all needed to log a 109-98 win in game seven so the Lakers could continue into the conference finals.

The Dallas Mavericks proved just as capable as the Jazz. The Mavs won all three games on their home floor behind great scoring from Mark Aguirre, Derek Harper, Rolando Blackman, and Roy Tarpley. The Lakers again won game seven at home with Worthy scoring 28 and Johnson leading his team in rebounds and assists with 11 and nine respectively, as the Lakers qualified for the finals with a 117-102 win.

The new challenge was Detroit's Pistons, who immediately won game one as Adrian Dantley scored 34. The Lakers won games two and three, but Detroit came back to crush Los Angeles in games four and five to take the series lead, three games to two.

In game six, Detroit had a 102-99 lead with a minute to play, but Abdul-Jabbar made two free throws with 14 seconds to play to earn a 103-102 victory. Detroit's Isiah Thomas poured in 43 points, but it wasn't quite enough.

The Lakers became the first team ever to play in three consecutive seven-game series when they came to the Forum for the final game. Detroit held a five-point lead at halftime, but Worthy scored 11 of his 36 points in the third quarter, and with major assistance from Scott, the Lakers pulled away to a 70-57 lead, extending it to 90-75 in the fourth quarter. However, the Pistons were relentless and closed to within two points twice in the final minutes before Green's breakaway dunk sealed the 108-105 win.

Back-to-back! Even the Lakers couldn't believe it. Even the always ebullient Johnson could only say, "I don't know what's left for us..."

There was one thing. At the official victory celebration at Los Angeles City Hall a few days later, the Lakers tied a handkerchief over Riley's mouth. No more predictions!

World Series:
Dodgers Win World Title over ChiSox, 4-2
Oct. 8, 1959

Who'd a thunk it?

After the move to Los Angeles (see Moment 10) for the 1958 season, the Dodgers settled into seventh place, their worst seasonal finish since 1944. The new city, the new stadium, additional travel, the loss of Roy Campanella (see Moment 29)—all contributed.

But 1959 was different. Yes, Gil Hodges, Duke Snider, Carl Furillo, and Johnny Podres were still there, but this team showed new spark in shortstop Maury Wills, outfielder Wally Moon, and pitcher Larry Sherry. No team had ever come from seventh place to first in a single year before, but the Dodgers celebrated their first Los Angeles pennant when they defeated the two-time defending champion Milwaukee Braves. It took 12 innings in the second game of a best-of-three play-off, on September 29 before 36,853 at the Coliseum, to do it, but when the game was over, the Dodgers were on top with a 6-5 win.

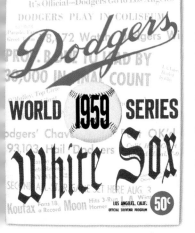

In the words of radio announcer Vin Scully, "And we go to Chicago!" The White Sox were waiting, having won 94 games, with All-Stars such as pitcher Early Wynn, second baseman Nellie Fox, and catcher Sherm Lollar. The Sox won the first game, 11-0.

But the Dodgers were much better in the second game at Comiskey Park, winning 4-3 behind Podres and three tough innings of relief from Sherry. Chuck Essegian, a Fairfax High graduate like Sherry, hit a pinch-hit home run to tie the game in the seventh. Charlie Neal's second homer was the margin of victory.

At home in the Coliseum, Los Angeles won two of three. Don Drysdale and Sherry were brilliant in a 3-1 win before an almost unbelievable crowd of 92,394. Sherry got credit for the win in relief as Hodges' home run in the eighth gave L.A. a 5-4 victory in game four. A brilliant effort by Sandy Koufax was wasted in game five in front of a new record crowd of 92,706 when Bob Shaw shut out the Dodgers, 1-0.

So it was back to Chicago for game six. Podres started and enjoyed the Dodgers' offensive onslaught against Chicago's Wynn. Los Angeles scored twice in the third and six times in the fourth to take an insurmountable 8-0 lead. Snider belted a two-run homer to open the scoring, and then singles by Don Demeter and Wills, a double by Podres, a walk to Jim Gilliam, another double by Neal, and a two-run homer by Moon settled the issue.

The White Sox got three runs back in the bottom of the fourth on a towering home run by first baseman Ted Kluszewski. That finished Podres and brought on Sherry to finish the game with 5 2/3 innings of scoreless relief. The 24-year-old was only called up in mid-season but had a hand in each of the Dodgers' World Series wins. The final exclamation point was added by Essegian, who slugged his second pinch-hit homer of the Series to close the scoring when he hit for Snider in the ninth. The final score: 9-3.

It was the perfect ending for the first world championship for the *Los Angeles* Dodgers.

Right: World Series MVP Larry Sherry (left) and Dodger legend Duke Snider are all smiles after Sherry's sixth-game relief effort led Los Angeles to the 1959 World Championship.

Opposite: "Big Game James" Worthy is unstoppable in the deciding game of the 1988 NBA Finals, leading the Lakers to back-to-back championships.

NBA Finals:
Lakers Hoist First Championship Banner against Knicks
May 7, 1972

There was always someone in the way. Either Boston's Bill Russell, or New York's Willis Reed, or someone else had kept the Lakers from winning an NBA championship despite seven tries since they moved to Los Angeles for the 1960-61 season.

But the 1972 Lakers were special. Special enough to win 33 games in a row (see Moment 18). Special enough to set a new record for most wins in a season, 69. Special enough to sweep aside play-off foes Chicago, 4-0, and then the defending world champion Milwaukee Bucks, led by Kareem Abdul-Jabbar, 4-2. And special enough to take a three-games-to-one lead over the New York Knicks in the 1972 championship series.

The Knicks, who had won the championship in 1970, were without the services of injured center Reed. Yet they stunned the Lakers by winning the first game by a score of 114-92 at the Forum. But rookie coach Bill Sharman rallied his team to three straight convincing victories: 106-92 at the Forum, and then 107-96 and 116-111 in New York's Madison Square Garden.

Now there were 17,505 screaming Lakers fans joining Owner Jack Kent Cooke in the Forum for game five, anxious to see Wilt Chamberlain, Jerry West, and the rest of the Lakers win their first title. But Chamberlain had a sprained right wrist from game four, and his effectiveness was in question.

No matter. After a 53-53 halftime score, the Lakers opened a small lead and nursed a five-point advantage going into the final quarter. Then the defense—and the 7-2 Chamberlain—took over.

Saying that he felt only a little pain, Chamberlain dominated the middle and grabbed every rebound in sight as New York managed only 41.5 percent shooting from the field, and was outrebounded for the game 76-47! Chamberlain also added 24 points on 10-of-14 shooting, and played 47 of the game's 48 minutes. He was, without question, the Most Valuable Player of the final series.

He had help, however. All-Pro guard Jerry West finally enjoyed that championship feeling. He had been with the Lakers since they began in Los Angeles, and his 23 points were an important part of the scoring, along with forward Jim McMillian's 20 and guard Gail Goodrich's 25. And don't forget forward Happy Hairston, who added 13 points and 14 rebounds to L.A.'s 114-100 win.

"It's an unbelievable feeling," said an excited West. "Now I know what it feels like to be a champion."

Chamberlain was equally proud, calling the championship his most satisfying achievement, even more so than the championship won by his Philadelphia 76er team of 1966-67. "That Philadelphia team was picked to beat anybody," he said. "At the start of the season, we weren't."

The Forum organist was playing "Happy Days Are Here Again" while the fans and players celebrated the first reason to rename Prairie Avenue in front of the Forum, "Avenue of the Champions."

The Lakers attack the lane against New York, with Happy Hairston (above) and Pat Riley (inset) joining Wilt Chamberlain (opposite) to help Los Angeles win its first NBA title.

16 World Series:
Dodgers Sweep Aside Yanks in Four Straight
October 6, 1963

By 1963, the Dodgers had regained their position as the National League's dominant team. After winning the World Series in 1959 (see Moment 14), Los Angeles had contended in 1961 and finished second. In 1962 they tied for the league title but lost the play-off to San Francisco. Then in 1963 the Dodgers won 99 games to take the crown, turning back a determined rush by St. Louis.

The Dodgers featured both speed and power. Shortstop Maury Wills again led the league in stolen bases, while Tommy Davis won his second consecutive batting title at .326, and big Frank Howard slugged 28 home runs.

And then there was the pitching. Sandy Koufax won his first Cy Young Award with a 25-5 record, a league-leading 306 strikeouts, and a 1.88 earned-run average. Don Drysdale was 19-17, and Ron Perranoski filled the stopper's role with a 16-3 mark and a 1.67 ERA out of the bull pen.

Waiting for the Dodgers were the New York Yankees, who had won their fourth straight pennant, with Whitey Ford, Mickey Mantle, Joe Pepitone, and crew winning 104 regular-season games.

It was an ironic homecoming for Koufax, as he returned to his native New York to face a Yankee Stadium crowd of 69,000 in game one. With a World Series record 15 strikeouts (including the first five Yankees in a row), Koufax cruised to a 5-2 win over Ford. A three-run homer from catcher Johnny Roseboro gave Koufax an early lead that stood up easily. After the game, Yankee catcher Yogi Berra was told of Koufax's seasonal record. "How'd he lose five?" replied the Hall of Famer.

In the second game, Johnny Podres returned to the site of his triumph in the 1955 World Series for the Brooklyn Dodgers. Thanks to a two-run homer from ex-Yankee first baseman Moose Skowron and Perranoski's relief effort, Podres won again, 4-1.

Down 2-0, the Yankees needed to mount a challenge to Drysdale in game three, but he shut them down on only three hits, 1-0. Tommy Davis' first-inning single off Jim Bouton drove in Jim Gilliam for the game's only run.

Koufax shut the door in game four. After six innings, the game was tied 1-1, thanks to home runs by Mantle and Howard. In the bottom of the seventh, Gilliam's high bouncer to third baseman Clete Boyer was fielded cleanly, but first baseman Pepitone let the throw bounce off his right forearm, and Gilliam was safe all the way to third on the error. Willie Davis followed with a sacrifice fly to center that allowed Gilliam to score standing up. The 2-1 lead was all Koufax needed, as his eight strikeouts were enough to ensure the sweep.

The ghosts of six Dodger losses in seven World Series with the Yanks were exorcised, as Koufax and company handed the Yankees their first four-game World Series loss since 1922.

Sandy Koufax is in the middle of a happy mob of Dodgers as they celebrate a sweep of the New York Yankees in the 1963 World Series.

Baseball: Hershiser Breaks Drysdale's Major-League Scoreless Innings Mark

September 28, 1988

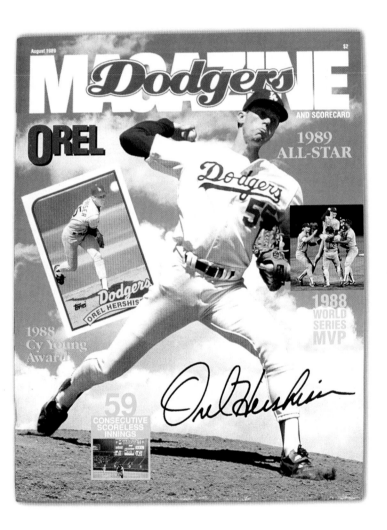

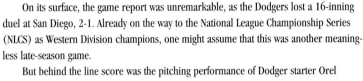

On its surface, the game report was unremarkable, as the Dodgers lost a 16-inning duel at San Diego, 2-1. Already on the way to the National League Championship Series (NLCS) as Western Division champions, one might assume that this was another meaningless late-season game.

But behind the line score was the pitching performance of Dodger starter Orel Hershiser. He entered the game not only with a 23-8 record and five consecutive shutouts behind him, but with a scoreless innings streak of 49. He was within reach of Don Drysdale's major-league record of 58, set back in 1968 (see Moment 27).

Hershiser had been on fire most of the season, but after the All-Star Game (in which he was the National League starter), his results were mixed. He had a 3-3 record from the break through August 14, when the Giants bombed him and the Dodgers for a 15-4 win at San Francisco. But he righted himself at Montreal on August 30, pitching a complete-game, 4-2 win over the Expos. Montreal failed to score in the last four innings.

Then Hershiser blanked the Braves in Atlanta on September 5, allowing only four hits and one walk while the Dodgers won 3-0. Back at Dodger Stadium five days later, the Cincinnati Reds were shut out 5-0 on a seven-hitter. Now the scoreless innings string was at 22 and attention focused on the Drysdale records of 58 scoreless innings and six straight shutouts.

On September 14, two days before his 30th birthday, Hershiser shut down Atlanta again, 1-0, at Dodger Stadium. If he was going to set any records, it was probably going to be on the road, where the Dodgers were set to play 11 of their next 14 games.

Hershiser pitched his fourth straight shutout at Houston, where the Dodgers needed all the help they could get to eke out a 1-0 victory. Things got a little easier at San Francisco on September 23, when Hershiser got three runs to defeat the Giants, 3-0, and run the scoreless-innings streak to 49.

In his five shutout wins, the Dodgers had averaged just 2.6 runs in support of their ace, but they didn't even do that well in San Diego, failing to score through nine innings. But Hershiser kept pace and equaled Drysdale's record of 58 with nine innings of shutout ball. Dodgers Manager Tommy Lasorda allowed Hershiser to pitch the 10th, and by retiring San Diego scoreless, he set a new mark of 59 scoreless innings and let Dodger relievers take over on the way to the 16-inning, 2-1 loss.

The epilogue is not only the 1988 Cy Young Award and the Dodgers' miracle World Series win (see Moment 1) but Hershiser's eight more innings of shutout pitching against the Mets in Game 1 of the NLCS, which extended his overall streak to 67 before a one-out, ninth-inning double by Darryl Strawberry scored Gregg Jeffries for the first run off Hershiser in 35 days.

Basketball:
Lakers Streak to 33rd Straight Win
January 7, 1972

Oh, those frustrating Lakers. Entering their 12th season in Los Angeles, this NBA powerhouse had reached the championship series seven times, without a single title. They had superstars Wilt Chamberlain, Elgin Baylor, and Jerry West, plus a good supporting cast of forwards Happy Hairston, rookie Jim McMillian, and guard Gail Goodrich to round out the team. And they had a new coach in ex-USC star Bill Sharman, who had guided teams in both the American Basketball Association and the American Basketball League to championships.

But after opening the season with a 6-3 mark, Baylor retired on November 5. Though one of the greatest players in the history of the sport (see Moment 85), he was averaging only 11.8 points a game and decided to end his career after just over 13 seasons.

The Lakers won for their retiring captain that night, 110-106 against the Baltimore Bullets, at the Forum. Neither Baylor nor his teammates could have known that it was the start of one of the most amazing feats in sports history.

With West, McMillian, and Goodrich averaging more than 70 points a game between them, as well as strong rebounding from new team captain Chamberlain (19.1 average) and Hairston (13.1), the Lakers ran, shot, and fast-breaked their way past a dozen opponents in 20 days. Most of the games weren't particularly close.

They went undefeated in the month of November, closing with a 138-121 drubbing of Seattle for their 14th win in a row. The all-time NBA record of 20 straight wins, set by Milwaukee the previous season, now seemed in reach.

The well-oiled Lakers machine was in full gear. Good defense led to rebounds, fast breaks, and blistering jump-shooting by Goodrich, West, and McMillian. Los Angeles opened the month of December on the road, crushing the Celtics in Boston, 124-111, and the 76ers in Philadelphia, 131-116.

On December 10, they polished off Phoenix at the Forum, 126-117, to tie Milwaukee's record at 20 straight wins. The tiebreaker came two nights later, also at the Forum, with a 105-95 win over the Atlanta Hawks. How far would the streak go?

By the end of the year, the Lakers had compiled two straight undefeated months and had 30 wins in a row to post a 36-3 record. Would they lose another game during the season?

They opened 1972 with another win over the Celtics, this time at the Forum, 122-113, then faced a six-game road trip over nine days.

The Lakers beat Cleveland, 113-103, and then clubbed Atlanta at the Omni, 134-90, to win their 33rd straight game, a total unmatched by any professional team in any sport. Jerry West had compiled a personal winning string of 41 straight games, having missed the Lakers' three losses earlier in the season. In the more than two months of the streak, the Lakers' average margin of victory was an astonishing 16 points per game.

But in a nationally televised game on Sunday, January 9, Milwaukee took advantage of Los Angeles' errors to post a 120-104 win and end the string. The Lakers had won 16 straight road games, plus 17 straight at home. But it was over.

Secure in their position as certain Western Division champions, the Lakers floundered a little in January, winning "only" five of the next eight games. Still, they were 13-4 in February and won 15 of their last 17 games to finish at 69-13, the best record in the history of the NBA. Their record-setting regular season was over, but the play-offs—and another chance at the Lakers' first-ever world championship in Los Angeles—remained ahead (see Moment 15).

World Series: Fernando-maniac Dodgers Win over Yankees

October 28, 1981

Nobody could have conceived of a story like this. It's too crazy.

The Dodgers started off the year brilliantly, paced by a rookie pitcher from Sonora, Mexico, named Fernando Valenzuela. He won his first eight games, five by shutout, and had an earned-run average of 0.50. The left-handed Valenzuela, who didn't speak English, used both a sneaky fastball and a fabulous screwball to baffle hitters. He even hit .250, with 16 hits and seven runs batted in. No wonder he was the National League's starting pitcher in the All-Star Game and won the Cy Young Award and Rookie of the Year honor at season's end.

Dodger Stadium filled for every one of his games, as the 21-year-old generated feverish enthusiasm among all sorts of fans, especially among the Spanish-speaking public. "Fernando-mania" was the catch-phrase of the early 1981 season, and English-speaking fans hung on every word of Dodgers Spanish-language broadcaster Jaime Jarrin as he translated Valenzuela's comments into English for radio listeners and television viewers.

The Dodgers were never out of first place, and by the All-Star Break were 36-21, thanks mainly to fabulous pitching from Jerry Reuss, Burt Hooton, Bob Welch, and Valenzuela. Then the strike came.

When a settlement was reached two months later, the division races were restarted, and a divisional play-off was held between the winners of the first and second halves of the season. The Dodgers faced Houston in a five-game series and promptly lost the first two games at the Astrodome.

But Hooton, Valenzuela, and Reuss allowed the Astros only two runs in the next three games at home, and Reuss' 4-0 shutout on October 11 allowed the Dodgers to face Montreal for the pennant in the five-game National League Championship Series. Each team won two of the first four games, with Hooton pitching brilliantly to win two games by 5-1 and 7-1 scores. In the decisive fifth game at Montreal's Olympic Stadium, Valenzuela held the Expos to one run through eight innings but was in a 1-1 tie. Then center fielder Rick Monday—who had scored the Dodgers' earlier run— ripped a home run off of Steve Rogers to give Los Angeles a 2-1 lead. Valenzuela and Welch combined to hold Montreal off in the ninth and give the Dodgers another pennant . . . and another World Series against the New York Yankees.

Two quick losses at Yankee Stadium put the Dodgers in a hole, but they won three straight at Dodger Stadium. Ron Cey's two-run homer and steady pitching by Valenzuela led to a 5-4 win in game three; Davey Lopes scored two runs and drove in two to overcome 4-0 and 6-3 deficits to eke out an 8-7 win in game four; and Reuss pitched a complete, five-hit game to win game five by a score of 2-1.

Back in New York for game six, the Yankees were tied 1-1 in the bottom of the fourth with two on and two out when manager Bob Lemon pulled ace pitcher Tommy John for pinch hitter Bobby Murcer, who popped out. The Dodgers then pounded the next four Yankee pitchers for eight runs in four innings and won going away behind Hooton and Steve Howe, 9-2. With a combined total of 18 hits and 17 runs batted in, Cey, Pedro Guerrero, and Steve Yeager were all named Most Valuable Players.

"We're the champs," shouted Dodgers Manager Tommy Lasorda. Whether in English or Spanish, no one could doubt it, no matter how improbable it seemed. Olé!

PART 4 ***Los Angeles Times*** SPORTS

VOL. LXXI MONDAY MORNING, DECEMBER 24, 1951

RAMS WHIP BROWNS, 24-17; WIN PRO TITLE

SPORT
SCRIPTS
BY PAUL ZIMMERMAN

Van Brocklin's Pass
to Fears Provides
Late Victory Spark

BY FRANK FINCH

20

NFL Championship:
Rams Return the Favor to Cleveland, 24-17
December 23, 1951

Three hundred and sixty-four days prior, the Los Angeles Rams lost a heartbreaking 30-28 NFL Championship decision to the upstart Cleveland Browns, the pride of the All-America Football Conference. Three of its franchises had been absorbed into the National Football League for the 1950 season, and Cleveland immediately became league champions.

The wounded pride of the old-guard NFL owners aside, the Rams sought their own revenge. Their 8-4 record was good enough to win the National Conference and face the 11-1 Browns, easy winners in the American Conference. A crowd of 57,522 poured into the Memorial Coliseum to see if Cleveland was as good as advertised and could outpoint the Rams for the 1951 title.

Cleveland had a 10-7 halftime lead, thanks to a 17-yard touchdown pass from quarterback Otto Graham to Dub Jones and a 52-yard field goal from Lou Groza.

But the Rams got a third-quarter touchdown on a one-yard run by fullback Dan Towler and extended their lead to 17-10 when quarterback Bob Waterfield kicked a 17-yard field goal.

The Browns tied the game in the fourth quarter, and the Rams handed over the quarterback responsibility to Norm Van Brocklin, in relief of Waterfield. Midway through the final quarter, Van Brocklin faced a third down and three-yards-to-go situation at his 27. Although Towler and Tank Younger had both been effective rushing the ball, Van Brocklin looked to pass.

"They figured sure I'd get another running play called, just to set up a first down," Van Brocklin said. "It was a perfect time to fool somebody."

So he faked a sideline pass to the Rams' featured receiver, Elroy "Crazylegs" Hirsch, then unloaded a bomb down the middle. Sandwiched between two defenders, the Rams' other receiver, Tom Fears, jumped for the ball at midfield, made the catch, and raced into the end zone untouched for a 73-yard touchdown and a 24-17 lead.

The Browns mounted one more rally, but rookie Norb Hecker—one of 13 rookies on the Rams' roster—dropped Jones for a loss on a fourth-down play starting at the Los Angeles 44.

The amazing Rams were champions, thanks to stingy defense and the pass catching of Hirsch and Fears, who combined for 212 receiving yards as the Rams piled up an impressive 334 yards of offense on the legendary Browns' defense.

Dick Hoerner (31) scores on this one-yard plunge to open a 7-0 lead for the Rams in the second quarter.

21

XV FIFA World Cup: USA 2, Colombia 1

June 22, 1994

When the 1994 World Cup, soccer's quadrennial world championship, was awarded to the United States, purists snickered. Not that the event would be poorly managed; the abilities of American organizers were well known. But a world championship in a country that hadn't won a World Cup game since 1950?

With opportunity, however, came the resolve to achieve success. In 1990 the U.S. qualified for its first World Cup since 1950. And when the 1994 tournament opened, American hopes were high after a dramatic 1-0 tune-up victory over highly regarded Mexico was played before 91,123 at the Rose Bowl.

But after an opening 1-1 tie with Switzerland at the Pontiac Silverdome, Bora Milutinovic's squad had to face Colombia, a team favored by many observers to win the tournament.

On a blisteringly hot Wednesday, 93,134 fans packed the Rose Bowl to cheer the American team. Alexi Lalas, Marcelo Balboa, and Thomas Dooley provided unexpectedly strong first-half midfield defense, while the best challenges to goalkeeper Tony Meola were rejected as Mike Sorber stepped in front of Colombian shots by Herman Gaviria and Anthony de Avila. One of these shots came so close to scoring as to bounce off the goalpost.

In the 35th minute, a U.S. advance started with Sorber's pass to John Harkes, who blasted up the left side, while forward Ernie Stewart moved toward the goal from the right. Colombian goalkeeper Oscar Cordoba moved to cut off Stewart's angle while defender Andres Escobar headed toward Harkes. Sliding to clear Harkes' crossfield pass, Escobar's foot hit the ball and sent it straight into his own goal for a 1-0 U.S. lead.

The American defense stiffened in the second half, opening occasional opportunities. In the 52nd minute, Stewart beat Cordoba off a lead pass from Tab Ramos to build the lead to 2-0 and send waves of disbelief, pandemonium, and shock both through the stadium and a worldwide television audience.

Even tighter defense fought off a desperate Colombian effort that included a 90th-minute goal by Jose Adolfo Valencia—too little, too late. The wild celebration, the waving and wearing of American flags, and the almost unthinkable reality of a U.S. World Cup victory was summed up perfectly by the orange-haired and -goateed Lalas: "It's an indescribable feeling to be part of such an historic day. It's incredible; it's historical; it's cool." It was all that and much more.

A sad epitaph: Escobar was murdered by deranged fans in his home city of Medellin on

College Basketball:
Bruins Streak past Irish for 61st Straight Win
January 27, 1973

It was widely anticipated that UCLA would surpass the legendary 60-game winning streak of the Bill Russell-led University of San Francisco (USF) teams of 1954-56. But the Bruins of Lew Alcindor, Lynn Shackelford, Lucius Allen, Mike Warren, and company rang up "only" 47 straight wins from 1966 to 1968 before losing to Houston 71-69 at the Astrodome in January 1968.

But with another 41 wins in a row after that, the Alcindor-era Bruins won 84 of 85 games over a three-year period: sensational, but not record-setting. And not as much was expected from the teams led by Curtis Rowe, Sidney Wicks, and Steve Patterson that followed.

But the 1969-70 and 1970-71 Bruins lost only three games on their way to two more NCAA titles. In the 1970-71 season, in fact, only Austin Carr's 46-point performance at Notre Dame—an 89-82 loss—spoiled a 29-1 season that ended with 15 straight wins.

Then the Walton Gang took over. Paced by Bill Walton—the 6-11, redheaded, sophomore center from La Mesa, California—and an excellent supporting cast of sophomores in Keith Wilkes and Greg Lee, junior forward Larry Farmer, and senior guard Henry Bibby, the youthful Bruins stormed to a 30-0 record and 45 straight wins in two years. UCLA crushed its opposition: only two of its wins were by less than 13 points, one of which was the NCAA final against Florida State (an 81-76 triumph).

So with Walton, Wilkes, Farmer, and Lee all back, plus Larry Hollyfield, Tommy Curtis, Swen Nater, and Dave Meyers, the Bruins were set to smash USF's 17-year-old mark. And smash it they did. Another 30-0 campaign ran the streak to 75 at season's end, which culminated in Walton's amazing 21-for-22 performance from the field in the 87-66 UCLA rout of Memphis State in the NCAA championship game (see Moment 38).

The record-tying win was against Loyola of Chicago, with Walton (32 points, 27 rebounds) and Wilkes (16 points, 15 rebounds) dominating the game en route to an 87-73 victory. Then came the record breaker, against Digger Phelps' Notre Dame team, at the Athletic and Convocation Center in South Bend, Indiana. Walton again dominated the boards with 15 rebounds, while he and Farmer each scored 16 points to complement Wilkes' 20-point performance as the Bruins cruised to an 82-63 triumph.

The streak reached 88 (including four wins over the Irish) by the middle of the 1973-74 season, when Notre Dame managed a 71-70 home victory on January 19, 1974. At that point, the Bruins had not only won 88 straight, but 107 of their last 108 and—over seven and a half seasons—a stunning 188 of 193 games, as well as seven consecutive NCAA championships.

After the season ended, Bruin coach John Wooden reflected on the achievement: "There was some pressure on us when we neared the magic 60 in a row set by the tremendous teams led by the great Bill Russell. But once we had broken their record, the only pressure was that which we imposed upon ourselves in an effort to play up to our capabilities." That unending quest to reach the highest possible level of performance was the hallmark of Wooden's brilliant Bruin teams, which not only reached for perfection but set new standards by which all that followed would be judged (see Moment 4).

The all-American duo of forward Keith (later Jamaal) Wilkes [52] and center Bill Walton [32] are two of the main reasons that UCLA compiled a record 88-game winning streak from 1971 to 1975.

Super Bowl XIV:
Rams Take Steelers to the Limit
January 20, 1980

The Pittsburgh Steelers entered the Rose Bowl for Super Bowl XIV ready to annex their fourth championship, having won three of the past five Super Bowls. They had rambled through the schedule with a 12-4 record and had stomped Miami and Houston in the play-offs. Quarterback Terry Bradshaw was still throwing strikes to wide receivers Lynn Swann and John Stallworth, and the running of Franco Harris and the Steel Curtain defense made Pittsburgh a formidable opponent.

Their challenge? The Los Angeles Rams, who had staggered to their seventh straight Western Division title at 9-7 and then eked past Dallas, 21-19, and Tampa Bay, 9-0. True, the Rams were playing what was essentially a home game, but against the Steelers. . . .

Despite predictions that this would be a walk for the Steelers, the Rams took a 7-3 lead on a one-yard run by Cullen Bryant and had a 13-10 halftime lead on two Frank Corral field goals.

Not appearing worried, the Steelers took the second half kickoff and marched to a 17-13 lead in less than three minutes. Bradshaw's bomb to Swann on the Rams' two-yard line—along with his acrobatic tumble into the end zone—completed a 47-yard play and a 61-yard drive.

But someone forgot to tell the Rams to fold their tents. Starting on their own 23, quarterback Vince Ferragamo completed a 50-yard bomb to receiver Billy Waddy, who ran to the Steelers' 24. On the first down, a halfback option play allowed Lawrence McCutcheon to loft a pass to the flag for receiver Ron Smith, who fell into the end zone for a 19-17 Rams lead. Corral missed the extra point, and the third quarter was history.

Now, though, the Steelers knew they were in a game. Trying again to get started early in the fourth quarter, Bradshaw began the Pittsburgh drive at the Steelers' 25. Two plays gained only two yards, but on the third down, Bradshaw found Stallworth deep over the middle at the Rams' 32, as the ball just eluded cornerback Rod Perry's outstretched hand. The result was a 73-yard touchdown and a 24-19 Steelers lead. It was the sixth time the lead had changed hands in the game.

With all 103,985 spectators at the Rose Bowl screaming, Ferragamo and the Rams tried to and come up with another miracle.

With 8:29 to play and the ball on his 16, Ferragamo completed passes for 24 and 8 yards to Preston Dennard, followed by two Wendell Tyler runs and a 15-yard pass to Waddy. The ball now lay at the Steelers' 32. But Ferragamo's pass for Smith was intercepted as linebacker Jack Lambert leaped in front of the receiver.

Two plays later, Bradshaw saw the Rams in the same coverage as when he threw the touchdown to Stallworth two series earlier. He called the same play, and it worked for 45 yards to the Los Angeles 22. A pass interference penalty took the ball to the one, and Harris' dive for the touchdown moved the Steelers out to a comfortable 31-19 lead. That's the way it ended.

The Rams were game, but not quite enough for the Steelers. "From the beginning, I thought we were going to win," said Rams Coach Ray Malavasi. "We ran on them; we threw on them, but we just didn't get the big play."

Steelers' free safety J. T. Thomas was certain he knew the difference in the outcome: "They only thought they could beat us. We knew we could beat them." After four Super Bowl titles in six years, Steelers Owner Art Rooney said what everyone was thinking: "This might be the greatest team of all time."

Pittsburgh's Jack Lambert stops Cullen Bryant on short yardage in the first half (top), but Bryant scores the first touchdown of the game (bottom) as Rams quarterback Vince Ferragamo (15) raises his arms in celebration.

Olympic Track and Field:
King Carl Crowned in Los Angeles

August 11, 1984

The four gold medals won by Jesse Owens in the 1936 Olympic Games in Berlin stood for nearly 50 years as a monument to greatness, unapproached by any of the great sprinters and jumpers who succeeded him.

But on the floor of the Los Angeles Memorial Coliseum, where Owens had thrilled 40,000 fans in a 1935 dual meet against USC (see Moment 91), a new challenger to the Owens legend was at work.

Carl Lewis, born in 1961 in Willingboro, New Jersey, entered the 1984 Olympic Games as a heavy favorite to duplicate Owens' feat: victories in the 100 and 200 meters, as well as the 4 x 100-meter relay and the long jump. Lewis had won three of these events a year earlier at the World Track and Field Championships in Helsinki, Finland, but now he faced an Olympic Games in his home country, under the scrutiny of more than 85,000 fans who awaited his history-making effort. They weren't disappointed.

Lewis blistered the field in the 100 meters, which began on the first day of track and field, August 3. He breezed through the heats, quarterfinals, and semifinals in 10.32, 10.04, and 10.14 seconds and lined up for the final in lane seven on August 4. Teammate Sam Graddy started best, but Lewis broke clear by 50 meters and hit the tape in 9.99 to Graddy's silver-medal-winning 10.19. Lewis was only warming up.

He was back on the track the next day, August 5, for qualifying in the long jump. Lewis was clearly the world's best long jumper, and his 27-2 3/4 mark on his first try easily led the field.

On August 6, Lewis' fourth day in a row of competition, he was the overwhelming favorite in the finals of the long jump, but had to run qualifying heats in the 200 meters in the morning. He won both, then came out in the afternoon to jump.

Because of a delay caused by the hammer throw, the Coliseum floor was cool by the time the long jump started. But Lewis' first try was a killer; at 28-0 1/4 (with the wind against him!), he not only took the lead, but he knew that no one in the field would mount any kind of challenge. He tried one more jump, a foul, and retired, secure in his second gold medal. Gary Honey of Australia won the silver medal at 27-0 1/2. The 200 meters, an event Lewis had run only infrequently, was next—after a rest day!

Lewis' teammate Kirk Baptiste won the first 200-meter semifinal in 20.29 and Lewis won the second in 20.27. For the final, Lewis drew lane seven and Baptiste, lane three, so Baptiste had the advantage of being able to see Lewis as they headed around the turn. No matter; Lewis wobbled slightly around the bend, but steamed home in 19.80, the third-fastest time ever, ahead of teammates Baptiste (19.96) and Thomas Jefferson (20.26).

After a day off on August 9, Lewis was back on the track for his sixth competition in eight days, an easy anchor leg in the qualifying heats of the 4 x 100-meter relay. The U.S. team of Graddy, Ron Brown, Calvin Smith, and Lewis won their heat in 38.89. Two days later they won the semifinal in a very fast 38.44, and Lewis equaled Owens' 1936 performance with a brilliant anchor on the world-record-setting final relay effort of 37.83.

"Two years ago, nobody thought I could do it," a tired, but relieved Lewis said afterward. "A year ago, I didn't know if I could do it. But now I have four gold medals, and that's one thing no one can take away." But now only he can share this experience with Owens.

Lewis takes off on the way to his 200-meter gold medal (left) and raises his arms in celebration of his final effort (above) as the anchor in a world-record-setting 4x100-meter relay.

Ice Hockey:
Gretzky Traded to the Kings
August 9, 1988

Imagine Babe Ruth, at the height of his powers, being traded from the Yankees.
Unthinkable? That's the shock that hit Edmonton Oilers fans when a tearful Wayne Gretzky
held a news conference to confirm his departure to join the Los Angeles Kings. One member of the Canadian Parliament said that trading Gretzky, a Canadian citizen born in
Brantford, Ontario, was like "selling a national symbol, like the Mountie or the beaver."

The Kings? An expansion franchise in 1967, the Kings had an up-and-down history,
often making the play-offs, but never making it to the Stanley Cup finals. Now they were
acquiring The Great One, perhaps the finest player ever to play the game. In his nine seasons in Edmonton, Gretzky won the Hart Trophy as the league's most valuable player eight
times and the Art Ross Trophy (scoring title) seven times. Most importantly, his Oilers won
four Stanley Cups.

That's what interested new Kings owner Bruce McNall. Gretzky was the game's marquee
player but was foremost a winner. McNall knew that the secret to making hockey a force in
warm weather Los Angeles was not only winning, but winning with style. In Gretzky, he got
both.

But he paid for it. With Gretzky came two other important, if less appreciated players—defenseman Marty McSorley and center Mike Krushelnyski. In return, Edmonton
owner Peter Pocklington accepted 55-goal scorer Jimmy Carson; rookie left wing Martin
Gelinas; first-round draft choices in 1989, 1991, and 1993; and a reported $15 million in
cash.

The impact was immediate. With Gretzky leading the charge, the Kings did an about-
face, improving from 30-42-8 (68 points) to 42-31-7 (91 points) in the 1988-89 season.
And their attendance jumped 28 percent in Gretzky's first Los Angeles campaign.

By the 1991-92 season, the Kings became the first Los Angeles franchise to sell out
each and every one of its home games. An unthinkable trade made the unbelievable a
reality: hockey has a home in Los Angeles (see Moment 12).

Rose Bowl:
Bruins Twice as Nice against Michigan State
January 1, 1966

As the 10-0 Michigan State Spartans got ready to win the national championship in the 1966 Rose Bowl, they didn't count on having much trouble with the 7-2-1 Bruins of UCLA. After all, the Spartans defeated the Bruins, 13-3, in the season opener at East Lansing, a game in which they outgained Tommy Prothro's team, 345 yards to 206.

But in front of 100,087, the Bruins struck back. Late in the first quarter, a fumble by MSU's Don Japinga was recovered by UCLA's John Erquiaga on the Spartan six. Two plays later, sophomore quarterback Gary Beban rolled into the end zone over the right guard spot. Kurt Zimmerman's conversion made it 7-0.

Then Prothro stunned Michigan State by ordering an onside kick, which Zimmerman executed perfectly, and the ball was recovered by UCLA's Dallas Grider on the Spartan 42. Beban gained three, and halfback Mel Farr shot through left tackle for 21 yards, but the Bruins suffered two delay-of-game penalties, leaving second down and 15 yards to go on the MSU 28. Beban then rifled a pass that somehow split two Spartan defenders and found the waiting arms of receiver Kurt Altenberg for a 27-yard gain to the one. Beban again sneaked into the end zone, this time over the left guard spot, and after Zimmerman's conversion, the Bruins had a 14-0 halftime lead.

Neither team scored in the third quarter, as the Bruins confounded the Michigan State offense with a defensive line that averaged a petite 203 pounds. Inevitably, the Spartans finally found a play that worked when reserve quarterback Jimmy Raye's option pitch to fullback Bob Apisa resulted in a 38-yard touchdown run with 6:13 left in the game. Spartan coach Duffy Daugherty then tried to fool the Bruins, as starting quarterback Steve Juday rose out of a conventional kicking formation, but his pass was incomplete under heavy pressure from Bruin defensive end Jerry Klein. UCLA 14, MSU 6.

Michigan State's Dwight Lee (34) is dragged down after a short gain (right); diminutive Bruin cornerback Bob Stiles shows the effects of his game-saving tackle of Bob Apisa on a two-point conversion try (bottom).

The Spartan defense then held UCLA, partially blocked a punt, and gave the ball to the offense at the MSU 49. With Juday and Raye alternating at quarterback, the Spartans drove 51 yards in 15 plays, with Juday diving over for an eight-inch touchdown with 31 seconds left. Now Raye came on the field for the two-point conversion try, sprinted to his right, and pitched again to the 6-2, 212-pound Apisa. Although slowed by Bruin left end Jim Colletto, Apisa leaned toward the goal line, only to be collared by 5-9, 175-pound defensive back Bob Stiles. With Stiles twisting him away from the goal while riding his back, Apisa was stopped inches short.

Stiles was knocked unconscious on the play, and so were the Spartans. The 14-12 win was UCLA's first-ever Rose Bowl victory.

Baseball:
Drysdale Sets Major-League Mark of
58 Scoreless Innings
June 8, 1968

The Dodgers of the 1960s will be remembered for light hitting and heavy pitching. With Sandy Koufax, Don Drysdale, Johnny Podres, Claude Osteen, and Don Sutton leading the way, Dodger teams finished first or second in the National League five times in the seven years from 1960-66.

By 1968, the Dodgers were rebuilding. Still, the pitching staff, led by Don Drysdale, was solid.

The 6-6, 239-pound, right-handed Drysdale was well known for his blazing speed and sidearm delivery. With Sandy Koufax, he was part of the finest 1-2 pitching punch in the game in the mid-'60s. But his greatest achievement came because he had to pitch almost perfectly to win any game for the light-hitting Dodgers.

Drysdale needed all of his skills to beat Chicago's Ferguson Jenkins, 1-0, at Dodger Stadium on May 14. While the Cubs managed only two hits, the Dodgers got six, but scored only once.

Los Angeles managed only five hits and another sixth-inning run in Drysdale's next start, four days later. But "Big D," as he was known, set down the Houston Astros and Dave Giusti, 1-0.

The dominant pitcher of the year, St. Louis' Bob Gibson, was waiting for Drysdale on May 22 at Busch Stadium. Despite Gibson's microscopic ERA of 1.12 that season, the Dodgers scratched him for a run in the third and one more in the ninth. Drysdale scattered five hits for a 2-0 triumph.

Drysdale was being watched now as he neared the major-league record of five straight shutouts, set by Doc White of the Chicago White Sox in 1904. The Dodgers knew it, too, and gave Drysdale better support with five runs against Houston and Larry Dierker on May 26.

To set the record, he would have to face the San Francisco Giants and old foes including Willie Mays, Willie McCovey, Jim Ray Hart, and Jesus Alou. Left-hander Mike McCormick faced Drysdale on a cool evening in Dodger Stadium on May 31, but two runs in the first three innings were enough support, as the Dodgers won, 3-0.

Drysdale then set down Jim Bunning and the Pittsburgh Pirates at Dodger Stadium on June 4, establishing a new record with his sixth consecutive shutout, and surpassing Carl Hubbell's National League scoreless string of 46 1/3 innings from 1933.

Only Walter Johnson's major-league mark of 56 scoreless innings was left to break. The great Washington Senators right-hander was unscored upon from April 10 to May 14, 1913. Drysdale faced the Philadelphia Phillies on June 8 at Dodger Stadium. Although seven of his first eight pitches were balls, he settled down. When Dodger third baseman Ken Boyer threw out Phillies shortstop Roberto Peña in the third inning, Drysdale had a new major-league record.

The Phillies finally scored the first run off of Drysdale in nearly two months when Tony Taylor crossed the plate in the fifth, ending the string at 58 2/3 innings. "I wanted the record so bad," Drysdale said later. "I could feel myself go 'blah' when the run scored. I just let down completely. I'm sure it was the mental strain."

Oh, yes, Hank Aguirre came in to relieve Drysdale in the seventh and the Dodgers went on to win, 5-3. But 55,017 screamed with joy and relief as Drysdale set a record that remains today a part of the Dodgers great pitching legacy (see Moment 17).

Baseball:
Nolan's Fourth No-No Knots Him with Koufax
June 1, 1975

When Baltimore's Bobby Grich stepped to the plate with two outs in the top of the ninth inning at Anaheim Stadium, he knew that history was looking in.

On the mound in front of him was Nolan Ryan of the California Angels, readying for another attempt at a no-hitter. Only the great Sandy Koufax of the Dodgers had thrown four no-hitters (see Moment 7). Ryan, only an out away from the no-hitter, was looking for his ninth win of the season, and the first win for the Angels after five straight losses.

Three minutes later, Grich watched Ryan's 147th pitch of the evening, a change-up of all things, go by him for a called third strike, leaving the Orioles a loser to Ryan's fourth no-hitter in a remarkable three seasons.

A flame-throwing power pitcher when he came up with the New York Mets in 1968, Ryan clocked the fastest pitch ever recorded up to that time with a 100.9 miles per hour fastball against Detroit in August 1974. His first two no-hitters came at Kansas City in May, 1973 (3-0, 12 strikeouts), and then two months later at Detroit in a 6-0 win with 17 strike-outs. He became only the fifth pitcher to claim two no-hitters in the same season.

There was no letup in 1974, as he no-hit Minnesota in his final start of the season, 4-0 (15 strikeouts). In just over 24 months—from May 15, 1973, to June 1, 1975—Ryan's heroics tied Koufax's major-league record of four no-hitters. In just his 109th major-league start, Nolan Ryan had his fourth no-hitter to go along with four one-hitters.

Ryan's reaction? "I think I'd prefer to have an outstanding year," said the 28-year-old. "You know, something like a 27-5 record. That way, people would know I was great all year, rather than just on one day."

Not everyone was so calm, however. "I feel like I pitched a no-hitter," said an excited catcher Ellie Rodriguez, who was activated only hours before the game after recovering from an injury. "I just want to catch his fifth."

Rodriguez didn't get the chance, but Ryan did. After a stint in Houston (NL), Ryan ended his career with Texas (AL). When he retired, Ryan took with him a remarkable major-league record of seven no-hitters, stretching from his first in 1973 to a final gem on May 1, 1991, as he no-hit Toronto's Blue Jays, winning 3-0.

Catcher Ellie Rodriguez (left) looks even happier than Angel pitcher Nolan Ryan after Ryan's fourth no-hitter, this time achieved against the Baltimore Orioles.

29 Baseball: Campanella's Night Lights Up Los Angeles
May 7, 1959

He was perhaps the noblest Dodger of them all. In his 10 seasons in Brooklyn, Roy Campanella became one of the bulwarks of the National League's premier team. As a catcher, he was named the National League's Most Valuable Player three times, in 1951, 1953, and 1955.

But he never got a chance to play in Los Angeles. A brutal automobile accident on January 28, 1958, ended Campanella's playing career and confined him to a wheelchair for the rest of his life.

Though denied a chance to see him play in Los Angeles, the area's fans paid him an astonishing tribute one season later.

A special benefit game was held between the Dodgers and their old Brooklyn nemesis, the world champion New York Yankees, at the Coliseum. The Bronx Bombers gave up two

days off and paid their own travel expenses to come to Los Angeles. For their part, the Dodgers had to fly back from San Francisco after defeating the Giants that afternoon, 2-1. Proceeds of the game went to Campanella and his family, including his wife and three children.

An all-time record crowd of 93,103 turned out to honor Campanella, not counting several hundred who broke down fences around the Coliseum or simply climbed over. The crowd stood for several moments in an extended tribute when Campanella was wheeled onto the field for pregame ceremonies by his old teammate Pee Wee Reese, accompanied by Dodgers manager Walter Alston and Yankee skipper Casey Stengel.

"I thank each and every one of you from the bottom of my heart," Campy said. "This is something I'll never forget as long as I live. I want to thank the Yankees for playing this game, and my old Dodger team, too. It's a wonderful tribute."

The unforgettable highlight of the evening came when play stopped between the fifth and sixth innings. Campanella was wheeled out and the Coliseum lights extinguished. Then the entire crowd lit up matches or lighters in salute to Campanella, turning the Coliseum into "a beautiful spectacle," according to Al Wolf of the *Los Angeles Times*.

The game was less spectacular as New York bombed Sandy Koufax for four runs in the top of the sixth on the way to a 6-2 win. But the night belonged to Campanella, whose only appearance as a Dodger in Los Angeles will always be remembered brightly.

Pee Wee Reese stands behind teammate Roy Campanella as matches light up the Los Angeles Memorial Coliseum in his honor. At left, Campy is honored before the game, with managers Walter Alston of the Dodgers and Casey Stengel of the Yankees.

Gretzky and the Great Western Forum crowd celebrate after his 802nd career goal, an all-time record that Gretzky achieved in 1994.

Ice Hockey:
Gretzky Becomes the Greatest One
October 15, 1989

As a childhood hockey player in Brantford, Ontario, Canada, Wayne Gretzky watched and studied the moves of his favorite player, Gordie Howe, star of the Detroit Red Wings.

Soon enough, Gretzky became the greatest player in the game, starring for the Edmonton Oilers and, after an improbable trade, for the Los Angeles Kings (see Moment 25). His prolific scoring (goals and assists) won him a cabinet full of National Hockey League scoring titles, including eight straight from 1980 to 1987, leaving him on the doorstep of Howe's all-time scoring record of 1,850 points, set during a 26-year NHL career. Gretzky, preparing for the sixth game of his 11th season, had 1,849 points as the Kings prepared to face Gretzky's old team, the Edmonton Oilers, at the Northlands Coliseum in Edmonton.

There was very little suspense. Gretzky equaled Howe's record early in the game but saved his record breaker for the dramatic close. With the Kings trailing 3-2 and only a minute left in the game, Gretzky led an all-out assault on Oiler goaltender Bill Ranford with the Kings' net empty and an extra forward on the ice for Los Angeles. With seven players, including Gretzky, swarming around the goal, he placed the puck in the upper-right-hand corner of the net, eluding Ranford and tying the game with 53 seconds to play. Naturally, he scored the winning goal in overtime for point number 1,852 and a 4-3 Kings win.

While still an Oiler during the previous season, Gretzky broke the all-time NHL record for assists, with his 1,050th assist on March 1, 1988, against . . . the Kings, of course. He had to wait a little longer to get Howe's all-time goal scoring record of 801.

But the moment came on March 23, 1994, against the Vancouver Canucks. Steaming down the ice on a power play, Gretzky slammed the puck past Kirk McLean at 14:47 of the second period to score number 802 and own all three major career scoring records in his 1,117th NHL game.

It was all the more remarkable that Howe's record had come in 1,767 games over many more years, a tribute to Gretzky's consistent brilliance during his entire career. And The Great One wasn't finished after number 802. He finished the season with one more goal for a total of 38 (803 total) and 92 assists for a seasonal total of 130 points, best in the league. With each season, he continues to add to his record-setting totals.

College Football:
Big Bad Bruins Bash Troy, 34-0,
to Win National Title
November 20, 1954

After a combined 16-3 record in 1952 and 1953, UCLA Coach Red Sanders knew he would have a powerhouse in 1954. The Bruins started against the San Diego Naval Training Center on September 18 and waltzed to a school record 67-0 victory, followed by a 32-7 drubbing of Kansas.

Then the first real test came, as the fourth-ranked UCLA took on sixth-rated—and defending national champion—Maryland at the Coliseum on October 1. In front of 73,376 fans, fullback Bob Davenport rushed for 87 yards and both Bruin touchdowns as UCLA edged the Terrapins 12-7 and advanced to second in the national polls. They fell back to third after Washington missed tying a 21-20 thriller because of an errant point-after-touchdown conversion.

But UCLA was just hitting stride. The Bruins then ran up 477 yards in total offense, intercepted eight John Brodie passes, and mauled Stanford, 72-0, with the most points ever scored by a UCLA team. The carnage continued unabated as UCLA mutilated Oregon State by a 61-0 count—while piling up 593 yards in total offense—and clubbed Oregon, 41-0.

That left only the season closer against USC. Because of the Pacific Coast Conference's "no-repeat" rule, UCLA could not play in the 1955 Rose Bowl, and there were no other bowls to go to. So the Bruins had to be content to slug it out with the seventh-ranked Trojans.

A monstrous crowd of 102,548 came out to see the game. They weren't disappointed. The Bruins held only a 7-0 lead going into the fourth quarter but exploded for 27 points on a one-yard Bob Davenport run and touchdown passes from Primo Villanueva to Terry Debay (12 yards), Doug Bradley to Rommie Loudd (8 yards), and Sam Brown to Bruce Ballard (17 yards) to win going away, 34-0. It was a perfect end to the Bruins' first undefeated, untied season: 9-0. UCLA led the nation in points with 367 and in scoring defense, yielding a mere 40 to its opponents. The average score for a Bruins' game was 41-4.

Davenport joined three other teammates—tackle Jack Ellena, halfback Villanueva, and guard Jim Salsbury—as first-team All-Americans, with eight other Bruins receiving honorable mention for All-American honors. UCLA finished at the top of the United Press International poll, while the Associated Press crowned Ohio State—also undefeated—which edged USC in the Rose Bowl, 20-7. But the Bruins received the coveted Grantland Rice Memorial Trophy from the Football Writers of America, a symbol of national supremacy and a fitting tribute to an overpowering team.

The unstoppable, undefeated, untied 1954 Bruin attack converges on USC's George Galli.

College Football:
Davis! Davis! Davis! Davis! Davis! Davis!
December 2, 1972

That was the headline in the *Los Angeles Times* as 5-9 sophomore tailback Anthony Davis raced in, around, and through an 8-1 Notre Dame team on the way to a 45-23 Trojan victory that ensured undefeated USC's place at the top of the college football polls, leading up to a national championship (see Moment 51).

Davis started with the opening kickoff, which he took at the three, and ran down the left sideline for a 97-yard touchdown and a 6-0 USC lead after 13 seconds. Ignoring a Bob Thomas field goal, Davis and the Trojans scored twice more on runs of one and five yards to run up a 19-3 lead at the end of the first quarter.

But Notre Dame used a Tom Clements-to-Willie Townsend touchdown pass to close the lead to 19-10 at the half.

Davis' fourth touchdown, a four-yard run, and a blown two-point conversion try extended the lead to 25-10 at the start of the third quarter, but the Irish still had plenty of fight.

Also just a sophomore, Clements quieted 75,243 fans at the Coliseum as he drove Notre Dame to two quick touchdowns and had Notre Dame within 25-23 when a two-point conversion try failed with 1:19 still to play in the third quarter. The Irish defense was then asked to hold the Trojans.

But Davis took the ensuing kickoff at his four-yard line. His brilliant 96-yard return for a touchdown solidified USC's lead at 32-23 and ended Notre Dame's hopes. On this day, USC would not be beaten.

The Trojans kept the pressure up in the fourth quarter. Davis scored again on an eight-yard run, his sixth score of the day, and Sam Cunningham finally went over from a yard out to close out the game at 45-23.

Davis had squeezed a career into a single game: 99 yards rushing, 51 yards receiving, and 218 yards on kickoff returns. He had etched his name into the annals of the USC-Notre Dame rivalry, but there would be plenty more to come in the future (see Moment 3).

An all-too-familiar nightmare for Irish fans: Anthony Davis on the sweep, followed by a celebration in the end zone.

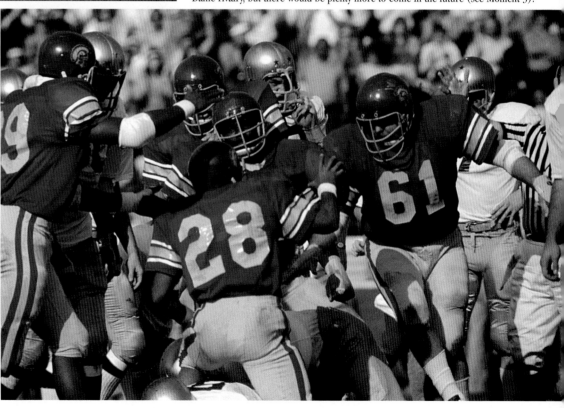

Baseball:
Wills Becomes the Top Thief in
Major-League History
September 23, 1962

The Dodgers were well known for their use of speed on the bases. Going into the 1962 season, they had led the National League in stolen bases for four straight seasons and 13 of the prior 16.

The 1962 season was altogether different, and the difference was named Maury Wills. The 29-year-old shortstop had led the National League in steals with 50 in 1960 and 35 in 1961 but was having his best season ever in 1962. His batting average was up, stronger Dodger hitting was giving him more chances at the plate, and he was stealing bases faster than ever before.

By the All-Star break, he already had 46 steals. By the end of July, he had 51. Even so, the National League mark of 80 steals in a season held by Bob Bescher of Cincinnati in 1911 was a long way away. But Wills kept going.

He stole and stole and stole. Whenever he reached base, Dodger Stadium reverberated with the cry of "Go, Maury, Go," and he rarely disappointed. In August, while the Dodgers spurted to the lead in the National League, Wills stole 22 bases and was caught only twice.

Maury on the move: Wills watches an opposing pitcher (left), then slides into third for his 104th steal of the 1962 season (above).

In September, the Dodgers played nip and tuck with San Francisco for the pennant and needed every advantage. Wills ran wild, surpassing Bescher by September 7 and heading for the major-league record of 96 stolen bases in a single season set by Detroit's legendary Ty Cobb in 1915.

But Cobb's 96 steals came in 156 games, including two replays of tied games; the Dodgers would play 162. Baseball Commissioner Ford Frick held that Wills would have to break the record in 154 games—the length of the regular season in Cobb's day.

It didn't matter. Cobb had stolen 94 bases in 154 games. Wills stole 95.

In his 156th game, Wills stole bases 96 and 97 against St. Louis, and even Frick had to relent: "It's a record. Whether we say it's a record in 162 games or not, there's no question it's a new record—the most bases ever stolen in a season."

Wills knew his place in history was secure: "I'm satisfied in my own mind that I broke the record. If 156 games was good enough for Cobb, then 156 games is good enough for me."

But the Dodgers were still playing. By the end of the regular season, they had been tied by the Giants for the league lead and had to face a three-game play-off.

Wills kept running, and although the Dodgers lost the play-off series, he completed the 165-game season with 104 stolen bases. He swiped 44 bases in his last 44 games and 28 in the final 25 games of the Dodger season. He was caught only 13 times, and the Dodgers as a team stole more bases (198) than any major-league team since 1918 and, in 1962, more than any two other major-league teams combined.

For his efforts, Wills was honored as the National League's Most Valuable Player. More importantly, he jump-started the reign of the "Go-Go Dodgers," leading to three pennants and two World Series championships in the next five years.

34

Rose Bowl:
USC's Longest Quarter Ends . . . in Victory!
January 1, 1963

Quarterbacks Pete Beathard (top right) of
USC and Ron VanderKelen (top left) of
Wisconsin have career days in the 1963
Rose Bowl; at bottom, USC halfback Willie
Brown (26) sweeps right against the
Badgers with help from Beathard's block
on James Nettles (26) and with Ron Paar
(63) and Roger Pillath (70) in pursuit.

Winning the Rose Bowl and securing the national championship was a dream come
true for USC's Trojans on New Year's Day, 1963. So how come nobody noticed?

In one of the most thrilling and unforgettable college football games ever played, USC
opened a seemingly insurmountable 42-14 lead, only to hang on for a 42-37 win over
Wisconsin. The game was completed in near darkness as the number one Trojans and number two Badgers battled for more than three hours.

After a 7-7 opening quarter before 98,698 spectators, USC opened the game up with
touchdowns by Ben Wilson and Ron Heller to take a 21-7 halftime lead. Then quarterback
Pete Beathard threw his second, third, and fourth touchdown passes of the day to Hal
Bedsole on a 57-yard play, to Bedsole again from 23 yards, and to Fred Hill for 13 yards.
Badger quarterback Ron VanderKelen matched one score with a 17-yard run, but with 14
minutes to play, Wisconsin trailed by 28 points.

VanderKelen then put on one of the greatest passing shows in college football history.
He completed eight of 10 passes on the next drive, hitting Lou Holland for a 13-yard score.
Then a recovered Trojan fumble led to a four-yard touchdown pass to Gary Kroner. Even an
interception by USC's Willie Brown in the end zone turned into Wisconsin points . . . when a
subsequent center snap went awry and earned the Badgers two points for a safety to make
the score 42-30.

VanderKelen got the ball again and raced down the field, hitting Pat Richter for a 19-
yard touchdown with 1:19 to play. With 23 points in 10:22, the Badgers were trailing only
42-37, and the Trojans were reeling. VanderKelen completed 18 of 22 passes in the quarter
and 33 of 48 for 401 yards in the game to set new Rose Bowl records.

But USC regained its composure, recovered the expected onside kick and ran out the
clock to save the victory and complete an undefeated, 11-0 season to win the national
championship. Bedsole said later, "There was no feeling of elation for winning the national
championship. It was really unfortunate. It was discouraging after they came back like that.

"We felt we were national champions before the Wisconsin game, and we knew we
were far superior to the Badgers. And we should have won by more. But that comeback
took a lot out of us."

An irritated Trojan coach John McKay was quoted after the game as telling his team,
"Wisconsin!? That's all they're talking about. We came in number one. They came in number two and lost.

"That makes us still number one." They were. . . they really were!

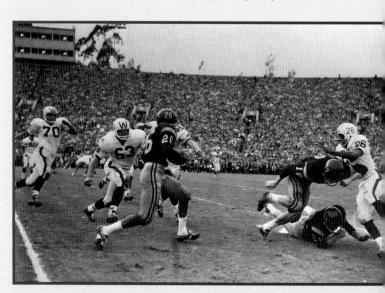

35

College Football:
Beban Bombs Bruins into Rose Bowl, 20-16
November 20, 1965

Garrett, Garrett, and more Mike Garrett. USC's brilliant senior tailback, and the 1965 Heisman Trophy winner, was having another career day in his final battle against 6-1-1 UCLA.

Forty times he carried the ball, gaining 210 net yards and helping his 6-1-1 Trojans to a seemingly insurmountable 16-6 lead with only 8:04 to play in the game. Although UCLA's Mel Farr had opened the scoring with a 49-yard sprint in the first quarter (the conversion try was blocked), the Bruins had gained just 85 other yards in the game. USC quarterback Troy Winslow had thrown two short touchdown passes, and Tim Rossovich's 10-yard field goal gave USC a 10-point lead with time running down.

The Trojans stopped UCLA's next drive, as Farr was inches short on fourth-and-two from midfield. Garrett then gained 20, but USC was called for clipping, followed by a Winslow fumble that was recovered by Bruin defensive end Erwin Dutcher at the USC 34.

This was the opportunity UCLA needed. Sophomore quarterback Gary Beban then found split end Dick Witcher deep in the end zone, and his perfect pass gave the Bruins a badly needed, 34-yard touchdown. Beban's two-point conversion pass to Byron Nelson was good, too, cutting the lead to 16-14 with 4:00 to go.

As 94,085 fans got nervous, Bruin Coach Tommy Prothro asked for an onside kick. Kurt Zimmerman's 11-yard dribbler was corralled by Dallas Grider at the USC 49. Two plays gained 11 yards, but Adrian Young sacked Beban for a loss of 14, back to the UCLA 48. On third and 24 from that spot, Beban arched a long pass toward the Trojan goal line which Kurt Altenberg caught at the five and ran into the end zone for a . . . 52-yard touchdown!

Beban's conversion pass for Nelson was broken up this time, but the impossible turn of events had given the Bruins a 20-16 lead in just 1:21, setting off a wild scene which was equal parts agony (USC fans) and ecstasy (incredulous UCLA supporters). If the Bruins could hang on, they would go to the Rose Bowl and USC, despite Garrett's heroics, would stay home.

With just 2:39 to go, Garrett took the kickoff at his 11 and ran it out to the 28. Three plays gained nine yards, but Garrett's dive over left tackle was just short on fourth down and one at the USC 37.

The Bruins took over, and Beban's 27-yard scamper around the right side ended the issue as UCLA ran out the clock, finishing at the Trojan six as the game ended. While the two teams had scored just 13 points in the first three quarters, there were 23 points in the fourth quarter alone as the Bruins beat their crosstown rivals for the first time since 1961 and headed to the Rose Bowl (see Moment 26).

USC's Heisman Trophy winner Mike Garrett runs wild against UCLA in 1965 (above), but Bruin quarterback Gary Beban has the fourth-quarter answers to lead the Bruins to a memorable, come-from-behind victory.

Rose Bowl:
USC 7, Duke 3
January 2, 1939

It was an unlikely ending by a pair of unlikely heroes that allowed USC to win its fifth Rose Bowl without a defeat against undefeated, untied, and unscored-upon Duke.

The 9-0 Blue Devils came to Pasadena to complete their perfect season against an 8-2 Trojan team coached by Howard Jones. With 89,542 watching, a scoreless battle was broken when Duke's Tony Ruffa kicked a 23-yard field goal at the start of the fourth quarter.

USC had moved the ball fairly well, with quarterback Grenville Lansdell gaining 96 rushing yards, but the Trojans were running out of time. With less than two minutes left, Lansdell's pass to fullback Bobby Peoples had USC in good field position again at the Duke 34.

While Braven Dyer of the *Los Angeles Times* drove away from the Rose Bowl toward his office in downtown Los Angeles, he listened to an amazing turn of events on the radio. Doyle Nave, a fourth-string quarterback championed for his passing ability all year long by Dyer, had entered the game. The truth is that Assistant Coach Joe Wilensky faked a telephone call from the Trojan coaches sitting in the press box to have Nave enter the game. Jones didn't stop him, and with reserve end Al Krueger, the Trojans set up shop on the Duke 39. In the confusion while Nave entered the game, USC was hit for a five-yard penalty for delaying the game.

Duke had been playing a "prevent" style of defense, rushing only E. L. Bailey and dropping 10 men into coverage. "Just fade back with the ball and throw it to me when I give you the sign by waving my arms, no matter where I go," instructed Krueger.

Nave's first pass hit Krueger for a 13-yard gain to the 26. A second strike gained nine more to the 17. The third pass lost two yards while the clock ran down to a minute to play.

From the Duke 19, Nave dropped back to the 31 while Krueger ran a stop-and-go pattern against Duke's great all-around back Eric Tipton. As Krueger raced toward the goal line, Nave heaved his last pass of the day into his teammate's arms for the first—and only—touchdown scored against Duke all season. Phil Gaspar kicked the point-after with 40 seconds to play, and USC held on for a 7-3 victory.

Before the game, the rarely used Nave had played only 28 1/2 minutes the entire season, and afterward, he sheepishly asked Trojan Trainer Doc Thurber if he'd win a letter for his Rose Bowl heroics. "Sure," replied Thurber, "and I'm in favor of giving you a whole alphabet!"

USC football coach Howard Jones (top) watches as Duke's Willard Eaves (24) helps to stop USC early in the game (bottom), but Al Krueger's touchdown catch (right) in the gathering darkness gives USC a heart-stopping 7-3 win.

37 Baseball:
Miracle Finish Lifts Angels
October 11, 1986

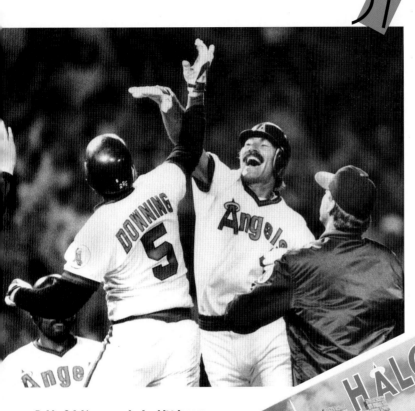

Bobby Grich's game-winning hit triggers this high five with Brian Downing as the Angels come back to win Game 4 of the 1986 ALCS, 4-3, over the Boston Red Sox.

The outcome was obvious. Here were the Boston Red Sox, behind ace right-hander Roger Clemens (24-4 for the year), leading the Angels 3-0 going into the bottom of the ninth inning of the fourth game of the 1986 American League Championship Series.

Clemens had pitched and lost the first game of the series, 8-1, in Boston. But the Red Sox won game two at home and lost a late-inning thriller to the Angels, 5-3 in game three at Anaheim Stadium. Working on three days' rest, Clemens looked overpowering as he mowed down the Angels on just five hits over eight innings.

But the Angels were full of surprises that night, as they had been all season. Although picked for last place, or close to it, prior to the season, California lurched through the first third of the season, sustained by the brilliant play of baby-faced rookie first baseman Wally Joyner. They caught fire once injuries healed enough to reassemble the talented pitching staff of Mike Witt, Kirk McCaskill, Don Sutton, and John Candelaria. In fact, it was Candelaria's return to the mound on June 16 that started the Angels on a brilliant 59-34 (.638) tear, leading to the division-clinching 8-3 win on September 26 against Texas. In all, they won 92 and lost 70 and charged into the ALCS against a Boston team that had won 95 games while losing only 66.

With Clemens on the hill in the ninth inning of game four, the Angels sent up third baseman Doug DeCinces, first baseman George Hendrick (subbing for Joyner), and shortstop Dick Schofield. After taking ball one, DeCinces clubbed the next pitch over the center field fence! Boston 3, California 1.

Hendrick grounded out, but Schofield singled to left, as did catcher Bob Boone. Red Sox Manager John McNamara watched Clemens throw 143 pitches in game one; after 134 in this one, he called for the sensational rookie reliever Calvin Schiraldi (1.41 earned-run average) to face center fielder Gary Pettis, while speedy Devon White ran for Boone.

With two on and one out, Pettis hit a high fly ball deep to left, which Boston's Jim Rice seemed to lose in the Anaheim Stadium lights as it sailed over his head for a double. Schofield scored, and White was on third with the score now 3-2.

Schiraldi walked Ruppert Jones intentionally, loading the bases. This move looked good when second baseman Bobby Grich struck out, but Schiraldi then hit left fielder Brian Downing on the leg. White trotted home with the tying run, and designated hitter Reggie Jackson came to the plate with two out and three on. He grounded to second to end the inning. Neither team scored in the 10th, and Angels Manager Gene Mauch watched his fifth pitcher, Doug Corbett, set the Sox down in order in the 11th. Now it was Schiraldi's turn again.

Reserve catcher Jerry Narron surprised Schiraldi with a leadoff single to right, and Pettis placed a perfect sacrifice bunt to move him to second. Jones was walked again to set up a double play. Grich, who had already struck out three times and was 0-for-5, was next. He lined the first pitch into left field, scoring Narron. The game ended as pandemonium erupted among the 64,223 fans at the Big A.

The Angels took a 3-1 series lead and looked ahead to a possible World Series date with the New York Mets. Although Boston rebounded to win the series 4-3, it did nothing to erase the exhilaration of an impossible comeback against the year's leading pitcher. For one, extra-inning night, the Angels were truly heavenly.

College Basketball Final:
Walton's Near-perfect 44 Defeats Memphis State

March 26, 1973

It was the high point of the college basketball reign of the Walton Gang.

In the NCAA basketball championship game of the 1972-73 season, John Wooden's amazing Bruins captured their seventh straight national title and won their record 75th game in a row, 87-66, over an outmanned Memphis State team coached by Gene Bartow.

A full house of 19,301 at the St. Louis Arena watched as Bill Walton, the 6-11 junior center, made 21 of 22 shots to score 44 points despite playing with four fouls for the last quarter of the game. An ankle injury forced him to leave with 2:51 to play, but the issue was already decided.

The Tigers gave UCLA strong opposition, and the game was tied at halftime at 39. A 1-2-2 zone defense helped keep the game close through the first part of the second half, but Walton and teammates Keith Wilkes (8 of 14 from the floor) and Larry Holyfield (4 of 7) tore up the Tigers, helped by pinpoint passing from Bruin guard Greg Lee, who ended the game with 14 assists.

Walton's 95.5 percent field goal shooting was in sharp contrast to his 2-for-5 free throwing, but he grabbed 13 rebounds and was named the tournament's Most Valuable Player for a second consecutive season. As a collegian, the red-headed Walton's record stood at a perfect 60-0.

Completely forgotten in the excitement over Walton were strong efforts from Larry Finch (29 points) and Larry Kenon (20), but Memphis State's 24-57 (42.1 percent) shooting and miserable rebounding performance from the field doomed them to defeat. The Bruins shot 63.6 percent from the field and outrebounded the Tigers, 40-21.

Beating a legend is sometimes nearly impossible. On reflection, Wooden noted that "this was one of the most cherished of all our championships." After the game, he told assembled reporters, "I think that, maybe, I've never had a greater team, considering both offense and defense."

Defending against a legend proved impossible for Bartow in St. Louis, as it would when he took over for Wooden following the 1974-75 season, in which UCLA won its 10th NCAA basketball crown (see Moment 4).

Opposite: Like medieval knights, these Angels lead the battle for the American League championship against the Boston Red Sox (left to right): reliever Donnie Moore, All-Star first baseman Wally Joyner, third baseman Doug DeCinces, catcher Bob Boone, and All-Star right-hander Mike Witt.

Baseball:
Jackie Robinson Breaks Baseball's Color Barrier
April 15, 1947

There were 26,623 Dodger faithful at Ebbets Field to see the Brooklyn boys win their seasonal opener 5-3 over the Boston Braves. They also saw history made as Jackie Robinson—most recently of the Montreal Royals of the International League after playing at Pasadena City College and UCLA—took the field as Dodger first baseman to become the first African-American to play major-league baseball in modern times.

His career brought honor to him and his team. Robinson was one of the most exciting players on one of baseball's showcase teams, and he won the National League's Most Valuable Player honors in 1949. In his 10 years as a Dodger, his team won six pennants as well as the 1955 World Series.

But those performances came as no surprise to Southern Californians who had followed his early athletic career. His family moved to Pasadena in 1940 when Jackie was one year old. By the time he graduated from Muir Technical High School, he was already known statewide as a great athlete. And at Pasadena Junior College in 1938, his broad jump (as the long jump was then known) of 25-6 1/2 at Claremont on May 7 was the best in the world that year.

So he had high expectations when he entered UCLA in the fall of 1939. Immediately, he took his place as an integral part of the Bruins' best football team to date, winning six, losing none, and tying four. He ranked third in the Pacific Coast Conference in rushing with 514 yards and averaged 12.2 yards per rush, caught six passes for an average gain of 24.2, and returned 14 punts for 281 yards and a 20.1-yard average.

In the winter, Robinson led the basketball team in scoring with 12.4 points per game (best in the PCC's Southern Division), and in the spring he won the NCAA broad jump championship at 24-10 1/4. On the baseball diamond, however, Robinson played poorly, hitting only .097 in the league season.

He was back for more football in 1940, however, and although the Bruins played poorly (1-9), Robinson was outstanding. He ranked second in the PCC in total offense (875 net yards), third in scoring (36 points), third in passing yardage (435), ninth in rushing (440) and second in punt returns (19 for 399 yards, a 21.0 average). He was, essentially, the entire team.

Back for more basketball, Robinson led the PCC's Southern Division in scoring in 1941 with 11.1 points per game on a 6-20 team. He left school in the spring but returned to graduate. He was the only Bruin ever to earn varsity letters in four different sports, with two each in football and basketball.

Robinson entered the army in 1942, was discharged in 1944, and joined the Kansas City Monarchs baseball club in 1945. One year later, he signed to play for the Dodgers' farm club at Montreal and was on his way to the major leagues.

Robinson's great talent and great humanity helped him to break down one of the many color barriers prevalent in segregated America in the 1940s. His fight for civil rights never stopped, and neither will the memories of Robinson, not only as a great baseball player but also as one of the greatest athletes ever to compete in college athletics. Today, UCLA's baseball stadium bears his name, complete with a statue in honor of one of the gutsiest Bruins of them all.

Known primarily for his contributions in baseball, Jackie Robinson is also the most exciting back in the West for UCLA in 1939 and 1940.

Official First Day Cover
Los Angeles Dodgers
Jackie Robinson Stamp

College Football Championship:
Troy's Baker Kicks Irish National Title Hopes, 16-14
November 21, 1931

Knute Rockne was ready to field one of his most powerful Notre Dame teams ever when he was killed in an airplane crash in March 1931. Coaching duties were assumed by Assistant Coach Heartley "Hunk" Anderson, who guided the Irish to a 6-0-1 record by the time USC came to South Bend for the sixth game in the series—all but one of which had been won by Notre Dame.

With a 26-game unbeaten streak behind them, Notre Dame looked to be quite a bit better than the 6-1 Trojans, coached by Howard Jones. And with touchdowns from halfback Marchy Schwartz and fullback Steve Banas, the Irish led 14-0 entering the fourth quarter.

But due to injury, the Trojans had substituted Orv Mohler for Jim Musick, with Mohler playing quarterback and Gus Shaver replacing Musick at fullback. Continuing a drive started late in the third quarter, left end Ray Sparling rushed 13 yards to the one. Two plays later, Shaver ran in for a touchdown. Although Johnny Baker's conversion kick try was blocked, Troy was on the board at 14-6.

On USC's next series, Mohler, Shaver, and an untimely penalty against the Irish put the ball on the Notre Dame 10. Mohler's fake into the line and subsequent pitch to Shaver fooled the Irish defense, and Shaver managed to dive into the corner of the end zone. The conversion left USC trailing 14-13 but with eight minutes still left.

The Trojans got their last chance with two minutes to play. Two key plays—a Shaver-to-Sparling pass for 33 yards and a tackle-eligible pass from Shaver to substitute left tackle Bob Hall that moved the ball to the Notre Dame 18—got USC into position to try for a field goal. Finally, the ball rested on the 15 and Mohler held for Baker, whose 23-yard field goal gave USC a 16-14 lead with a minute to play.

That margin held up, and USC had not only its first-ever victory in South Bend, but a national championship to boot. The team celebrated with the purchase of smart-looking derbies in Chicago and posed for a smug victory photograph on Sunday. Nothing could prepare them, though, for the coming carnival in Los Angeles.

"S.C. Heroes Welcomed by Cheers of 300,000" boomed the headline in the *Los Angeles Evening Herald* on Wednesday, November 25, under the banner heading of "Trojan Madness." A wild parade on Spring Street honored the returning Trojans, who were overwhelmed by the noise, confetti, and streamers that poured out of the office buildings on both sides of the street and from well-wishers who lined the street. Writing in *The Trojan Heritage*, Mal Florence of the *Los Angeles Times* noted quite correctly that "no one in sophisticated Los Angeles has seen anything like it since."

41

Olympic Track and Field:
Bruin Generations Face Off in Tokyo
September 6, 1960

RAFER JOHNSON WINS DECATHLON TITLE

Los Angeles Times
Sports
PART IV

Rafer's Win---Teacher Over Pupil

Otis Davis and Elliott Set Marks

(newspaper clipping — additional articles: "HERE'S THE PITCH — Parseghian Tabs Illinois to Win," "DRYSDALE BLANKS GIANTS IN FINALE," "BOX SCORE," "STANDINGS," "Groat's Wrist Broken by Pitch; Bucs Win, 5-3," "TODAY IN SPORTS")

Ducky Drake (left) and star pupil Rafer Johnson (right) triumph in the 1960 Olympic decathlon, overcoming another Drake pupil, C.K. Yang.

Rafer Johnson, a perfectly proportioned, 26-year-old, 6-3, 200-pound decathlete, already knew success. He had a silver medal from the 1956 Olympic decathlon, and now he was ready to assume the mantle of Olympic champion in the Games of the XVII Olympiad in Rome. At the final Olympic trials, he smashed the world record with his total of 8,683 points.

But bronze medalist Vasily Kuznyetsov of the USSR posed a threat, as did Johnson's good friend C.K. Yang of Taiwan. Both Johnson and Yang attended and trained at UCLA under Bruin Coach Elvin "Ducky" Drake.

Kuznyetsov was held back by injury, and Yang zoomed ahead in the 100 meters, running 10.7 seconds to Johnson's 10.9. And Yang outjumped Johnson, 24-5 3/4 to 24-1 1/2 in the second event, the long jump. But the shot put was Yang's weakness, and Johnson knew it.

Rafer exploded to 51-10 3/4 on his second put, and Yang could only answer with 43-8 3/4. Johnson gained 273 points to be put in front by 143.

Yang kept up the pressure with a 6-2 3/4 high jump to Johnson's 6-0 3/4 and ran the 400 meters in 48.1 seconds to Johnson's 48.3. Yang won four of the five first-day events against his fellow Bruin but trailed by 55 points.

But Johnson crashed through the second hurdle of the 110-meter hurdles to begin the second day, and he staggered home in a horrible 15.3 seconds, losing 193 points as Yang cruised to a 14.6 clocking. Yang led by 138.

Johnson threw the discus a good 159-1, though, gaining ground as Yang threw 130-8, and Johnson retook the lead by 144 points.

Johnson pole-vaulted like never before, setting a personal record of 13-5 1/4 and losing only 122 points to the much-better-vaulting Yang, who cleared 14-1 1/4. Only the javelin and 1,500-meter run remained.

Johnson was a better thrower, but Olympic rules required that they use unfamiliar equipment. He threw 228-10 1/2 to Yang's 223-9 1/2 and held a 67-point lead against Yang, who was a much better 1,500-meter runner. Johnson had to stay within 10 seconds of Yang to win, but Yang's best was 17.3 seconds better than Johnson's.

At 9:20 p.m. they started. Yang was out strongly, and Johnson just hung on, running at a faster pace than he had ever attempted. He staggered on the home straight, but with eyes fixed on Yang, he finished only six meters back in 4:49.7 to Yang's 4:48.5, four-and-a-half seconds faster than his four-year-old best of 4:54.2.

Johnson was mobbed in the locker room, while Yang sat on a nearby bench and wept, alone. "I wavered in the stretch," he said, "but I knew he was as tired as I was. Victory obliterates fatigue."

Yang won seven of the 10 events from Johnson and yet still lost by a score of 8,392 (a new Olympic record) to 8,334 (better than the old Olympic record). He reflected later, "There was nothing I could do. Rafer was the better man . . . I had little or nothing left."

There was little—almost nothing—that separated these two men at the end, and they are still close friends to this day.

Rose Bowl:
USC 18, Ohio State 17
January 1, 1975

The immovable object met the irresistible force when USC and Ohio State got it on in the Rose Bowl for the third year in succession. The Buckeyes were ranked second nationally; USC was fourth. Hence the game had national championship implications, but the issue between the two combatants was more compelling.

USC had capped a perfect, national championship season by throttling OSU 42-17 in the 1973 game (see Moment 51). But Ohio State got revenge in 1974, winning 42-21. Now both teams were ready to prove themselves to be the best in what had grown into an intense New Year's Day rivalry.

The tension was palpable among the 106,721 spectators at the Rose Bowl, as well as on the field. Despite some sloppy play, Ohio State managed a 7-3 lead by halftime and carried that edge into the fourth quarter.

USC quarterback Pat Haden marched the Trojans to a go-ahead touchdown with a nine-yard pass to tight end Jim Obradovich for a 10-7 lead. Then the Buckeyes erupted.

Cornelius Greene led Ohio State on a determined march for a touchdown, sprinting in for the final three yards himself and a 14-10 lead. Then the Bucks recovered a Haden fumble, and Tom Klaban's 32-yard field goal put Ohio State up 17-10 with six minutes still remaining.

USC got the ball back on its 17-yard line. Mixing runs by Allen Carter—who replaced the injured Anthony Davis in the second half—and fullbacks Dave Farmer and Ricky Bell, Haden moved USC to the Ohio State 38. Once there, he launched a rainbowlike pass into the corner of the end zone where J.K. McKay, son of Trojan Coach John McKay, caught the ball and triggered a stadiumwide celebration that rocked the Rose Bowl. But USC still trailed 17-16 with only 2:03 left on the clock.

Now Coach McKay gambled. Rather than kick the point-after for a tie, he tried for a two-point conversion. The entire stadium knew that the play would be a Haden pass for J.K. McKay, who lined up on the right side in tandem with flanker Shelton Diggs. While McKay curled deep into the end zone, Diggs came across the middle, dove, and caught Haden's throw for an 18-17 lead.

Greene, however, wasn't done. Scrambling, running, and improvising, he moved Ohio State to the USC 45, but Tom Skladany's 62-yard field goal try was short as the game ended. Still shaking with emotion as he came off the field, USC's Coach McKay deadpanned, "It was quite a game."

USC coach John McKay savors his team's 1975 Rose Bowl win at top; his son, Trojan receiver J.K. McKay [25], signals victory as Shelton Diggs (on the ground) clutches the two-point conversion pass that won the game.

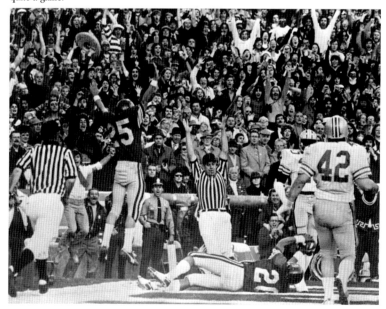

Super Bowl I:
McGee Puts the Hammer on Kansas City, 35-10
January 15, 1967

The inevitable clash of the powers of the National and American Football Leagues came to pass in Los Angeles on a sunny Sunday in 1967. Called the "AFL-NFL Championship Game," it pitted the powerful, bruising NFL champion Green Bay Packers against the wildly entertaining, lightning fast Kansas City Chiefs in the Los Angeles Memorial Coliseum.

The patented Green Bay sweep, here featuring fullback Jim Taylor, and Bart Starr's passes to Max McGee (pictured right), are too much for Kansas City in Super Bowl I.

This was not a meeting of divisional rivals. These were two totally different leagues meeting on the same field for the first time. Even the television rights were split; CBS—as a part of its NFL commitment—carried the game, and so did NBC, the broadcast partner of the AFL.

A curious, but well-below-capacity crowd of 61,946, came to the Memorial Coliseum to see how well Kansas City's Fred "The Hammer" Williamson would do against the Packers. Williamson's nickname came from his trademark clothesline-style tackle using the forearm.

But Vince Lombardi's Packers hung Hank Stram's Chiefs out to dry. Although Green Bay quarterback Bart Starr suffered two sacks on the initial series of the game, he had the Chiefs on their heels quickly. Starting his second series at the Packers' 20, he completed passes to tight end Marv Fleming, running back Elijah Pitts, split end Carroll Dale, and, finally, Max McGee for a 37-yard touchdown and a 7-0 lead. McGee had caught only four passes all year and was better known for breaking curfew than breaking tackles. But when Boyd Dowler was hurt on the first series, McGee stepped up, making a one-handed catch of Starr's pass at the Kansas City 23, and romped into the end zone for the first touchdown of the game.

The Chiefs tied the game at 7-7 and trailed at halftime only 14-10. But on the first series of the second half, Chiefs quarterback Len Dawson's pass intended for tight end Fred Arbanas was intercepted by Packers cornerback Willie Wood, who raced 50 yards to the Kansas City five. One play later, Pitts was in the end zone, and Green Bay led 21-10.

After two Chiefs' series went nowhere, Starr and McGee got going again. Starting with good field position at his 44, Starr mixed runs with passes, throwing to McGee for 11 and 16 yards and, finally, a juggling catch in the end zone for a 13-yard touchdown. Green Bay 28, Kansas City 10.

Starr was named Most Valuable Player for his 16-of-23 passing performance for 250 yards and two touchdowns. McGee caught seven passes for 138 yards and made the cover of *Sports Illustrated*. And Williamson? Starr picked on him often; late in the game, he was knocked out and had to be helped from the field. It was reported that Green Bay offensive guard Fuzzy Thurston looked over the fallen cornerback and hummed the chorus from "If I Had a Hammer."

44

World Series:
Welch Juices Jackson to Save Dodger Win
October 11, 1978

Reggie Jackson put on one of the greatest displays of power hitting in the pressure-packed history of baseball's World Series in 1977, when his three home runs in three swings downed the Dodgers, 8-4. That effort won another World Series for the Yankees, four games to two.

One year later, the scene was almost identical. The Dodgers and Yankees were at it again in the Series, with the Dodgers leading one game to none. Jim "Catfish" Hunter and Burt Hooton faced off, with Jackson tagging Hooton for a two-run double in the third inning to give the Yanks a 2-0 lead.

The Dodgers scratched out a run in the fourth, but Ron Cey hammered a 2-0 delivery from Hunter over the left-center-field wall for a three-run homer and a 4-2 Dodger lead.

Terry Forster took over for Hooton one batter into the seventh, and Jackson's ground-out scored Roy White to close the Dodgers' advantage to 4-3.

Rich "Goose" Gossage relieved Hunter and set the Dodgers down in the seventh and eighth; Forster did the same. Entering the top of the ninth, Forster gave up a single to Bucky Dent, got White to bounce out, and walked Paul Blair on a 3-1 pitch. Then Dodger Manager Tommy Lasorda executed his preconceived plan by bringing in rookie Bob Welch, who had won seven games. Welch's assignment was immense: he was going to face catcher Thurman Munson and then Jackson. Munson hit an 0-1 delivery into center field, but Reggie Smith made the catch for the second out of the inning.

Now Jackson came up and the Dodger Stadium crowd of 55,982 tensed. A rookie against Reggie? "The first pitch I threw him was the one he really had a chance to hit," said Welch afterward. Jackson swung and missed.

Welch's second pitch was high and tight, and Jackson fell away. He fouled on the third pitch, another fastball. "He missed it just enough," said Welch. Two more fast ones produced two more fouls, but the sixth straight fastball was high, for a 2-2 count.

"I was just trying to relax," said Jackson after the game. "I had never seen Welch pitch before, but I knew what to look for. I was looking fastball all the way, thinking I would just try to fight everything else off."

Another fastball was outside for ball three. On the 3-2 pitch, Dent and Blair ran and Welch's 11th straight fastball of the inning flew past Jackson, who swung hard and missed for strike three. YES!

Welch's riveting duel with Jackson had taken just seven minutes, but it seemed an eternity. The Dodgers were up 2-0 but lost the Series in six games. Still, Welch won the respect of baseball players and fans everywhere, and he earned himself a moment in baseball history.

Welch (left) wins this duel with Reggie Jackson in Game 2 of the 1978 World Series, as Dodger catcher Steve Yeager exults after Jackson's miss for strike three.

NBA Finals:
West's Ultimate Clutch Shot
April 29, 1970

Jerry West's Los Angeles Lakers were in yet another championship series. This time, it was against the New York Knicks, who had the Lakers on the ropes at the Forum with the series tied at one game each.

This was a great Knicks team, with Willis Reed at center, supporting forwards Dave DeBusschere and Bill Bradley, and smooth guard play from Walt Frazier and Dick Barnett. But the Lakers were no slouches, with West in his usual unbelievable play-off form (he had once *averaged* 40.6 points a game in the play-offs), and future Hall of Famers Elgin Baylor at forward and Wilt Chamberlain at center.

The Lakers looked to take a two-games-to-one lead at the Forum after a solid first half, when they led the Knicks 56-42. But New York enjoyed spectacular second half performances from Reed, Barnett, and DeBusschere, and they closed the gap to five points by the end of the third quarter. They evened the game at 100-100 with 13 seconds left.

Frazier looked to create a shot from the perimeter but instead found DeBusschere down low, and his short jumper gave the Knicks a 102-100 lead with three seconds left. Out of timeouts, the Lakers had to inbound the ball and take their chances.

Chamberlain tossed the ball into West, who took three dribbles to get by Reed and let fly a 63-footer from near the right sideline, as the buzzer sounded.

SWISH!

The game was tied, 102-102 (this was long before the three-point rule existed in the NBA), and overtime loomed. The Knicks' Reed hit a free throw, and when the Lakers could not respond, Barnett's 15-foot jumper sealed the victory 108-105. West had played all 53 minutes and scored 34 points, but it wasn't enough.

The Lakers lost that series, four games to three, on Reed's seventh-game heroics at Madison Square Garden. West averaged 31.3 points per game for the series and 31.2 points a game for the play-offs. It was another brilliant, if heartbreaking, performance for West, whom Celtics guard Larry Siegfried called "the only guard. They can talk about the others, build them up, but he is the one. He is the master."

Nonetheless, West hungered for a championship. As he continued what would be a 14-year career, all played with the Lakers, he wondered whether he would get another chance to be a champion. He didn't have to wait long for an answer (see Moment 15).

Golf:
Hogan Lives It Up on the Riviera
January 5, 1948

The magnificent Riviera Country Club course has challenged and confounded members, guests, and even the world's finest golfers since it opened in 1927. The design of architect George Thomas was consistently mastered, however, by one of golf's greatest names, Ben Hogan.

Hogan entered the 1947 Los Angeles Open already a past champion, having won at the Hillcrest Country Club course in 1942. After an opening round of one-under 70, he ripped through the course for a five-under round of 66, making four putts of more than 30 feet in length. His final two rounds were both one-over 72s, but his tournament total of 280 (-4) was a course record and an easy winner by three stokes.

He couldn't have been happier when he saw the 1948 tournament schedule. Not only would he be able to return to Riviera to defend his L.A. Open title, but the U.S. Open would be held on the same course.

More than 400 golfers tried to qualify for the 1948 L.A. Open, which necessitated qualifying rounds spread over nine different courses to narrow the field to 150. Not that it made any difference to Hogan. He blistered his competitors from the start, shooting a three-under-par 68 in the first round and then extending his lead with rounds of 70, 70, and a final round of 67 to set another course record of 275, or nine-under-par for the four-round tourney.

Hogan was almost as good at that year's U.S. Open, where his 276 total dispatched Jimmy Demaret and the rest of the field for Hogan's first U.S. Open title. Thanks in part to his two titles at Riviera, Hogan was named as the PGA's Player of the Year for 1948.

After a severe automobile accident almost ended his life, Hogan returned to the Open at Riviera in 1950 and nearly pulled out another victory. His four-round total of 280, which would have won every other Open previously held at Riviera, was equaled by Sam Snead, who won a one-day, 72-76 play-off to take his third Los Angeles Open title. Even in defeat, Hogan showed his rare mastery of one of golf's great courses.

College Football:
Trojans Bring Tears to Irish Eyes, 20-17
November 28, 1964

The Era of Ara had awakened the echoes of Notre Dame's glorious past when the top-ranked, 9-0 Irish came west to face USC in its season finale. A win over the 6-3 Trojans would sew up Notre Dame's first national championship since 1949, and the Irish were favored by a dozen points.

Notre Dame's new coach, Ara Parseghian, had taken a 2-7 squad of the year before and given it new leadership. Most importantly, he had recognized the talent of its players. Quarterback John Huarte was promoted to the first string and responded by directing a quick-strike offense featuring split end Jack Snow. Meanwhile, USC Coach John McKay relied on the running of improving tailback Mike Garrett and the passing arm of quarterback Craig Fertig.

Both teams moved the ball well, but the Irish executed more crisply and took the lead. At the half, the scoring summary showed three entries, all for Notre Dame: a field goal, Huarte's 21-yard touchdown pass to Snow, and Bill Wolski's five-yard touchdown run late in the half for a 17-0 lead. An undefeated season and national championship were within reach for Notre Dame.

Rod Sherman [12] catches Craig Fertig's touchdown pass, giving USC a thrilling 20-17 win over Notre Dame in the first meeting between USC's John McKay and Notre Dame's Ara Parseghian.

But the Irish did not score again. USC scored on its first possession of the second half, as Garrett thundered over from the one-yard line. Troy scored again midway through the fourth quarter when Fertig found wide receiver Fred Hill for a 23-yard touchdown, but the missed conversion left USC trailing, 17-13.

In the meantime, the Irish sputtered. A Huarte third-quarter pitchout went awry and was recovered by USC on its nine-yard line. Early in the fourth quarter, the Irish scored an apparent touchdown from the one, but were penalized for holding.

USC got a last chance when a short Irish punt gave the Trojans excellent field position on the Notre Dame 40 with 2:10 left. Energized by the opportunity, Fertig found Hill for 23 yards and a first down at the Irish 17. Garrett gained two yards on the first down play, but two incomplete passes left USC at the 15 with a fourth down and eight yards to go and just more than 1:30 remaining.

USC's other receiver, sophomore flanker Rod Sherman, then entered the game. He gave the call to Fertig—84-Z Delay—which was designed to let Sherman get open over the middle after a fake to the outside. Irish cornerback Tony Carey fell for the fake, and Sherman caught Fertig's bullet at the three and tumbled into the end zone for the winning touchdown and a 20-17 victory.

Immortalizing the 84-Z Delay in his day-after story in the *Los Angeles Times*, John Hall wrote, "It's the one that beat unbeaten, unbeatable Notre Dame Saturday to climax another dramatic, unbelievable USC [finish] and touch off a mass nervous breakdown at the Coliseum. . . . It's also the play that one day will have the 83,840 stunned spectators telling their grandchildren about the time they saw Craig Fertig pass to Rod Sherman."

Years later, many times that number claim that they were there to see 84-Z Delay and the end of another Notre Dame national championship bid.

50

Rose Bowl:
Wrong-Way Riegels Runs Wreck into Roses
January 1, 1929

California's Golden Bears brought a 6-1-2 record into the 1929 Rose Bowl game against an undefeated and possible national champion Georgia Tech team. The game was scoreless in the second quarter when Tech took over on its own 20-yard line.

Right halfback Stumpy Thomason swept left end but fumbled when hit by California's star back, Benny Lom. The ball bounded into the arms of Cal center Roy Riegels on the 35, who moved toward the Georgia Tech goal line, only to get confused when he turned to elude Thomason and start running toward his own goal.

In the confusion of the play, and the screams of 65,000 fans, Riegels steamed toward his own goal as the Bears blocked expertly, giving him a clear path to . . . a safety? Lom finally got hold of Riegels by the arm at the Cal one-yard line, but Tech end Frank Waddey knocked them down at that point. California had to start from there.

Lom then tried to punt to get the Bears some breathing room, but tackle Vance Maree blocked the kick, and it bounded off Cal quarterback Harold Breakenridge and out of the end zone for a safety and a 2-0 Georgia Tech lead. That's the way the half ended. Tech extended its lead to 8-0 in the third quarter when Thomason scored on a 15-yard touchdown run. Despite freak mishaps like a punt in which the air popped out of the ball—with the referee awarding

the ball at the point where it fell to the ground—California battled back.

Late in the fourth quarter, the Bears finally hit pay dirt. Riegels blocked a Tech punt to give California the ball, starting a drive which culminated in Lom's pass to Irv Phillips for a touchdown. Stanley Barr's conversion was good, but at 8-7, California fell short at game's end.

Cal outgained Georgia Tech, 276-180, and led in first downs, 11-5. But Riegels, who went on to captain the Bears to a very successful 7-1-1 season in 1929, will always be remembered for his 64-yard scamper in the wrong direction. Years later, he used his experience to inspire youngsters: "I gained true understanding of life from my Rose Bowl mistake. I learned you can bounce back from a misfortune. At first it bothered me any time I heard the words 'wrong way,' but it doesn't bother me any more."

As Riegels runs toward his own goal (top), California's Benny Lom runs just as hard to stop him at the California one-yard line. As the correspondent at left so aptly expresses, "[we] . . . saw things you never see but read about."

Rose Bowl:
Sam Bams OSU for 4 TDs as Trojans Win National Title
January 1, 1973

There wasn't any doubt that USC's 11-0 Trojans were looking forward to their New Year's Rose Bowl battle against Ohio State. It was to be the crown on their undefeated season and final claim to the national championship. The Trojans had won their regular season games by an average score of 39-11, and only Stanford had been as close as nine points at the final gun of any game.

But the third-ranked, 9-1 Buckeyes weren't impressed. After shoving the camera of *Los Angeles Times* photographer Art Rogers back into his face during pregame warm-ups, Buckeyes Coach Woody Hayes watched his squad roll up 151 yards rushing and battle USC to a 7-7 halftime score.

But in the second half, USC took advantage of Ohio State's short kickoffs, which were designed to neutralize returns by dangerous sophomore Anthony Davis (see Moment 32). Starting on their own 43, USC mixed runs by Davis with a clutch 23-yard pass by Mike Rae to Lynn Swann on a third-and-17 to position fullback Sam "Bam" Cunningham for a perfectly executed high dive from the two-yard line to put USC ahead, 14-7.

OSU answered with a field goal and then kicked off short to avoid a long return by Davis. USC started with great field position again at its 44 and moments later, Davis ripped off a 20-yard touchdown run that extended Troy's lead to 21-10 and changed the complexion of the game.

The Trojans didn't let up as they began to pile up yardage against the Ohio State defense. Cunningham scored on three straight series that covered 32, 67, and 41 yards, and with scores on their first five possessions of the second half, USC breezed to a 42-10 lead, cementing their national championship season. A late Buckeye touchdown made the final score 42-17, but the largest crowd in Rose Bowl history—106,869—left the Arroyo Seco quite clear about the Trojans' place in history as one of the finest teams of all time.

Asked whether the Trojans were the best team he'd ever played against, Hayes responded, "Yes, I'd say so." The 42 points scored by USC were the most ever against a Hayes-coached club.

The Trojan stars included Davis, who rushed for 157 yards in 23 carries; underrated quarterback Rae, who completed 18 of 25 passes for 229 yards; and receivers Charles Young and Swann, who each had six receptions. How good was this squad? Trojan Coach John McKay, who won four national titles at USC, said later, "I've never seen a team that could beat it."

A familiar and unstoppable sight: Sam (Bam) Cunningham (39) flies into the end zone for another USC touchdown.

College Basketball Final:
Small Bruins Take the Big Trophy against Duke, 98-83
March 21, 1964

A group of very happy Bruins, including Gail Goodrich, Walt Hazzard, Jack Hirsch, and Coach John Wooden (front row, left to right), clutch UCLA's first national basketball championship trophy.

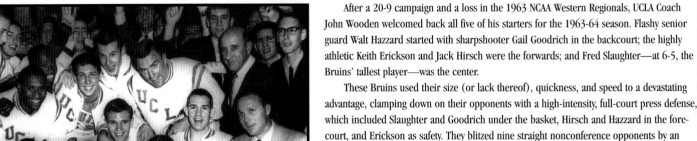

After a 20-9 campaign and a loss in the 1963 NCAA Western Regionals, UCLA Coach John Wooden welcomed back all five of his starters for the 1963-64 season. Flashy senior guard Walt Hazzard started with sharpshooter Gail Goodrich in the backcourt; the highly athletic Keith Erickson and Jack Hirsch were the forwards; and Fred Slaughter—at 6-5, the Bruins' tallest player—was the center.

These Bruins used their size (or lack thereof), quickness, and speed to a devastating advantage, clamping down on their opponents with a high-intensity, full-court press defense, which included Slaughter and Goodrich under the basket, Hirsch and Hazzard in the forecourt, and Erickson as safety. They blitzed nine straight nonconference opponents by an average of 22 points, then ripped through a 15-0 AAWU schedule and finished the regular season with 26 wins in all and a number one national ranking.

The NCAA Western Regionals were held at Corvallis, Oregon, and the Bruins escaped with wins over Seattle University (95-90) and University of San Francisco (76-72) to reach their second Final Four. Two years earlier, a Gary Cunningham-led UCLA team lost to Cincinnati in the national semifinals, 72-70, and the third-place game to Wake Forest, 82-80. Playing in Kansas City this time, the Bruins outlasted Kansas State, 90-84, and qualified to meet third-rated Duke for the national championship. In a performance which epitomized the entire season, the Bruins blew apart a close game in the first half. Mal Florence of the *Los Angeles Times* wrote: "UCLA turned the taller, proud Blue Devils into a jittery, frantic club late in the first half when it scored 16 points without retaliation. The splendid spurt, which consumed 2 min. 33s., left the Bruins with a 43-30 advantage, and they easily held off the disenchanted Devils the rest of the way."

In his 16th year as Bruin coach, Wooden savored his first national championship as the Bruins cruised home with a 98-83 win to cap a 30-0 season. Hazzard was named the tournament's Most Outstanding Player with Goodrich leading the final-game scoring parade with 27. Typical of the team's ability to perform under pressure was the brilliant play of reserve forward Kenny Washington. Entering the game late in the first half, he made 11 of 16 field goal attempts and all four of his free throw tries for 26 points, plus a game-high 12 rebounds.

After the season, the soft-spoken Wooden could barely contain his enthusiasm for what his team had accomplished. "Comparatively speaking, it was the shortest of all NCAA champions," he noted, "but it used the exciting press defense exceptionally well, it was a very colorful and fascinating team, and it was one of the few undefeated teams. It exemplified unselfish team play to a remarkable degree, and it came closer to realizing its full potential than any team I have ever seen."

The dynasty was born.

Football:
The Year of the Ram Indeed!
December 9, 1967

The Rams' Tony Guillory blocks Donny Anderson's fourth-quarter punt, setting up the climactic finish of Los Angeles' improbable 27-24 win.

As the 1967 NFL season started, the vastly improved Los Angeles Rams, led by hyperactive second-year Coach George Allen, dreamed of a division championship and play-off berth. No Rams team since 1955 had done as much, but for Allen, anything seemed possible.

After a 3-0 start, Los Angeles lost to the San Francisco 49ers, 27-24, at the Coliseum, and then tied both Don Shula's Baltimore Colts, 24-24, at Baltimore and Washington at home, 28-28. But the Rams ran off six straight victories after that—including a payback 17-7 win at San Francisco—to stand 9-1-2 after 12 games. The only problem was that Baltimore was 10-0-2, and quarterback Johnny Unitas was having one of his best seasons ever.

The Rams filed into the Coliseum on Saturday morning, December 9, knowing they would have to defeat defending World Champion Green Bay to earn a shot at the Coastal Division title the next Sunday, December 17.

The 9-2-1 Packers were cruising to another Central Division championship behind quarterback Bart Starr, defensive end Willie Davis, and Coach Vince Lombardi. They had won the first NFL-AFL Championship game (later called the Super Bowl; see Moment 43) over Kansas City in the Coliseum, and Starr was ready as he tossed a 30-yard touchdown in the first quarter to split end Carroll Dale.

But the Rams had weapons, too. Quarterback Roman Gabriel found crafty wide receiver Jack Snow in the end zone twice for 16-yard and 11-yard touchdowns, and the Rams took a 17-10 lead on a 23-yard Bruce Gossett field goal in the third quarter. But Packers' rookie Travis Williams returned Gossett's ensuing kickoff from four yards deep in the end zone all the way for a 104-yard touchdown, his fourth kickoff return for a touchdown that season and a new league record. The game was tied.

The Rams responded with another Gossett field goal from 16 yards, but Starr guided the Packers down the field for a go-ahead touchdown late in the final quarter, as Chuck Mercein carried over from four yards to go. Packers 24, Rams 20.

The Packers then held the Rams and regained possession for what looked like the final series with less than two minutes remaining. But the Rams, led by their "Fearsome Foursome" defensive line of Deacon Jones, Merlin Olsen, Roger Brown, and Lamar Lundy, held Green Bay, and Donny Anderson lined up to punt from his 41-yard line with 54 seconds to play.

The Rams gambled, rushing nine men on the line of scrimmage, and Tony Guillory blocked the kick. Safety Claude Crabb picked up the loose ball on the 25 and raced to the five before being hauled down. Now Gabriel had to withstand the pandemonium from 76,637 Coliseum fans and find a way to get Los Angeles a touchdown. He threw his first pass too high, but the incompletion stopped the clock. On second down, he dropped back, faked to running back Tommy Mason, and arched a high pass into the left corner of the end zone for 6-5 receiver Bernie Casey. The ball spiraled perfectly into Casey's waiting arms, well behind the Packers' defense, for a touchdown and an exciting 27-24 win.

Baltimore's easy 30-10 defeat of New Orleans the next day, December 10, meant that their regular-season-ending rematch against the Rams would decide the Coastal Division title. The regular season ended perfectly for Los Angeles, as a Gabriel-to-Snow touchdown of 80 yards on the Rams' first play from scrimmage started a 34-10 rout that gave the Rams a brilliant 11-1-2 record and the Coastal Division title; Baltimore finished with the identical record, but went home empty.

The brilliant season came to an end at Green Bay in the conference semifinals the following week, as the Rams lost 28-7. But nothing could top the miracle finish against the Packers two weeks earlier for sheer drama in a season that the Chinese calendar had properly declared as the Year of the Ram.

54 Super Bowl XXVII:
Dallas 52, Buffalo 17
January 31, 1993

Whether on offense with Kelvin Martin (83) or on defense against Buffalo's passing attack of Jim Kelly to Kenneth Davis (23), Dallas is unstoppable in Super Bowl XXVII.

Although the Super Bowl began its journey to *de facto* national holiday status in Los Angeles in 1967 (see Moment 43), the area's abilities were challenged as never before by the National Football League ownership in 1991.

The owners awarded the right to host the 1993 game to the Los Angeles area. They also told the leadership of the Host Committee that the area's famous indifference could make it the last Super Bowl to ever be held there.

But there was new energy in this effort. For the first time, all of the area's stadiums—Anaheim Stadium, the Los Angeles Memorial Coliseum, and Pasadena's Rose Bowl—had come together under the banner of the Los Angeles Sports Council to offer a unified bid. For the first time, a separate Host Committee was created with responsibility to self-fund the required expenses and bring the area to a fever pitch for the NFL's ultimate game.

When doubting NFL executives and owners arrived, they found 3,500 brightly colored street banners welcoming them and the game. And they found youth clinics; 4-on-4 flag football tournaments; two major golf tournaments; a Punt, Pass & Kick competition; the NFL Experience theme park; a Governor's Dinner; a Media Party at Universal Studios; a giant pep rally called "Touchdown Downtown"; festival and shopping events such as "Pasadena Celebrates" and the "Taste of the NFL"; and much more. An ad hoc Host Committee group had overseen contract distribution to ensure that participation in Super Bowl events had been truly communitywide.

Perhaps the most impressive of its innovations was that the Host Committee had arranged for 750 underprivileged youngsters to attend the game via the novel "Touchdown for Youth" program, with underwriting provided by local corporations.

All of this was produced without public funding, through the sale of 2,500 Host Committee hospitality packages, which included game tickets sold to it by the NFL.

The game? Oh, yes, a triumph for the Dallas Cowboys of the NFC, who defeated the Buffalo Bills 52-17. Led by ex-UCLA quarterback Troy Aikman, Dallas led by 28-10 at the half and 31-17 at the start of the fourth quarter, when they scored 21 more points to make the game a rout.

But the triumph was equally shared by the Host Committee, whose efforts had not only landed the Super Bowl and a $183.8 million economic impact, but earned NFL Commissioner Paul Tagliabue's respect as "the best" Super Bowl ever.

Baseball:
Angels Win the West as Baylor Collects
MVP Trophy

September 25, 1979

Here was the dream ready to come true. As the Angels trotted out to face Kansas City in the 158th game of a 162-game season, they knew they could wrap up the first championship in the club's 19-year history. As a second-year expansion club in 1962, the Angels shocked the American League by being in first place on July 4, but they faded to third overall. They had third-place finishes in the Western Division in 1969 and 1970, and a second-place tie in 1978. But now the crown was at hand.

A big Anaheim Stadium crowd of 40,631 was in attendance, and Frank Tanana did not disappoint them. The tall left-hander pitched a complete game, scattering five hits as the Angels won 4-1 over Craig Chamberlain. Tanana even made the final putout on a toss from first baseman Rod Carew to retire Darrell Porter of the Royals.

A big reason for the Angels' rise was the explosion of designated hitter Don Baylor. In his 10th major-league season, Baylor dominated the American League with 36 home runs and 139 runs batted in (RBI) to go with a .296 average as he played in all 162 games. He led the majors in runs scored with 120 and in runs batted in. Just as important was his leadership in the clubhouse, which reflected his experience and maturity.

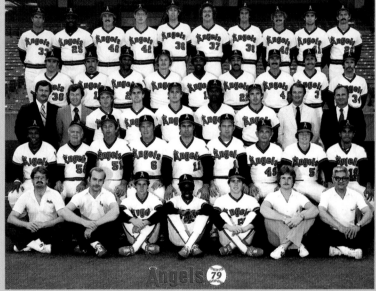

"When I came here in '77, there was no leader," he noted after the season. "It was chaotic; they were changing managers and players all the time."

But Baylor settled down and so did the team. Winter acquisitions of Carew and Dan Ford from Minnesota helped to power the Angel offense, which produced the most runs in the majors, 866. Carew hit .318. Ford scored 100 runs, drove in 101, and hit 20 homers. Bobby Grich hit .294, with 30 home runs, and batted in 101. Willie Aikens had 21 homers. And Brian Downing hit .326 with 12 home runs and 75 RBI. Among the pitchers, Nolan Ryan and Dave Frost both won 16 games, but Mark Clear had 11 wins (and 14 saves), and Jim Barr had 10 as the Angels won the West with an 88-74 record.

It was no surprise when Baylor won the Most Valuable Player award, becoming the first member of the Angels to be so honored. He received 20 of the 28 first-place votes.

Although the Baltimore Orioles won the American League Championship Series in four games, Baylor's home run in the third game helped the Angels on the way to their only win, 4-3. The Angels lost but earned the respect they had sought for so long.

"When people sit down and talk about the good ballplayers," Baylor said later, "I want my name to come up. You spend money, and it goes quickly. Respect lasts a lot longer."

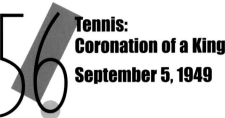

Tennis:
Coronation of a King
September 5, 1949

Richard "Pancho" Gonzales wasn't even a blip on the radar screen of American tennis until 1948. But the 20-year-old, 6-3 right-hander from the east side of Los Angeles rose from 17th in the 1947 rankings to become the youngest U.S. Nationals' champion since 1931. He did so when he battled past four opponents before meeting South Africa's Eric Sturgess in the final and winning an exhausting 6-2, 6-3, and 14-12 match that ended only minutes before darkness would have halted play.

His overwhelming talent impressed the tennis establishment. The Official United States Lawn Tennis Association Guide for 1949 noted, "His unusual size, his suppleness, and the manner in which he smoothly covers [the] court with little apparent exertion is panther-like—repressed power under control."

Even though he was the defending champion, Gonzales was seeded only second for the 1949 tournament, with Wimbledon champion Ted Schroeder (of La Crescenta) seeded first. Gonzales zipped through his first three matches in straight sets, then outlasted Arthur Larsen in five sets in the quarterfinals and two-time Nationals' champion Frank Parker in the semifinals. Gonzales would now meet Schroeder in an all-Southern California final.

But Gonzales had more than pride on the line as he defended his title. Some thought his 1948 win was a fluke, and Schroeder was top-seeded. But if Gonzales won, a lucrative professional contract loomed.

The first set, played in front of a capacity crowd of 13,800, was one of the great battles in tennis history. In a time long before tiebreakers were introduced to the sport, Gonzales and Schroeder battled for an hour and 18 minutes until Schroeder finally broke Gonzales' service in the 33rd game with a controversial shot down the sideline and then held service for a pulsating 18-16 win.

After the exhausting, 204-point opening set, Schroeder continued to win the second set, 6-2, and his victory seemed assured. After all, he had won seven of the previous eight matches against Gonzales.

But the inner strength of the defending champion was now being tested. Gonzales roared back to win the next two sets, 6-1 and 6-2. The fifth set was a matter of desire. In the ninth game, with the set even at 4-4, Gonzales won three of the first four points, Schroeder closed to 40-30, and then let a Gonzales forehand go by, only to see it land fair in the corner. Game to Gonzales, for a 5-4 lead. When Gonzales held his serve, as he had every time in the fourth and fifth sets, he had his second straight title, 6-4.

So much for seedings. Gonzales proved to be one of the enduring greats of tennis, playing brilliantly in the first U.S. Open in 1968 at age 40 and outlasting 25-year-old Charlie Pasarell in a five-set, five-hour, 12-minute match in the 1969 Open.

The final thrill for his home fans came in 1974, when Gonzales won the Pacific Southwest title again, 20 years after his first victory in that tournament. "Somebody had to lose," he said years later, "but I didn't want it to be me."

Basketball:
Abdul-Jabbar Points to the Sky
April 5, 1984

It was oh so familiar. A lob pass into the low post, where the captain of the Lakers swung to the right and arched a soft shot toward the basket.

But when this 14-foot, right-handed skyhook against Utah settled through the basket with 8:52 to play in the game, its author became the greatest scorer in the history of professional basketball. All 18,359 people at the Thomas & Mack Center in Las Vegas came to their feet to honor Kareem Abdul-Jabbar as he surpassed former Philadelphia, San Francisco, and Lakers great Wilt Chamberlain, whose career total of 31,419 points had been considered a difficult assignment for anyone to reach.

But Abdul-Jabbar became the most difficult defensive assignment in basketball immediately upon entering the league in the fall of 1969. In his second of six seasons with the Milwaukee Bucks, he led his team to the 1971 NBA title and topped the league in scoring at 31.7 points per game. He repeated as scoring champion in 1972 (34.8) and was named the league's Most Valuable Player in 1971, '72, and '74 while at Milwaukee.

Abdul-Jabbar could score from anywhere, but especially in the lane with his patented skyhook, as he does at the right, over Rick Robey (8) and Jay Humphries (24) of the Phoenix Suns.

On June 16, 1975, the Lakers and Bucks shocked the basketball world as Los Angeles sent Elmore Smith, Brian Winters, and first-round draft choices Dave Meyers of UCLA and Junior Bridgeman of Louisville to Milwaukee for Abdul-Jabbar and center Walt Wesley. It brought Abdul-Jabbar back to the city of his all-conquering college career at UCLA (see Moment 47) and set the foundation for the great Lakers teams of the 1980s.

Abdul-Jabbar continued his brilliant play, winning MVP honors in 1976, 1977, and again in 1980, when he teamed with rookie Magic Johnson for a second NBA title for himself and the Lakers (see Moment 6). With Abdul-Jabbar at center, the Lakers won a total of five championships. After 20 years in the league, he retired at the end of the 1988-89 season. In all, he had scored 38,387 points, nearly 7,000 more than Chamberlain's second-place total, in an amazing 1,560 games—the most games played of any NBA player in history.

As a Bruin, as a Buck, or as a Laker, the 7-2 Abdul-Jabbar was unique, as was his patented skyhook, which will forever be burned into the collective memory of basketball fans everywhere as perhaps the game's most unstoppable weapon.

58 Olympic Gymnastics: Only You, Mary Lou!
August 3, 1984

At 4-9, it's hard to call Mary Lou Retton a giant. But that's how she stood at UCLA's Pauley Pavilion after winning a dramatic duel with Romania's Ecaterina Szabo in the women's all-around competition at the 1984 Olympic Games.

The 16-year-old Retton had been brilliant in the team all-around and led all competitors by 0.15 points going into the final all-around session. But Szabo, a calm and elegant competitor, scored a perfect 10 on her first event, the balance beam, while Retton had to settle for a 9.85 on the uneven parallel bars. After one event, they were tied.

The race for the gold was clearly going to be settled by these two alone. Szabo poured on the pressure, scoring a brilliant 9.95 with an error-free floor exercise routine, but Retton could manage only a 9.8 on the beam. Advantage Szabo, by 0.15.

Szabo's vault was well received and scored 9.9, but Retton was now in one of her favorite events, the floor exercise. Tumbling with a vigor that is hard to comprehend from one so small, Retton's acrobatics—and what one writer called "a smile that revealed what must have been hundreds of the whitest teeth you ever saw"—held the capacity crowd of 9,023 and the judges enraptured for a perfect score of 10.00. Only 0.05 separated first and second place, with one event left.

Szabo was first to go, on the uneven parallel bars, but her dismount included a small hop and a small deduction: 9.9. Now Retton had her destiny in her hands: a 9.95 on the vault would produce a tie; a perfect 10.00 would give her sole possession of the all-around gold medal.

Retton's speed was evident as she dashed down the runway, struck the takeoff board, and executed a Full Twisting Tsukahara, landing solidly— without a hop—on the Pauley Pavilion floor.

"Little Body, we did it!" screamed her coach, ex-Romanian Bela Karolyi, who had trained Nadia Comaneci and had started Szabo's rise to world class. The crowd exploded with approval. The judges agreed, posting a score of 10.00 that brought Retton the ultimate prize, by 5/100ths, 79.175 to 79.125.

"I knew the takeoff was good," Retton said afterward, "and I knew the vault was good. And I knew I'd stick it.

"I guess I work best under pressure."

Johnnie Morton's touchdown catches, like this one in front of Dion Lambert (26), prove decisive for USC.

College Football:
USC 45, UCLA 42

November 17, 1990

Unlike so many of the matches between the UCLA and USC football teams, this game did not determine national, conference, or Rose Bowl honors. But the 60th renewal of the crosstown series may have been the most entertaining of them all.

The 7-2-1 Trojans were led by colorful sophomore quarterback Todd Marinovich. The 5-5 Bruins had found new energy in freshman quarterback Tommy Maddox.

Maddox opened the game with two touchdowns, the first to Trojan cornerback Stephon Pace for 27 yards and then a scramble for a nine-yard score. When Marinovich finally got his hands on the ball, he drove the Trojans to a go-ahead score when tailback Mazio Royster dove in after a seven-yard run. Back and forth they went; by the start of the final period, the scoreboard showed USC ahead 24-21.

But Maddox was only warming up. He pitched another interception, returned for a 34-yard touchdown by USC cornerback Jason Oliver with 12:02 to go. USC 31, UCLA 21. Five plays later, he threw a 29-yard touchdown strike to flanker Scott Miller. USC 31, UCLA 28 with 10:46 to play. Four plays later, he got another chance and bombed the Trojans with a 38-yarder to Miller with 9:17 to go. The conversion gave the Bruins a 35-31 lead.

The gigantic Rose Bowl crowd of 98,088 began screaming when Marinovich found split end Johnnie Morton from 21 yards out for a 38-35 lead with just 3:09 left. Maddox's response: passes to Miller (for 29) and split ends Reggie Moore (14 and 11) and Sean LaChapelle (9), all leading to Kevin Smith's one-yard dive. UCLA 42, USC 38.

But 1:19 remained and Marinovich started a final drive at his own 25. On third down and seven from his 28, he found the magic: 27 yards to Gary Wellman over the middle, then another 22 yards to Wellman to bring the ball to the UCLA 23. After a time-out, he threw a perfect pass to the far corner of the end zone and the glue-fingered hands of Morton for a touchdown and a wild on-field celebration. At the end: USC 45, UCLA 42.

Said Marinovich: "I was getting tired of hearing that UCLA fight song. I just wanted to shut them up. I never get tired of our fight song." He who played last had won.

60

Olympic Track and Field:
The One-Woman Show
August 4, 1932

In his marvelous book, *Track's Greatest Women*, Jon Hendershott of *Track & Field News* reported a quote from a member of the U.S. women's track-and-field team from the 1932 Olympic Games in Los Angeles: "Babe thinks she is the whole show, the star attraction—and, of course, she is."

Mildred Didrikson, a slight 21-year-old from Port Arthur, Texas, was the Babe. She captured the nation's fancy during the Games of the X Olympiad. A natural athlete, she only took up track and field in 1930 and first heard of the Olympic Games in 1931. By 1932, she was full of fury. She entered eight events in the National AAU Championships in Evanston, Illinois, that also served as the U.S. Olympic Trials.

Didrikson won the 80-meter hurdles, shot put, javelin, and baseball throw outright, tied Jean Shiley for the high jump title, and placed fourth in the discus. She made no impact in the 100 or 200 meters but won the team championship for her employer, the Employer's Casualty Insurance Company of Dallas.

At the Games she was in full flower. On the first day of competition, she won the javelin with a throw of 143-4, which was incorrectly reported at the time as a world record. "Mildred (Babe) Didrikson, 128 pounds of feminine dynamite, came through yesterday when all competitors of the so-called stronger sex failed in their world-record wrecking attempts" was the story line in the *Los Angeles Times*.

She tied the world record of 11.8 in the heats of the 80-meter hurdles, then lined up for the final on Thursday, August 4. Her teammate Evelyne Hall got out best, but Didrikson closed at the tape and the two crossed together, both timed in a new world record of 11.7. The judges awarded Didrikson the victory and Hall the silver medal in a decision which Hall contested to her final days more than 60 years later. "Babe had so much publicity it was hard to rule against her," she noted. "I do know, though, that I had a welt on my neck for a week from the finish string when I broke it."

Didrikson was the toast of Los Angeles. She bemoaned the limit of three events per person, but three days later she was in the Coliseum again for her final competition, the high jump.

Shiley was the fourth-place finisher in the 1928 Games in Amsterdam and the cofavorite. Both cleared 5-1 on their first tries, then an Olympic Record of 5-3 and then both equaled the world record at 5-3 3/4. The bar was raised to a new world mark of 5-5 and Shiley cleared on her first try, while Didrikson cleared on her second. Eva Dawes of Canada had settled for the bronze medal at 5-3, but the Babe and Shiley were still at it. The rules at that time looked only to height and not to which trial was successful. So they proceeded to another world record height of 5-6 1/4, and as both missed three times, a jump-off was arranged at 5-5 3/4.

Shiley cleared on her trial, as did Didrikson. But the judges ruled that her head had led the rest of her body over the bar, a violation known as "diving" at the time, and Shiley was awarded the gold medal. No one had ever taken exception to Didrikson's jumping style until that moment, but the decision was final. Asked later if she knew her technique was illegal, she replied, "Nope."

But the Babe had two gold medals and a silver and achieved a feat that may never be duplicated: she won Olympic medals in the same Games in a running event, a jump, and a throw.

61 Football:
Dickerson Runs past Simpson into Record Books
December 9, 1984

In 1983 former USC football Coach John Robinson joined the Los Angeles Rams as head coach. Not coincidentally, Eric Dickerson of SMU joined the Rams as a first-round draft choice at running back and second pick overall. Robinson was well known for his fondness for slashing, tireless running backs from his days as Trojan headmaster. In the 6-3, 218-pound Dickerson, he found the perfect vehicle to help push the Rams back toward the top of the National Football League's Western Division. When Dickerson gained 1,808 yards in his rookie season, another goal came into view: O.J. Simpson's single-season record of 2,003 yards, set in 1973.

Dickerson started brilliantly, gaining 138 yards against Dallas in the season opener, then 102 against Cleveland in a 20-17 win at Anaheim Stadium. He had only three games under 100 yards and big days against New Orleans (175 yards), St. Louis (208), and Tampa Bay (191). After 14 games, he had piled up 1,792 yards, 211 short of the record, as the Rams got ready to face Houston at home in front of 49,092 fans.

Most observers thought Dickerson would have to try for the record breaker at San Francisco in the final game of the season, but by halftime, he already had 106 yards as the Rams raced to a 17-3 lead and a 20-13 halftime advantage.

The Oilers brought the score to 20-16 at the end of the third quarter, but Dickerson was still charging. Midway through the fourth quarter, he carried for the 25th time, and his two-yard advance gave him 200 yards for the game. More importantly, he slipped into the end zone at the end of a six-yard run three plays later, giving the Rams a comfortable 27-16 lead with less than six minutes to play. Dickerson had 1,998 yards, and everyone—including the Oilers—knew it.

While the frenzied crowd and the Rams offensive line yelled at the defense to give Dickerson some more chances, Houston gained 22 yards in the next three plays as the clock ran below four minutes. But Warren Moon's long pass for Herkie Walls was intercepted by Rams safety Vince Newsome at the five and returned to the 36. Dickerson would have his chance.

The play call was for 47-gap, a classic sweep. Off the snap, center Doug Smith, right tackle Bill Bain, right guard Dennis Harrah, and tight end David Hill held their opponents in place, while Irv Pankey and Kent Hill pulled from left to right, opening the hole for Dickerson, who ran out of a one-back set. The man in the number 29 uniform dashed through the hole, broke outside, and gained nine yards to the 45. He had 215 yards for the day—his best ever as a professional—and a record-breaking 2,007 for the season.

"It's fantastic," he said afterward, "but I'm glad it's over." After being mobbed by his teammates and ending a self-imposed media blackout, Dickerson went back to running and winning, as the Rams posted their best record (10-6) in five seasons. At the end, Dickerson had piled up 2,105 yards in 379 carries, with the promise of many more yards to come. Most agreed with Harrah's postgame assessment: "There's no telling what this man can do."

Golf:
Venturi's Final-Round Surprise Wins L.A. Open
January 11, 1959

Art Wall was having a career year in 1959. He would win the Bing Crosby National and the Masters, and he looked like the winner of the 1959 Los Angeles Open. After three rounds, that is.

Wall charged into the lead with his second straight 68, after opening with a par 71 on the 6,827-yard Rancho Park municipal course. He was well behind first-day leader Johnny Bulla, the 1941 champion, who shot a 64. But his three-under second-day round closed the gap, and at the halfway point, Wall stood at 139, just four shots back of the leader, Doug Sanders, who had shot 135.

With a three-round total of 207, Wall was six under par but was in a scramble with Sanders (208), Billy Maxwell (209), Tommy Bolt (210), and Mike Souchak (210) for the lead.

Ken Venturi, who had won four PGA Tour events in 1958, was expected to contend for the title but had shot indifferently during the first three rounds. His one-over first round of 72 was followed by a par 71 on Friday and another 72 on Saturday. At 215 (+2), he was well back of the leaders.

But he was on fire on Sunday. By the time he shot consecutive eagles on the eighth and ninth holes, he had turned the front nine in a six-under-par 30, which brought him to four-under for the tournament. He continued his hot shooting with three more birdies on the back nine and a bogey on the 12th hole. His eight-under-par round of 63 was the best ever in the final round of the tournament and put him in the clubhouse at a six-under 278.

Ken Venturi is honored for his memorable 1959 triumph with a color portrait on the cover of the 1995 Nissan Open program (opposite).

Wall and the rest of the leaders became chasers, but they couldn't match Venturi's magic. Wall's final round was a two-over 73; Sanders shot 74; Bolt and Souchak, 73; and Venturi won by two shots to Wall's 280.

The 27-year old Venturi won his seventh Tour title and took home $5,300 while Wall collected $3,400, with Maxwell claiming $2,200 for third (281), with Sanders fourth (282, $1,900), and Bolt, Souchak, Paul Harney, and Al Geiberger tying for fifth at 283 ($1,533.33 each).

In 1995, 36 years after his L.A. Open triumph, Venturi was honored at the Open for his remarkable final round charge in one of the most unpredictable Opens ever.

63
Olympic Diving:
McCormick Double Good for Double Gold
December 7, 1956

Pat McCormick was worried. The defending double Olympic diving champion was trailing teammate Juno Irwin with only two dives remaining in the platform competition of the 1956 Olympic Games in Melbourne, Australia. Both attempts would have to be near perfect.

But the 5-4 McCormick, a Long Beach native, was used to challenges. As a 22-year-old in Helsinki four years earlier, she dove brilliantly to win both the springboard and platform titles, bringing the gold medals back to the Los Angeles Athletic Club. Now married and a mother of one, she was trying to duplicate the feat and become the first diver to win both events in two successive Games. She bore her son, Timothy, eight months prior to the Games but continued training until two days prior to giving birth.

That kind of determination brought her another gold in the springboard competition. She easily outclassed the other 16 competitors and piled up a 142.36 to 125.89 advantage over silver medalist and U.S. teammate Jeanne Stunyo.

But the platform was another matter. McCormick was only fourth in qualifying, 1.68 points behind the surprise leader, Paula Jean Myers of the U.S. (and USC and Glendora), and two Soviet divers. The four-dive totals from the preliminary round carried over into the final session, where each diver had two final tries.

When McCormick climbed the platform for her fifth effort overall and her first of the finals, she also knew she would have to overtake a brilliant fifth-dive effort of Irwin, also of the U.S., also from Southern California (Glendale), and a mother of three. Irwin was the bronze medalist in Helsinki four years earlier, competing while three and a half months pregnant with her second child. Now, she mastered her fifth try and scrambled into the lead.

But McCormick's last two dives were special. She had chosen a two-and-a-half somersault for her fifth dive and executed it perfectly, a feat which moved her into a precarious lead. Then she nailed her final effort, a one-and-a-half somersault with full twist, to seal the victory, 84.85 to 81.64, over Irwin. Myers came in third at 81.58 to complete an American and Southern California sweep.

"I knew I had to do those last two dives better than I ever did before," said McCormic to reporters afterward. "I guess I did. They were my best—and my last." With that, McCormick retired from competitive diving at age 26, with four gold medals and more than 30 national diving championships, and leaving a legacy that would be hard to match—for achievement or for grace under pressure.

64

College Track and Field:
UCLA 75, USC 70
May 3, 1975

The intensity of exertion, struggle, and sheer force of will that has marked virtually any competition between UCLA and USC was never demonstrated more vividly, or with greater flair, than in the 1975 UCLA-USC dual track-and-field meet.

The combination of world-class talent, the feverish recent history of their dual battles, and the raw fervor of this crosstown competition combined to set the stage for the most remarkable local meet ever.

Drake Stadium filled with a record 15,069 fans, and the fire marshal closed the gates. At least 2,500 more lined the fence along the back straight to watch the meet.

The fans saw USC's 1972 Olympic long jump champion Randy Williams soar 25-3 1/2, only to be beaten by Bruin freshman Willie Banks (26-2 1/4 wind-aided), whose mother, Georgia, had to watch from the back-straight fence.

The Trojan 440-yard relay team of Guy Abrahams, Mike Simmons, Ken Randle, and James Gilkes steamed to a world-leading 39.1 clocking. Randle then upset Bruin legend Benny Brown in the 440, 45.1 to 45.2. Next, Gilkes sprinted 100 yards in 9.3 and won the 220 in 20.4, while Brown (20.6) took revenge on Randle (20.6).

As the meet wound down, the Bruins clung to a 71-69 lead with only the last round of the triple jump and the mile relay left. USC had the better relay team, especially with Brown exhausted after running in three events already. Banks stood third in the triple jump and, entering the final round, knew that to give his team points to win, he would have to move up to second and jump seven inches better than his lifetime best of 53-2.

As USC's leading duo of Tom Cochee (54-3 wind-aided) and Don Bryson (53-9) looked on, Banks readied. Suddenly, cheerleaders led the U-C-L-A 8-clap, the band played the Bruin fight song, and the crowd roared as the 6-2, 190-pound freshman charged down the runway . . . and hopped, stepped, and jumped . . . .

55-1! A new personal, meet, stadium, and school record. More importantly, the jump won the meet, as Banks was carried aloft on the shoulders of delirious teammates.

USC won the mile relay in a school record 3:07.2 after a spent Brown fell on the final straight. It was the last measure of emotion; as Bruin Coach Jim Bush said later, "USC was just as good as we were, but I'll take it. This has to be the greatest dual meet ever held." It was and still is.

Track and Field:
Barriers Fall for Bannister . . . and O'Brien
May 8, 1954

The four-minute mile and the 60-foot shot put. These were two of the "unbreakable" barriers in track and field, magical marks which would never be reached.

Roger Bannister ended the mile watch with his 3:59.4 effort at Oxford on May 6, while the shot record stood at 59-9 3/4, a record set by Parry O'Brien at the Drake Relays in Des Moines, Iowa, on April 24.

But while Bannister planned his attack on the record with the cooperation of friends Chris Brasher and Chris Chataway, O'Brien—already the Olympic champion from 1952—was watching his back nervously.

That's because in a meet at Asbury Park, New Jersey, on May 1, Stan Lampert had put the 16-pound ball 59-5 7/8, dangerously close to O'Brien's world standard and the first 60-foot shot put he had been dreaming of for four years.

So O'Brien came home to compete in his favorite event. The occasion was a special shot put competition added to the USC vs. UCLA dual meet scheduled for the Los Angeles Memorial Coliseum on Saturday, May 8.

His first try was a foul, but he used the glide-and-explode technique he had invented to launch the ball into the air—and watched it land at 60 feet, 5 1/4 inches, the first 60-foot put in history. O'Brien and Bannister had done the "impossible" in two events on two continents in less than two days.

Two weeks later at the Coliseum Relays on May 21, O'Brien extended his world record to 60-5 3/4 and then rewrote the event's history at the Southern Pacific AAU Championships on June 11—also at the Coliseum—with world records of 60-6 and 60-10. At the end of his short 1954 season, he had set five world records and owned the top 10 throws ever.

From his freshman year at USC in 1950 until his retirement after the 1967 season, O'Brien set the standard by which all shot putters must be measured. He competed on four U.S. Olympic teams, winning the gold medal in 1952 and 1956, the silver in 1960, and fourth in 1964, at age 32. He set 16 world records in all, but he will always be known as the man who reached beyond the 60-foot barrier.

66 Track and Field:
The World's Fastest Human
April 23, 1921

A French physician with a keen eye for athletics, Berlin de Coteau, examined the world-record holder for 100 yards and reported: "His chest is round, and his shoulder blades are too prominent. He has defective nasal respiration and breathes through his mouth most of the time.

"He is plainly fat. . .A racing horse would not be considered in condition if he carried such excess weight. But [his] arms and shoulders remind one of a 40-year-old matron in décolleté. In short, I have never seen any sprinter so poorly set up for speed. But, nevertheless, he is the fastest man in the world."

You got it right, doc. Charley Paddock was the original "World's Fastest Human" and proved it in a remarkable afternoon in Redlands, California.

USC's Paddock zipped down the straight in a combined 100-yard/100-meter race. Then, according to Maxwell Stiles of the *Los Angeles Examiner*, "15 feet from the tape, Paddock gave a mighty bound and fairly flew over the finish line [of the 100 yards] two yards ahead of [Vernon] Blenkiron. He came down heavily. Recovering, he took two quick strides, and leaped for the tape at 100 meters.

"Two such leaps as these made it appear that the boy must have wings or a kangaroo hoof."

Regardless of how his feet were configured, Paddock equaled the world 100-yard record of 9.6 seconds and set a new 100-meter world record of 10.4 seconds.

Later that afternoon, Paddock ran a four-distance race over 300 meters with finish tapes set at 200 meters, 220 yards, 300 yards, and 300 meters. Totally unpressed by any other competitor, he finished the 200 and 220 in 21.5 seconds, and then set world records of 30.2 for 300 yards and 33.2 for 300 meters. He had set three world records and tied a fourth in the space of 43.6 seconds. At the time, his 200-meter mark was incorrectly believed to also be a world record.

Stiles reported that at the end, "pulling with eyes half shut and mouth open, he passed the finish line and fell in a heap into the arms of waiting friends. . . .

"To break one record is to make history. To break four in one day is to crystallize it." And Paddock did, earning forever his place in history as the "World's Fastest Human."

67
College World Series:
Unbelievable Trojan Comeback Just Part of the Dedeaux Tradition
June 12, 1973

Minnesota pitcher Dave Winfield, the Most Valuable Player of the 1973 College World Series, walked to the mound for the ninth inning of a final-series game against USC. The Golden Gophers were leading 7-0. Winfield had 15 strikeouts but had also thrown 168 pitches. The Trojans were unbeaten up to this point in the double-elimination College World Series, but they were looking at their first loss unless something miraculous happened.

USC had the pitcher's spot up first and pinch hitter Ken Huizenga singled, followed by Creighton Tevlin's force-out. But Rich Dauer, Fred Lynn, and Ed Bowman singled, and Winfield left the game, leading 7-3 with one out and one on.

Four singles and a passed ball led to a 7-6 score as Marvin Cobb went in to run for pinch hitter Dennis Littlefield. A Huizenga sacrifice fly was the second out of the inning, but catcher Ed Putnam scored to tie the game. With Tevlin now up again and facing the third Gopher pitcher of the inning, Gordon Peterson, Cobb stole second and came home on Tevlin's single to bring the Trojans all the way back, and more, for an improbable 8-7 victory.

"That's a good example of Trojan tradition," said USC baseball Coach Rod Dedeaux afterward. It was a tradition which he was primarily responsible for.

The Trojans squeezed past Arizona State the next night, 4-3, to win their fourth College World Series title in a row. First baseman Daryl Arenstein knew why: "We've had good hitting and defense, but the biggest difference is that we have the greatest coach in the world. Whoever is second best isn't even close."

Dedeaux's success was dynastic. He played at USC from 1933 to 1935, then won his first national title at USC as a co-coach with Sam Barry in 1948. Then he won on his own in 1958, 1961, 1963, 1968, five times in a row from 1970 to 1974, and a final title in 1978.

In 45 seasons, Dedeaux-coached teams had winning records in 41 and enjoyed 37 winning seasons in a row from 1954 to 1981. They played in 17 College World Series and won or shared in 28 conference championships. Dedeaux won 1,332 games as a Trojan coach, losing only 571, with 11 ties.

The quality of his work is also illustrated by the dozens of major-league baseball players his program produced. Big league stars including Don Buford, Rich Dauer, Ron Fairly, Randy Johnson, Steve Kemp, Don Kingman, Fred Lynn, Mark McGwire, Hall of Famer Tom Seaver, and Roy Smalley all played for, and learned from, Dedeaux. First baseman Arenstein, the first player ever to start on four consecutive national championship teams, was absolutely right about the remarkable record of USC's coach; no one else is even close.

Marvin Cobb scores the winning run in USC's unbelievable 8-7 victory over Minnesota in the 1973 College World Series as Rich Dauer [24] celebrates. The win is another triumph for long-time Trojan Head Coach Rod Dedeaux (right).

College Football:
Davis Finally Recognized
December 3, 1946

It's hard to say that a college football player "deserved" the Heisman Trophy, the sport's greatest honor. But Glenn Davis clearly did, and in 1946, he finally and fittingly received the honor.

He was "Mr. Outside" on a two-time national championship team at the U.S. Military Academy at West Point, N.Y. Originally from Claremont and Bonita High School, Davis attended Army during the difficult World War II years from 1943 to 1946. Because of the skill of Coach Earl "Red" Blaik, Army dominated college football. And Davis dominated the Army team.

Davis was allowed to play as a freshman because of the manpower shortage due to the war, and he gained 634 rushing yards on 95 carries (a 6.7 average!) and scored eight touchdowns. But he blossomed as a sophomore, winning consensus all-American honors in 1944. His performance bordered on the incredible, averaging 11.5 yards per carry. He gained 667 yards on just 58 carries, scored 20 touchdowns to lead the nation in scoring, passed for two touchdowns, and caught four. He finished second in the Heisman balloting to Ohio State's Les Horvath. Army won its first national title with a 9-0-0 record and, more importantly, defeated Navy, 23-7, for Army's first win after five straight losses to the Middies.

Davis was even better in 1945. He again led a 9-0-0 Army team to the national championship. He gained 944 yards rushing in 82 tries, again an 11.5 yards-per-carry average. He scored 108 points on 18 touchdowns and passed for two touchdowns. In the Heisman balloting, he finished second again, this time to teammate Felix "Doc" Blanchard, known as "Mr. Inside," who gained 718 yards rushing and scored a nation-leading 19 touchdowns and 115 points.

When the 1946 season opened, the nation braced for the return of wartime veterans and the showdown between Army and a re-energized Notre Dame team under the direction of new coach Frank Leahy. Army stomped seven consecutive opponents and met the 5-0-0 Irish at Yankee Stadium in New York before 74,121 spectators on November 9. Both teams were brilliant, but the game ended in a 0-0 tie, the first blemish on Army's record after 26 consecutive wins. Both finished unbeaten: Army at 9-0-1 and Notre Dame at 8-0-1, but Notre Dame was voted the nation's best team, with Army second. It was the end of an era, as Davis and Blanchard closed out their Army careers with a 21-18 win over Navy. Davis' pass to Blanchard from 26 yards out in the second quarter provided the winning points.

Davis' statistics were not as stunning as in previous seasons, although they were still sensational by any standard. He gained 712 yards in 123 carries (5.8 average), threw four touchdown passes, caught 20 passes for 348 yards and five touchdowns, and had five interceptions on defense. But he was voted the Heisman Trophy as the nation's finest player, for 1946 and for the years before. No one else had ever finished *second* twice and then won the trophy in three consecutive years. Blaik summed it up best when he wrote, "Anybody who ever saw Davis carry a football must realize there could not have been a greater, more dangerous running halfback in the entire history of the game."

Don't look so glum, Glenn. You're the 1946 Heisman Trophy winner!

Following the 1984 NCAA championship, UCLA's Al Scates (above, at far right) shows the victory sign for his 11th NCAA volleyball title as coach of the Bruins. The Bruin reign of four straight titles in the early 1980s is helped by all-Americans like Karch Kiraly (right, 31) and Doug Partie (opposite, 20).

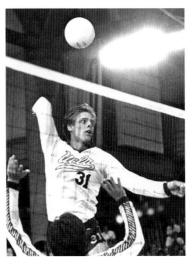

College Volleyball Championship: Bruin Magic Rubs Off on America's Gold Medal Spikers

May 5, 1984

Winning championships is the hallmark of Al Scates' UCLA volleyball program. It's hard to comprehend that his Bruins have *continuously* dominated U.S. collegiate volleyball since the inception of UCLA's program in 1970. But it's true.

As the 1984 Olympic Games (see Moment 2) neared its opening in Los Angeles, Scates and his Bruins rocketed to a new level of brilliance.

In 1982 team catalyst Karch Kiraly, a senior, made his fourth straight all-American team, leading the Bruins through an undefeated season and into the NCAA Championship match against Penn State on the Nittany Lions' home floor. Kiraly and his all-American teammates Doug Partie and Dave Saunders were much too good, and they spanked the home team in straight sets, 15-4, 15-9, and 15-7, to finish a 29-0 season and achieve a second consecutive championship for UCLA.

Could a new core of all-American players bring another NCAA title in 1983? Not to worry: the 27-4 campaign produced four first-team all-Americans, including Steve Gulnac, Ricci Luyties, Partie, and Reed Sunahara . . . and another title. This time Pepperdine fell in straight sets, 15-10, 16-14, and 15-7.

In 1984 UCLA looked for a fourth straight title, this one to be decided at Pauley Pavilion in May, just two months before the Olympic Games would begin. The Bruins were awesome and were paced by first-team all-Americans Luyties, Partie, and Asbjorn Volstad, as well as second-teamer Sunahara. Before a raucous crowd of 9,809, they overcame a very good Pepperdine team in the final, 15-11, 15-13, 16-18, 15-12, and Sunahara had 17 kills, Luyties had 16, and Partie and Volstad had 14 each. A sensational 38-0 season was in the books as the season ended.

On August 11 another familiar team stood on the top of the victory platform at the Long Beach Arena to receive gold medals symbolic of the Olympic championship. The United States team had defeated Brazil, 15-6, 15-6, and 15-7, in an hour and 19 minutes to win its first Olympic tournament. There, receiving their medals, were Kiraly, Saunders, and 1978-1979 Bruin all-American Steve Salmons, still in championship form.

The Bruins provided the core of the 1988 Olympic squad as well, as Kiraly and Saunders were joined by teammates Partie and Luyties. The Americans won seven consecutive matches and breezed to their second consecutive Olympic triumph. With so many Bruin stars on the team, what else could be expected . . . but continuing dominance?

College Track-and-Field Championship:
Bruins Graduate to Bush's League
June 9, 1973

UCLA's dignified, quotable, and forthright track-and-field coach, Jim Bush, was determined to be remembered for more than dropped relay batons.

His Bruins defeated perennial NCAA champion USC for the first time in track and field in 33 tries in 1966, later winning the school's second NCAA track-and-field championship. But as the 1970s opened, his luck was ebbing.

Injury, misfortune, and especially dropped passes in the 440-yard relay kept the Bruins out of the winner's circle at the 1968 and 1969 NCAA meets, but they did win the mile relay at the 1969 and 1970 meets. By 1971 Bush's assembly of a team that could not—and would not—be beaten was complete.

Quarter milers Wayne Collett and John Smith were dominant; sprinter Warren Edmonson was a sure national scorer; and jumpers Finn Bendixen (long jump), Denny Rogers (triple jump), James Butts (triple jump), and Francois Tracanelli (pole vault) were all going to be high scorers. And they would win the mile relay again.

The Bruins rolled up 52 points, casting aside USC, which scored 41. In addition to winning the mile relay for the third year in a row, Smith won the 440-yard dash, Bendixen was third, Rogers and Butts went 3-4, and Tracanelli was second.

In the Olympic year of 1972, Bush guided one of the most powerful collegiate teams ever seen. In addition to an undefeated dual meet season, 12 individual Bruins, including champions Edmonson (100m), Smith (400m), and Butts (TJ), scored NCAA points. UCLA had two scorers in the 400 (Smith and third-place freshman Benny Brown) and three in the triple jump (Butts, Harry Freeman in third, and Milan Tiff in fourth), and they scored points in 10 separate events, including another victory in the mile relay—an unprecedented fourth straight. UCLA's 82 points was 33 better than runner-up USC and completed a banner season. Could anyone beat UCLA?

By 1973 the talent had thinned slightly, but there was no letup. Victory had brought confidence and toughness to Bush's Bruins, and they stomped nine dual-meet victims in a row (including USC, 89-55), won the Pacific-8 title with a runaway 156 points, and entered the NCAA meet as the favorite again.

Their fifth straight mile-relay win closed out a wild and steamy NCAA championship in Baton Rouge, Louisiana, with UCLA's third title in a row. Bendixen was an upset winner in the long jump (with James McAlister third), Tiff won the triple jump, and Brown was second in the 440 (with Maxie Parks fifth). The Bruins scored in seven events, and their 56 points trumped Steve Prefontaine and his Oregon teammates, UCLA's closest pursuers, who had only 31.

Bush's gracious demeanor hid the fearsome determination to win that his athletes embraced and intensified on the track. "These teams were not only talented," he said years later, "but they were great people who wanted to win together."

His short relay teams never could get it together, but the unmatched string of six NCAA mile-relay championships (1969-74) is a fitting tribute to a coach who preached togetherness and whose teams handed him five national championships in his 20-year tenure at UCLA.

John Smith led a parade of world-class Bruins to three straight NCAA track-and-field championships in the 1970s. Here, he wins the 1972 NCAA 400 meters, with teammate Benny Brown (to Smith's right) placing third. USC's Edesel Garrison, on the far right, finished fourth.

High School Football:
Touchdown Twins Meet for Title
December 14, 1956

In a city marked by magnificent successes in college, professional, and Olympic sports of all kinds, it is hard to imagine that a high school football game could command the attention of the entire area. But it often did, never more so than when the remarkable "Touchdown Twins"—Mickey Flynn of Anaheim High School and Randy Meadows of Downey High—faced off for the CIF Southern Section championship at the Los Angeles Memorial Coliseum.

Both schools were 12-0-0, with Downey outscoring its opponents 428-112 and Anaheim, riding a 24-game winning streak, scoring 423 points to 101 for its victims.

Downey's Meadows had set a California Interscholastic Federation record with 190 points (29 touchdowns and 16 points after) while rushing for 2,016 yards on 126 tries (a 16.0 average!). Anaheim's Flynn was no slouch either, having scored 20 touchdowns and gaining 1,232 yards on only 77 carries, while missing most of three games with injury.

A record high school football crowd of 41,383 poured into the Coliseum on a cool and foggy Friday evening to watch the championship battle.

Both players were ready. Halfway through the first quarter, Flynn raced 62 yards for a touchdown and a 7-0 lead. Meadows responded with a 69-yarder for Downey on the next series, but Jack Trumbo's conversion kick try was wide.

Anaheim still led, 7-6, in the third quarter, when Flynn got hot again. On a 12-play drive that covered 65 yards, he carried six times for eight, twenty, three, nine, seven, and, finally, one yard for a touchdown, but John Baker's conversion try was kicked wide, leaving Anaheim ahead by only 13-6.

With Meadows suffering the effects of an injured elbow—incurred while tackling Flynn in the first quarter—reserve halfback Ron Russell took over in the fourth quarter. As the clock wore down, Downey moved from its own 23 for a touchdown in 12 plays as quarterback Brent McDowell ran for 17 and nine yards and Russell ran for 13 yards and the final yard for the score. Trailing only 13-12, Russell then took the handoff on the point-after try and raced around left end for the tying conversion with only 3:02 to play in the game.

Meadows piled up 112 yards in 10 attempts but had to leave the game with injuries; Russell subbed admirably, running for 51 yards in 11 tries, while McDowell added 85 yards in 15 attempts. Flynn played the entire game and gained 134 yards in 17 attempts, but his two touchdowns were not enough to untangle two evenly matched teams that had to settle for a 13-13 tie and the cochampionship.

Key play in the first quarter: Randy Meadows of Downey tackles Mickey Flynn of Anaheim and is injured, while Stan Perumean of Downey closes in.

72 Little League Baseball:
Long Beach Little Leaguers Are Big-Time Players
August 28, 1993

In the 1992 Little League World Series, a very good Long Beach team was overwhelmed, 15-4, by Zamboanga City of the Philippines in the championship game. But Zamboanga City had stocked its team with several players older than the age limit of 13 and forfeited the title three weeks later. The Long Beach All-Stars were happy to be recognized as the best legitimate team there was, but they would have preferred to prove it on the field.

The Long Beach team knew they would get another chance the following season. With the nucleus of the 1992 team returning, there would be an opportunity to show how good they could be in 1993. And in late August Manager Larry Lewis sent out his ace pitcher, 12-year-old Sean Burroughs, to face Bedford, New Hampshire, in the U.S. championship game to determine one-half of the Little League World Series final matchup. Burroughs responded with his fifth straight shutout and third consecutive no-hitter, striking out 16 batters en route to an 11-0 victory. Long Beach would face Panama, a 5-0 winner over Kaiserslautern, Germany, in the international championship game.

More than 40,000 fans showed up at Lamade Stadium in Williamsport, Pennsylvania, for the final, a remarkable total for a town with a population of 33,401. A national television audience looked in as Brady Werner took the mound for Long Beach (23-1 for the season) and held Panama scoreless for the first two innings.

Abel Navarro gave Panama a 1-0 lead in the top of the third with a run-scoring single, but Long Beach tied it in the fourth, and both teams scored runs in the fifth.

At 2-2 in the sixth inning—the last inning of regulation Little League games—Werner retired Panama without scoring. Long Beach could win it with a run in the bottom of the inning, but no U.S. team had ever won back-to-back championships in the history of Little League baseball. And Panama's Alex Beitia was pitching a two-hitter.

Left fielder Timmy Lewis singled. First baseman Ken Miller bunted and reached first safely as Lewis was caught at third. Charlie Hayes pinch-ran for Miller and ended up on third after singles by right fielder Chris Miller and third baseman Brent Kirkland.

With the bases loaded and one out, Panama Coach Carlos Botello replaced Beitia with Navarro, and Navarro fanned catcher Billy Gwinn. But pinch hitter Jeremy Hess liked Navarro's fastball pitches to Gwinn. "I expected the fastball," he said. "I really wanted to hit the ball instead of getting a walk." Hess got his fastball and ripped an 0-1 pitch into the right-center-field gap, scoring Hayes for a 3-2 win and the absolute, unquestioned, unchallenged, undeniable, and unbelievable repeat championship of Little League baseball. Viva Long Beach!

The celebration is on as Manager Larry Lewis (left) raises his arms in victory and Coach Jeff Burroughs is overrun by happy Long Beach Little Leaguers following their 3-2 win in the 1993 Little League World Series.

College Track and Field Championship:
Troy's Four-of-a-Kind Wins NCAA Hands Down
June 12, 1943

It was wartime, and America's young men were engaged in the brutal business of winning World War II. Priorities were changed, and the sports world was turned upside down while the nation's finest athletes donned khaki or olive green uniforms.

Dean Cromwell, the veteran track-and-field coach of the USC Trojans, had the same problems. After winning eight consecutive NCAA track-and-field championships from 1935 to 1942, he could field only four entrants for the 1943 meet at Evanston, Illinois.

Hal Davis of the University of California was the favorite in both the 100-yard and 220-yard events, and he won easily in 10.0 and 21.4. But, USC's Jack Trout came in second in both the 100 and the 220 while Cliff Bourland placed third in the 220 and first in the 440, completing it in 48.5 seconds. Edsel Curry nabbed second place in the broad jump, and Doug Miller was third in the javelin. Voilà!

The Trojans had 46 points, their lowest total since 1932, but it was enough to win their ninth title in a row. It was another triumph for Cromwell, who virtually owned the national collegiate championship.

Cromwell began at USC in 1909, 12 years before the NCAA championships began in 1921. But he had a championship team by 1926 and titles in 1930 and 1931. Beginning in 1930, Cromwell's teams won 11 championships and finished second five times over the next 19 years until his retirement following the 1948 season. There's no way to know how many additional titles his teams would have won between 1909 and 1920.

His domination of intercollegiate track and field was naturally accompanied by his development of some of the greatest athletes in American history. Charley Paddock, the original "World's Fastest Human" (see Moment 66), was a Cromwell student, as were NCAA champions including sprinter Frank Wykoff (1930-31); miler Lou Zamperini (1938-39); long jumper Al Olson (1934); pole vaulter Bill Graber (1931, 1933); and the "Heavenly Twins," Bill Sefton and Earle Meadows (1935 and 1936). Olympic discus champions Bud Houser (1926) and Ken Carpenter (1935-36) also won NCAA championships for Cromwell and USC.

The man with the stylish bow tie was the cream of college coaches during his 39-year tenure at USC. He established the Trojan track-and-field dynasty, a tradition that not only continued with his successors, but spread to USC's next generation of coaches in baseball (see Moment 67), football (see Moment 34), and swimming (see Moment 86).

Cliff Bourland (above) leads the four-man USC contingent to a remarkable win in the 1943 NCAA Championships by winning the 440-yard dash. The entire team stands with Coach Dean Cromwell, including (left to right) Bourland, Jack Trout, Edsel Curry, and Doug Miller.

Horse Racing:
The Last Ride
March 12, 1966

There he was, the 59-year-old gentleman riding in the saddle as he had for the past 40 years, entering his first mount of the day in the fourth race, this time on the favorite, Chiclero. And when he finished—with another winner—he accepted the cheers of an over-sized crowd of 60,792 who had come to Santa Anita to watch him one final time.

It was Johnny Longden's last day in the saddle.

His brilliant riding career had also included many injuries, including a recent kick from a filly that had caused considerable pain, in addition to a pinched nerve in his right leg. So, at the Pasadena Sports Ambassadors dinner on Tuesday, March 8, Longden announced that Saturday's $125,000 San Juan Capistrano Handicap would be his last race.

The interest in seeing the final ride of the winningest jockey of all time spread quickly, and the cheers were heavy for his fourth-race win, although less so for his out-of-the-money mount in the sixth race and a close third in the seventh. Then it was time for the San Juan Capistrano moment.

Longden and the horse, George Royal, were both defending champions, and the five-year-old was noted for fast finishes. As the race started, George Royal was a 6-1 choice, third-best in a field of nine. Plaque, ridden by Bobby Ussery, raced to the front; George Royal ran easily in last, but close to the pack.

Longden crowded the second choice, Cedar Key, ridden by Bill Shoemaker, then took off after the favorite, Hill Rise. Both horses moved strongly down the back straight, making up almost all of the 15 1/2 lengths between them and Plaque. Longden's careful positioning stilled Hill Rise for just a moment, allowing George Royal to make an unobstructed charge at Plaque.

At the head of the stretch, George Royal had the lead by a nose, and he and Plaque raced side by side, inching forward and back, right to the finish. When they crossed the line together, the crowd was silent for the only time all day, waiting for the judges to determine the winner.

And then, the number 10 for George Royal went up and so did the yells from the crowd as Longden brought home his 6,032th win in a career of 32,413 races. It was the storybook finish to his career that was already filled with highlights: his Triple Crown ride aboard Count Fleet in 1943 and his amazing run aboard the unheralded Noor in 1950 at the San Juan Capistrano, when he upset the 1948 Triple Crown winner Citation and Calumet Farms running mates Ponder and Two Lea.

"Fantastic," was all he could manage when he entered the press box. "Wasn't it fantastic!" It was, and so was he.

Olympic Swimming:
High Schooler Evans Mines Gold in Seoul
September 19, 1988

While her classmates at El Dorado High School in Placentia, California, were going back to school to start their senior year, a 5-4, 105-pound windmill named Janet Evans was standing on the starting platform for the 400-meter individual medley at the 1988 Olympic Games in Seoul, Korea.

The 17-year-old swim sensation was already the world-record holder in the 400-meter, 800-meter, and 1,500-meter freestyle events and was chasing the first U.S. swimming medal of these Games.

Her success was not assured. She was third best in the qualifying heats, and she had to face Romania's Noemi Lung and Kathleen Nord of the German Democratic Republic (GDR).

Evans stood only fourth after the butterfly leg but charged into the lead with a brilliant two laps of backstroke that left only Lung close. Two laps later, the lead was a body length and a half as Evans' strong breaststroke pulled away from Lung.

Two laps of freestyle swimming from the front was no problem for the triple freestyle world-record holder, and Evans touched with an American Record of 4:37.76, the first gold medal in any sport for the United States during the 1988 games. Evans flashed the famous toothy grin that signaled the joy of victory. "There are no words to describe it," she said afterward; Evans had known that the gold medal was hers as she pulled into the lead on the backstroke.

Two days later, Evans was in the pool for one of her world-record events, the 400-meter freestyle. But she had never faced defending world and European champion Heike Friedrich (GDR), who had already won the 200-meter freestyle. Evans sprinted to the lead and at the halfway mark, in 2:02.14, had a half-body length on Friedrich and teammate Anke Mohring.

Friedrich closed to within 0.16 after 300 meters, but Evans was awesome in the final two laps. She swam 100 meters in 1:00.45 and sped away from the German to a gold medal and a new world record of 4:03.85, a hard-to-believe 1.6 seconds under her old world mark. She had swum the last half of the race faster than the first half, an amazing feat of discipline for any swimmer. No wonder she wore another big grin.

Now the biggest star of the U.S. team in the early days of the Games, Evans had one more challenge in another of her record events, the 800-meter freestyle, the longest event on the women's program. She was burning to make up for her only long-course defeat over the past two years, to Australia's Julie McDonald. No one was even close. Evans led by two body lengths at 300 meters and was five meters ahead by the midway point. She sprinted home in a new Olympic Record of 8:20.20 and said later, "I thought it was going to be tougher than it was; I looked around at the 100, and no one was there."

Not bad for a high schooler; after Seoul, Janet returned to school to earn her high school diploma to go along with her *summa cum laude* (with triple gold medal cluster) in swimming and the most stunning exhibition of worldwide dominance by any prep athlete in the long history of sports in Southern California.

Familiar sights in Seoul for U.S. swimming fans: first the touch, then the winning smile of Janet Evans.

Tennis:
The Best of the Best, Twice Over
September 14, 1947

Ranked three times in the first half of the 1940s, John A. Kramer—known at the time as "Jake" and later as "Jack"—assumed the mantle of the nation's finest amateur tennis player in 1946.

He did so by storming through the 1946 United States Lawn Tennis Association Championships, held at the West Side Tennis Club in Forest Hills, New York. He destroyed his first three opponents in straight sets, then overwhelmed Robert Falkenburg, 6-3, 6-2, 1-6, 6-2 in the semifinals. The third set against Falkenburg was the only set Kramer lost during the entire championship.

The final was another straight set masterpiece but with an element of suspense. Twenty-three-year-old Tom Brown of San Francisco held a 7-6 lead in a very closely contested first set, with Brown serving. But as he often did, the 6-1 Kramer turned aggressive on his returns, broke Brown for a 7-7 tie, held service, and broke Brown again for a 9-7 win in the first set. Brown never recovered and lost the last two sets, 6-3 and 6-0. The Associated Press report was succinct: "For one set, it was a tremendous match."

Could Kramer repeat? On September 14, 1947, the 26-year-old from Los Angeles had the chance to become the 10th man to win two consecutive titles at the "Nationals" and to add the U.S. title to his Wimbledon triumph earlier in the year. He had breezed by his first two opponents in straight sets, lost one set in the fourth round, then crushed Falkenburg, 6-2, 7-5, 6-1 in the quarterfinals. But he had plenty of problems with Jaroslav Drobny of Czechoslovakia in the semis. He lost the first set, 3-6, then rallied to win, 6-3, 6-0, and 6-1, to meet the 1944 and 1945 champion, Frank Parker, before a packed house of 13,800.

The second-seeded Parker, who had lost only one set in his five qualifying matches, stunned the crowd and Kramer with quick set wins of 6-4 and 6-2. Facing a straight-set loss, Kramer regained his composure, ripped a series of winners against the sidelines, and won the third and fourth sets, 6-1 and 6-0. In the decisive fifth set, the 31-year-old Parker had too few answers for Kramer's furious ground strokes, and Jake returned to the top with a 6-3 final set win.

Having conquered all that the amateur ranks could throw at him, Kramer turned professional in October 1947, beginning an important career as professional player, promoter, and broadcast commentator.

77

Olympic Track and Field:
A Female Answer to Rambo
September 24, 1988

Jackie Joyner-Kersee had been anxiously waiting for her chance at an Olympic gold medal since a sore hamstring during the 800 meters relegated her to the silver medal in the 1984 heptathlon in Los Angeles. As the Games of the XXIV Olympiad loomed in Seoul, Korea, she was the prohibitive favorite, having set three world records in her last five heptathlons, including a 7,215 score at the U.S. Olympic Track and Field Trials. No other heptathlete had even broken the 7,000 barrier.

Joyner-Kersee started well enough, with a 12.69 in the 100-meter hurdles, a new American record for the heptathlon. Her toughest competition was expected to come from Sabine John, of the German Democratic Republic (GDR), who held the heptathlon hurdles record (12.64). But John could manage only 12.85, and the issue was essentially settled.

The high jump was next, and although Joyner-Kersee strained her left knee on one approach, she cleared 6-1 1/4 and was running away from the rest of the field. She was, however, 76 points behind her own record pace from the U.S. Olympic Trials.

Joyner-Kersee heaved the shot put out to 51-10 and ran a speedy 22.56 in the 200 meters, but finished the day with 4,264 points, 103 points behind her own record pace. GDR's John (4,083) and Anke Brehmer (3,986) trailed badly.

After a sleepless night, Joyner-Kersee knew the key to reaching for a world record would be her best event, the long jump. Her coach and husband, Bobby Kersee, knew that most observers had written off another record. "They were people," said Bobby, "who don't know Jackie."

Joyner-Kersee reached out to an amazing 23-10 1/4 on her fifth jump. It wasn't just the best long jump ever in a heptathlon competition; it was better than the Olympic record for the women's open long jump, and it put her within 11 points of her own record pace.

She lost ground to her record totals in the javelin, her most inconsistent event. She threw only 149-10 and trailed her record total by 97 with her least favorite event, the 800 meters remaining.

"If there's a female answer to Rambo," noted Bobby Kersee, "Jackie is it. She's looking for perfection, and she's willing to pull every muscle in her body to achieve it."

The 800 meters might require that; she needed to run 2:13.67 to set a new mark. She ran evenly for as long as she could, finally finishing in a new personal best of 2:08.51 and setting the record out of sight at 7,291. She was defiant as she warmed up: "I felt like, 'If I can't give these people a world record, I don't deserve to be out here,'" she said afterward.

But she did, in the first of two gold medal performances. Five days later, she won the long jump with another Olympic record of 24-3 1/2.

College Basketball Championship: Trojans Horse Around Long Enough to Win NCAA Title
April 1, 1984

The sisters McGee shot big smiles at each other and at their teammates. And why not? Didn't the McGee twins—Pam and Paula—have twin championships to celebrate after a 72-61 win over Tennessee in the NCAA basketball championship game?

Trojan coach Linda Sharp had molded a durable spirit in her sixth team in 1983 with Pam, two-time all-American Paula McGee, and freshman all-American Cheryl Miller leading the way. Only tough losses in midseason to Louisiana Tech (58-56) and Long Beach State (74-73) marred an otherwise perfect regular season. Then the Trojans swept through the NCAA tournament, reaching the finals against two-time defending national champion Louisiana Tech, whom they had met two other times that season. The Lady Techsters built a 37-26 halftime lead while the Trojans shot only 42 percent. A withering second-half rally led by Miller, Cynthia Cooper, and Paula McGee, though, produced a 69-67 win that capped a 31-2 season with USC's first national basketball title.

The McGees, Miller, and Cooper were back in 1984; in all, nine of the 12 players from the 1983 championship team returned. Although they were not quite as sharp in the regular season, they still rolled up a 24-4 record and steamed past BYU, 97-72; Montana, 76-51; Long Beach State, 90-74; and their old nemesis, Louisiana Tech, 62-57, to reach the final game against Tennessee's Lady Vols at UCLA's Pauley Pavilion.

The challengers used a slow pace and good play from forwards Mary Ostrowski and Tanya Haave to forge a 28-26 halftime lead, which expanded to 43-38 with 11:47 to go. But as she had in the 1983 championship game, Cooper brought the spark that ignited the Trojans. She led an 8-0 run that put the Trojans ahead, 46-43, only to see Tennessee come back and take a 49-48 lead before she decided to end the suspense.

"I told them, 'Let's get pumped,'" Cooper recalled. Her teammates responded. Pam McGee made a three-point play and followed a Yolanda Fletcher miss for two more. Next they watched point guard Amy Alkek score a lay-in and a right side jumper, and USC led 57-51.

Tennessee's Paula Towns tipped in a missed shot, and the Vols trailed, 57-53. Then the roof fell in. Paula McGee's jumper started a 9-0 streak that included points from Miller, Cooper, and Alkek. The Trojans had it won, with a 66-53 lead and only 1:17 to play. The game ended at 72-61.

Pam McGee gained all-American honors as the Trojans finished with a 29-4 record; Miller was also named all-American for the second straight year (she would finish as a four-time A-A selection). The difference in USC's back-to-back titles? Tennessee Coach Pat Summitt summed it up after the game: "USC has the experience," she noted, "and they have Miller."

Pam McGee (left), sister Paula McGee (above), and four-time all-American Cheryl Miller (right) are three of the main reasons why USC won consecutive national basketball titles in 1983 and 1984.

79

Olympic Diving:
Diminutive Lee Stands Tallest on the Platform
August 1, 1952

Sammy Lee was a 28-year-old U.S. Army physician who stood five feet, two inches tall. He also stood head-and-shoulders better than any platform diver in the world at the 1948 Olympic Games in London.

Lee won the gold medal convincingly, ending his 10-dive program with a near-perfect forward three-and-a-half somersault that provided his final margin of victory: 130.05 points to 122.30 for his teammate and silver medalist Bruce Harlan. Two days earlier, Lee completed an American sweep by winning a bronze medal in the springboard competition, watching Harlan take the gold, also by a comfortable margin.

Born in Fresno and raised in Los Angeles, Lee continued in the army and continued diving. Nonetheless, his road to the 1952 Games was a rocky one. His exceptional grace off the platform made him the favorite to pull off a repeat championship, a feat that had never been accomplished in either the men's springboard or platform event. But he had challengers.

Sammy Lee accepts the gold medal in the 10-meter platform diving event at the 1948 Olympic Games in London, with silver medalist Bruce Harlan on his right and bronze medalist José Capilla Perez on his left.

At the inaugural Pan American Games in Buenos Aires, Argentina, in 1951, all diving honors were delivered to Mexico's José Capilla Perez. He edged Miller Anderson of the U.S. and Lee for the springboard title by just 2.65 points, and then defeated Lee, 159.966 to 153.533, with Anderson third, for the platform championship. If Lee was going to repeat at Helsinki, he was going to have to be almost perfect.

Lee blistered the field at the U.S. Olympic Trials, winning the platform competition by a staggering 56.20 points. Now an army major, he was ready to celebrate his 32nd birthday and a gold-medal-winning performance on August 1.

He didn't simply win. He gave a clinic. Lee overwhelmed Capilla and the rest of his competition, and became the first man to ever win back-to-back Olympic diving titles. His 10-dive scoring total of 156.28 points was far ahead of silver medalist Capilla (145.21) and bronze medalist Gunther Haase of Germany (141.31), and was the largest margin of victory in Olympic platform diving history.

"I came here to avenge the defeat at the hands of Capilla in the Pan American Games a year ago," Lee told reporters afterward. Having succeeded, he declared his retirement. "I'm getting too old for this sort of thing, you know."

Lee left Helsinki with his legend assured and enjoyed a European holiday with his wife Rosalind, before returning to complete his residency as an ear, nose, and throat specialist at Letterman General Hospital in San Francisco. But his place in Olympic history was already assured; in any discussion of history's greatest platform divers, this diminutive graduate of Franklin High School and Occidental College is sure to stand tall.

College Basketball Championship:
Bruin Dreams Come True at Home for AIAW Title
March 25, 1978

This was too good to be true. Ann Meyers, UCLA's four-time all-American basketball star, would end her career in front of a home audience and play for the national championship.

After three straight disappointments in regional or sectional finals, Meyers' Bruins had made it through to the national finals of the Association for Intercollegiate Athletics for Women (AIAW) at Pauley Pavilion. Best of all, the 26-3 Bruins were riding a 20-game winning streak and a 31-game home winning streak in Pauley.

First-year coach Billie Moore had molded UCLA into a multifaceted club that had strong scoring from 6-1 freshman forward Denise Curry (20.3 points per game) and 5-8 junior guard Anita Ortega (18.4) to complement the 5-9 Meyers, who started at forward and averaged 18.6 points and 9.6 rebounds per game.

The championship game was not going to be a coronation, however. Maryland (27-3) had already beaten UCLA at College Park early in the season, 92-88, and had won its tournament games by an average of 10.3 points.

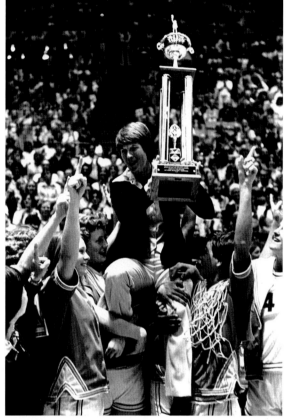

But the Bruins, lifted by an AIAW record crowd of 9,351, came out firing; a 16-3 run after the first three and a half minutes put UCLA ahead, 24-11, with 11:21 to play. The speedy Ortega had seven points, and senior center Heidi Nestor contributed five.

Maryland responded with a 14-2 run of its own to close the score to 26-25 with 5:29 to play in the half, but the Bruins zoomed again. Four points from Meyers keyed a 9-2 spurt, and UCLA ran off the court at the half leading by 10, 43-33.

The issue was settled midway through the second half when another UCLA blitz, this time 13-2 with Meyers scoring six, left Maryland trailing 74-55, and the Bruins cruised home for their first national women's basketball title, 90-74. Ortega had 23, Meyers had 20, Curry scored 18, and Nestor added 13 to lead the delirious, almost disbelieving Bruins.

"It's an indescribable feeling," said Meyers, who left to a standing ovation with 1:09 on the clock. "This team has a specialness that kept it together and took us all the way."

Moore recognized what made the Bruins special. "Annie did a fantastic job," she said afterward. "It gets so you expect a superb performance every game, and sure enough she delivered."

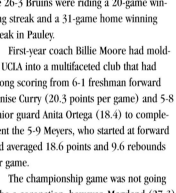

UCLA Coach Billie Moore lifts the AIAW national championship trophy as Bruin teammates (left to right) Beth Moore, Denise Curry, and Ann Meyers (wearing the net) celebrate.

81 Auto Racing:
Takin' It to the Streets of Long Beach
September 28, 1975

Walt Disney is often quoted as having said, "If you can dream it, you can do it." Chris Pook would agree.

Originally from Somerset, England, Pook was a travel agent in the Long Beach area in the 1970s. Listening to the Indianapolis 500, he dreamed of bringing big-time auto racing to the streets of Long Beach, just as he had seen in Europe. "Predictably," he said later, "people thought I was nuts." But after lots of meetings, and with a lot more faith than funding, he got his chance in 1975.

The streets of the city were converted into a wild, Formula 5000 racecourse featuring fast cars and tight turns. A crowd of more than 75,000 showed up to watch, cheer, and ultimately celebrate the emergence of Long Beach into one of the important venues in auto racing.

The big names were there: England's Brian Redman, the defending Formula 5000 champion, in a Lola; Al Unser and Mario Andretti in identical Viceroy-Lolas; and many more who hoped for a large share of the richest Formula 5000 race ever.

Unser and Andretti took off from the start and shared the lead with Tony Brise, a 23-year-old Englishman, navigating carefully around the 2.02-mile course. But the strain of the difficult course on the cars took their toll and left Redman with a comfortable advantage 35 laps into the 50-lap race.

Redman continued on a sensible pace, easily lapping everyone except Australia's Vern Schuppan as he took the checkered flag, winning with an average speed of 86.325 miles per hour and clinching his second straight Formula 5000 championship. Eppie Wietzes of Canada finished third as the top six places all went to foreign drivers.

But the big winners were Long Beach and Pook. His gamble on the Grand Prix format, which only grew in importance as the years passed, had turned up a winner. Racing's international governing bodies awarded Pook the right to stage a Formula One Grand Prix race in 1976. The Toyota Grand Prix of Long Beach was on the way to becoming one of the most famous races anywhere.

In 1984 when the format switched to Indy cars, familiar faces—including Michael Andretti, Bobby Rahal, and Al Unser, Jr.—mounted the victory stand to the applause of crowds in excess of 85,000. Purses climbed well over the $500,000 mark.

Springtime in Long Beach is now marked by the roar of engines and the sound of more than 200,000 spectators who annually enjoy a week's worth of racing, Long Beach-style.

Rose Bowl:
Point-a-Minute Wolves Humble Stanford, 49-0
January 1, 1902

When the Tournament of Roses began in 1890, the parade was the primary focus of attention. As the program grew in popularity, sports events were added as a secondary attraction for primarily local amusement.

But new Tournament president James Wagner was determined to add a sporting event of national significance to the New Year's Day program. So, an invitation was sent to the University of Michigan, whose team had outscored its 10 opponents, 501-0. The best of the western teams, Stanford, agreed to match up with the Wolverines.

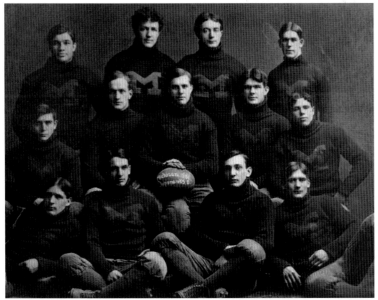

Both teams marched in the Parade and, following the procession, attention turned to Tournament Park (now part of the California Institute of Technology), where one policeman and a few ticket sellers/ushers were set to handle the crowd, which the Tournament hoped would fill the 1,000 seats available.

But a near-mob of more than 8,000 showed up to see the two schools in action and overpowered the staff. Even so, the gate receipts from those who did pay totaled a tidy $6,000, and the Tournament turned a profit of more than $3,100.

The game started at 2:57 p.m., with the teams playing two 30-minute halves. Touchdowns counted for five points, field goals the same, and conversions, one. The playing field was 110 yards long, and first downs were earned by gaining five yards in three downs. And, of course, forward passing was illegal.

A scoreless punting duel was finally broken at the 23-minute mark of the first half, as Michigan's Neil Snow bulled over from the five-yard line, followed quickly by an Everett Sweeley 20-yard field goal and Chris Redden's 25-yard touchdown return of a short Stanford punt. Michigan had a 17-0 halftime lead.

The tired Stanford 11 had no answer to Michigan's second-half charge. Snow scored four times on short runs of two, eight, seventeen, and four yards; Redden returned a fumble 25 yards for a touchdown; and Al Herrnstein ran 21 yards for another score as Michigan took a 49-0 lead with eight minutes remaining. At that point, Stanford captain Ralph Fisher conceded defeat, and Michigan agreed.

Michigan's Willie Heston ran 18 times for 170 yards; Snow gained 107; and Herrnstein added 97 as Fielding Yost's squad piled up 527 yards of offense in 90 plays to Stanford's 67. Of course, Stanford was hurt by its nine fumbles in the game.

Although a success, the mismatch and the crowd problems returned the Tournament to chariot racing and other amusements until football returned to stay in 1916.

College Softball World Series:
Fernandez Mows Down Wildcats for NCAA Title
May 25, 1992

It is said that good pitching will always beat good hitting. If so, the Arizona Wildcats had essentially no chance to win the 1992 NCAA women's softball championship when they faced off against UCLA at the College World Series in Oklahoma City.

The reason? Lisa Fernandez, the Bruins' junior batting and pitching sensation. Entering the title game, Fernandez had already won all three of her College World Series starts, shutting out Massachusetts, California, and Fresno State, and giving up only five hits in 19 innings.

But Debby Day, Arizona's pitching ace, was equal to the challenge. Through six innings, neither side could score. In the seventh, Fernandez set down Arizona, giving the Bruins a last chance to score in regulation play. Finally, UCLA freshman Jennifer Brewster got hold of a Day delivery and powered it over the left field fence for a two-run homer that won UCLA's eighth national softball championship, 2-0. Fernandez's four-hitter completed her 1992 College World Series with a 4-0 record, four straight shutouts, and 26 strikeouts in 26 innings. She ended the season with a 65-inning scoreless streak. Oh, yes, she also batted .500 with eight hits in the series. The Bruins finished at 54-2.

It was like that for Fernandez during her brilliant career at UCLA. By the time she finished up in 1993, she had compiled a career record of 93-7, with 42 wins in a row from February 1992 to April 1993. And she had 74 career shutouts, a career earned run average of 0.22, three perfect games, and 11 no-hitters. In her last three seasons as a Bruin, she won 20, 29, and 33 games.

Fernandez was tough at the plate, too. In her senior season, she became the first player to lead the nation in both batting average (.510) and earned run average (0.25) in the same year. In her career, she batted .382 and had 287 hits in 240 games, scoring 142 runs and batting in 128 runs.

No softball player had ever exhibited this kind of dominance. It was no surprise that she earned three consecutive Honda Awards as the nation's top player for 1992, 1993, and 1994.

"Lisa Fernandez is the best all-around softball player in the history of the sport," said Bruin Coach Sharron Backus. "She just spoils you rotten. She does whatever is necessary and does it so classy, so effortlessly."

"She has everything," agreed her roommate, catcher Kelly Inouye. "When she's on, batters just go up there hoping."

Against Fernandez, there was virtually no hope for her opponents as her Bruins won 222 games during her four-year career and two national championships.

84

Track and Field: Dumas Does It!

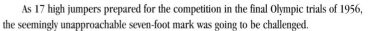

June 29, 1956

As 17 high jumpers prepared for the competition in the final Olympic trials of 1956, the seemingly unapproachable seven-foot mark was going to be challenged.

But it wasn't going to go without a fight. The existing world mark of 6-11 1/2, set by Walter Davis (USA) at the 1953 national AAU championships in Dayton, Ohio, had held up for more than three years.

More than 34,000 were in the Los Angeles Memorial Coliseum to watch the first day of the two-day Trials, but the high jump was working its way well into the evening. By 9 p.m., the bar was at 6-9 1/2, and only five men remained to chase the three spots on the U.S. team that would compete in Melbourne, Australia, in late November.

Bernie Allard, Ernie Shelton, and Compton College freshman Charles Dumas missed on their first tries at 6-9 1/2, but little Phil Reavis—who stood only 5-9 3/4—rolled over. Verne Wilson cleared easily on his first try, and Dumas, who had to buy a $3 ticket to get into the meet because his coach forgot to give him a participant's credential, made it on his second try. Allard missed a second time, and Shelton grazed the bar on his way over, causing it to fall off.

Allard missed on his third try and was eliminated. When Shelton lay face down in the pit after his third miss, the American team for Melbourne was set. But the bar was going higher.

Although the "western roll" was the accepted technique of the day, Dumas used an updated technique known as the "float"—which would later be known as the "straddle." He cleared 6-10 1/2 on his first trial, but Wilson missed three times. Reavis was close on his third try, but missed, and he had to settle for third.

Now after 10 p.m., the 19-year-old Dumas ordered the bar to a new world record of 7-0 5/8 and promptly missed on his first trial. He then rested for about five minutes, readjusted his bright red Compton uniform, and at 10:17 p.m., headed for the bar.

Cordner Nelson, writing in *Track & Field News*, described the try: "Halfway to the bar he speeded his run, threw up one green shoe in a powerful kick over his head, and floated gracefully over without even touching the crossbar. A tremendous roar rose from the thousands who had remained to watch, and immediately Dumas was mobbed by high jumpers and photographers."

Seven feet, five-eighths of an inch, which was later rounded for record purposes to 7-0 1/2. Dumas had done it but took it in stride.

"I wasn't nervous," he said afterward. "By that time, I knew I had made the plane. I've had lots of other tries at seven feet; maybe I was so relaxed that I did everything right."

He did everything right, straight through to Melbourne, where his all-conquering season culminated in the gold medal and an Olympic record of 6-11 1/2.

85

Basketball:
Baylor's Garden Party: Record 71 vs. New York
November 15, 1960

The unstoppable Elgin Baylor (22) is so good that even his teammates sometimes stop and watch.

"Give it to Baylor!" was the cry from 10,000 screaming fans . . . at Madison Square Garden in New York! The brilliant third-year All-Star from Los Angeles was entertaining the fans with the greatest scoring display ever seen.

Elgin Baylor already held the record for most points scored in an NBA game: 64, set in the 1959 season when the Lakers were located in Minneapolis, Minnesota. But now he was on a pace to catch and surpass even his own great performance.

Baylor had 34 points by halftime, as the Lakers led the Knicks 65-58. But he poured it on in the second half as the fans forgot the home team and yelled at the Lakers to ignore their "other" scoring threats, rookie guard Jerry West and veteran forward Rudy LaRusso.

"During the warm-up, I didn't miss a shot," said the 6-5 Baylor afterward. "That has happened before. But this time, it just continued during the game."

With Baylor pouring in the points, his teammates clamped down on the Knicks and outscored New York 25-15 in the third quarter to take a commanding 90-73 lead going into the final period. That allowed Baylor to continue his assault on the record books until he finally left the game with 28 seconds to play, having scored a new record of 71 points in a single game. He made 28 of his 48 field goal attempts and 15-19 free throws; almost unnoticed was his 25-rebound performance. The Lakers won easily, 123-108, as LaRusso added 15 and West scored 10. Willie Naulls' outstanding 35-point output for the Knicks was, well, overlooked in the excitement.

West knew something special was happening. "About the middle of the third quarter, I began to get the idea I was seeing something unusual," he said many years later. "Elg missed a shot, and it rebounded all the way to the free throw line. When Elg tipped it in from there, I realized anything could happen."

Afterwards, Baylor was unfazed, as always. Riding back to the Lakers' hotel in a taxi, he turned to roommate Rod Huntley, who had scored seven points that night. "Well, our room scored 78 tonight," said Baylor with a smile. "That's pretty good."

Baylor was much more than pretty good in his Lakers career, which stretched from the 1958-59 season in Minneapolis to the 1971-72 campaign in Los Angeles. In 14 seasons, he scored 23,149 points, averaging 27.4 per game. He was named to the All-NBA first team nine times and had the respect of his teammates and opponents as captain of the Lakers. And he was the king of all basketball for one night in New York that cannot be forgotten.

86 College Swimming Championship: Awesome Trojans Win Fourth Straight NCAA Title
March 26, 1977

There was no doubt in anyone's mind that Peter Daland's sensational USC swim team would win the 1977 NCAA championship. Before the season started, Bob Hammel of the *Bloomington* (Indiana) *Herald-Telephone* wrote, "No one even talks of pulling off that upset—and no one will until USC and Daland say goodbye to a remarkable group of seniors."

The Trojan class of '77 included world-class swimmers like John Naber (see Moment 95), Joe Bottom, Rod Strachan, Scott Brown, Mark Greenwood, and Rod Stewart. USC crushed the rest of the collegiate field by 161 points—the biggest margin ever— at the 1976 meet, and at Cleveland State University in 1977, they did even better.

Naber and Bottom each won two events, Strachan and sophomore Bruce Furniss each won one, and Troy won both freestyle relays to pile up a mind-boggling total of 385 points, a ridiculous 181 points better than Alabama's 204 in second place. In all, 15 Trojans won all-American honors.

It was Daland's ninth and final NCAA championship, a remarkable feat at a school that had never finished better than 10th prior to his arrival for the 1958 season. Within three years, he had USC at the top of the platform, winning the 1960 NCAA title with junior Charles Bittick leading the way with victories in both backstroke events. USC finished second in the 1961 and 1962 NCAA meets, mostly thanks to the brilliant Murray Rose, who won five NCAA championships in those two years, and then USC ascended to the top for four straight years from 1963 to 1966. Sophomore John Konrads won the 500-yard and 1,650-yard freestyle events to pace the 1963 team, while Roy Saari dominated the next three championship teams.

Saari won the 440-yard freestyle, 1,650-yard freestyle, and 200-yard individual medley in 1964, as well as the 200-yard, 500-yard, and 1,650-yard freestyles in 1965. The next year, he repeated the feat for a total of nine individual championships in three years. He also swam the anchor leg on two NCAA champion relay teams. He had plenty of help, however, in classmates William Craig (three breaststroke titles in two years) and Rich McGeagh (the 1964 400-yard individual medley champion and nine-time all-American in his three years).

From 1967 to 1973, Daland guided his teams to five second-place and two third-place finishes until he took possession of the national championship for the four years ending in 1977. At the end of that streak, Naber owned 10 NCAA individual event championships, plus five relay titles. Bottom had five individual titles and four relay wins, and Strachan had two individual championships to his credit.

At the time of his retirement in 1992, Daland's team had won nine national titles, finished second nationally 11 times, won 17 conference championships, and compiled a dual meet record of 318-31-1 in 35 seasons. Daland was almost as dominant as his 1977 team, perhaps the greatest collegiate swim squad that will ever be assembled.

The two worlds of Peter Daland: at the pool (opposite) and accepting NCAA championship trophies, as here in 1976. Celebrating USC's third championship in succession are
(front row) Athletic Director Dr. Richard Perry, Assistant Athletic Director Dr. Jim Dennis,
Joe Bottom, Mike Nyeholt, Rod Strachan, and Mike Bottom. In the second row are Ron Orr
(hidden), Daland, Mark Smith (with arm raised), Dave Hannula, Bob Shearin (hidden),
Allen Poucher, Rod Stewart, Steve Furniss, Bruce Furniss (bending over), and Scott
Brown.

Horse Racing:
Big 'Cap Puts Santa Anita on the Map to Stay
February 23, 1935

In 1934 the Dodgers were playing in Brooklyn, and the Angels were a Pacific Coast League team. Professional sports teams called the "Rams," "Lakers," and "Kings" were figments of someone's imagination. But there was racing at Santa Anita.

On a lovely Tuesday, December 25, 1934, the four red-jacketed trumpeters announced the coming of the horses for an eight-race program. A strong crowd of 30,777 attended the first meeting, a tribute to the determination of Dr. Charles G. Strub, who had masterminded the idea of the place with help from movie studio head Hal Roach and who had sold $5,000 shares (in the depths of the Depression!) to build it.

The technical wizard behind the entire enterprise was the brilliant Gwynn Wilson, who had helped to inaugurate the USC-Notre Dame football series and who joined the project after his triumph as associate manager of the 1932 Olympic Games organizing committee. One of his many contributions, almost too amazing to be believed today, was the planning and construction of Santa Anita for a mere $800,000.

The inaugural day was a success, but the following days were less so, as the whole idea of racing was a new one to the area. Something special was needed, a promotion that would fire the imaginations of people all across Southern California. The nation's first regularly scheduled, $100,000 handicap race—another brainchild of Strub and Roach—was launched. There had been one other race with a $100,000 purse, but that was a one-time-only match race in 1923. Santa Anita would offer this purse annually.

Considering that the Kentucky Derby and Preakness Stakes were offering barely half as much, racing know-it-alls told Roach and Strub they were crazy. Still, the Santa Anita Handicap was scheduled for Saturday, February 23, 1935. It cemented the Southland's interest in horses forever.

Horse owners were enthusiastic, so much so that 20 horses started the race in front of a cheering crowd of 34,269 (who bet a remarkable $802,553). The favorite was Equipoise, carrying top weight at 130 pounds, but it was Ted Clark who ran to the front and stayed there for much of the race, leaving Time Supply in second and Ladysman in third at the three-quarters mark. The former steeplechase racer Azucar ran hardest down the straightaway, with Ladysman clear for second as Ted Clark and Time Supply tired.

George Woolf, the jockey on Azucar, took away a mammoth purse of $108,400 for Fred Alger, Jr., of Detroit, Michigan, as Ladysman finished second by two lengths, with Time Supply rounding in third and Equipoise coming in seventh.

The success was apparent for all to see. The vision of Strub and Roach had been realized. Roach could see success coming: "There was something about the people of Los Angeles in those days, that if you did something absolutely first class, they would go for it every time." Santa Anita and the Big 'Cap were first class in every way, and Southern Californians have been going for it ever since.

Swimming:
Chadwick Conquers Catalina
September 21, 1952

Florence Chadwick was already a world-famous distance swimmer by 1952. Two years earlier she had crossed the 20-mile English Channel for the first time, setting the fastest time ever recorded by a woman; in 1951, she became the first woman to swim the distance both ways (to and from Dover).

But while growing up in San Diego, Chadwick also had her eye on the difficult and dangerous 21-mile swim between Catalina Island and Point Vicente near Palos Verdes. In July of 1952, she tried to swim across and break the standing record of 15 hours, 44 minutes, set by George Young in 1927, but she ended her quest about two miles short of the shore.

For her September effort, Chadwick changed her plan. The 34-year-old wore 10 pounds of grease to aid her through the water and ate solid food along the way. At 6:16 p.m. on a balmy Saturday evening, she set off from Emerald Cove at a steady pace, accompanied by support boats and approximately 75 sightseeing craft, which formed a virtual alley as she began.

She swam in a school of candlefish off and on for nearly four hours; one fish even slipped into her swimsuit, and another bit her on the chin. A seal swam beneath her part of the way, and two small sharks had to be scared off by shotgun fire. But the water remained at an even 60 degrees throughout the night.

Stomach cramps set in, and Chadwick began to flounder two miles from shore. One of her trainers, Myron Cox, jumped in to swim with her, followed by two training pals, Doug and Dick Hume, as well as an unidentified girl.

Chadwick made it to a rocky beach south of Point Vicente at 8:03 a.m., completing a record swim of 13 hours, 47 minutes, 32 4/5 seconds, almost two hours better than Young's standard. "I extended myself in this swim more than ever before," she said during her recovery at the San Pedro Community Hospital.

The only serious injury of the evening came to a spectator. A crowd of nearly 2,000 had gathered at the shore, some for many hours, to wait for the result of Chadwick's effort. As the enthusiastic spectators surged forward to greet her as she emerged from the water, numerous photographers found their feet in the shallows of the Pacific Ocean, and one woman, 36-year-old Josephine Wright, suffered a mild heart attack and was taken to Harbor General Hospital.

For Chadwick, it was another in a lifetime of magnificent performances. Fred Cady, the official starter of her Catalina Channel swim, grasped the obvious when he called her "the greatest feminine swimmer of all time."

Olympic Track and Field:
Benoit Wins First Olympic Marathon for Women
August 5, 1984

Marathon runners are supposed to be long and lean, able to move effortlessly, like Grete Waitz and Ingrid Kristiansen of Norway, two of the favorites to win the first-ever women's marathon at the 1984 Olympic Games in Los Angeles.

America's best hope was a petite New Englander, Joan Benoit, who held the world's best time of 2:22:43, run at the 1983 Boston Marathon. When 50 women started off at Santa Monica College at 8 a.m. on a cool, overcast Sunday morning, the confrontation between Waitz and Benoit was widely anticipated.

But it never happened. "I did not want to take the lead," said Benoit afterward. "But I promised myself I'd run my race and nobody else's."

Benoit's race was a seemingly leisurely pace of 18:15 for the first 5,000 meters and 35:24 at the 10km mark. But no one followed. Waitz, nursing a back injury and concerned about the midmorning heat that she knew would come, was 11 seconds back at the 10km mark, and a shocking 1 1/2 minutes behind at the 20km mark. For all intents and purposes, the race was over.

The 27-year-old Benoit ran easily, enjoying the sunshine under a large white baseball-style cap. The large crowds that lined the 26.2-mile course cheered her on, and she waved her hat happily when she entered the Coliseum to the roar of 70,000 spectators. She was on the way to finishing in 2:24:52, the third-fastest marathon of all time.

"I was surprised I wasn't challenged at all," she noted. "Nobody came with me—and I didn't complain."

Despite her pain, Waitz held on for second in 2:26:18—still excellent time—and the surprising bronze medalist was Portugal's Rosa Mota, in 2:26:57. Forty-four of the original 50 runners (88 percent) completed the marathon, proof positive of the fitness of women to compete in the longest race on the Olympic program. Silly predictions of dire consequences for the competitors should have been reserved for the men's race on August 12, when only 72 percent of the starters (78 of 108) finished the course.

Benoit was brilliant, but her achievement hadn't quite sunk in after the race was finished. "This is something very, very special, something I've dreamed about, something that hasn't hit me yet," she said. "I can't believe I've won this marathon."

Boxing:
Sugar Ray Too Sweet for Bobo
May 18, 1956

In 1956 Sugar Ray Robinson was acknowledged as one of the great fighters in boxing history. He held the world welterweight crown, relinquishing it only when he stepped up in weight to win the world middleweight crown from Jake LaMotta in 1951. He nearly won the light-heavyweight crown in 1952 before he retired.

Carl "Bobo" Olson was the beneficiary of Robinson's retirement, winning the tournament for Robinson's vacated middleweight crown in 1953. But when Robinson returned to the ring in 1955, Olson was knocked out in the second round on December 9 as Sugar Ray again ascended to the middleweight throne.

So the rematch was scheduled at Wrigley Field in Los Angeles—an unusual venue for a fight of this magnitude—on a pleasant Friday evening. Approximately 18,000 spectators paid up to $25 to see the matches, and a national television audience looked in on NBC. The champion, Robinson, who was 35 years old by then, stood 5-11, and weighed 160 pounds for the fight, tried to improve his overall record to 143-4-2. Olson was only 27, and stood 5-10 1/2, weighed 160, and had a 65-8 record, including three defeats at the hands of Robinson: in 1950 (knocked out in the 12th round), 1952 (a 15-round decision), and in 1955.

Olson's day started badly. A court order from Redwood City, California, arrived in the morning, which held up Olson's share of the purse (more than $75,000!) thanks to a separate maintenance, community property, and custody proceeding filed by his wife. Once the fight started, a court hearing might have been more pleasant.

This fourth-round left hook by Sugar Ray Robinson ends the evening—and any title hopes—for Carl "Bobo" Olson in their 1956 middleweight title tilt at Wrigley Field.

Olson's plan was to concede the first five rounds or so, then bank on his stamina to pile up the points toward a possible 15-round decision. Robinson stung Olson in the first two rounds, but the third was even as Olson clinched continually.

Olson started the fourth round with a right to the head and a solid left to Robinson's body. One minute later, though, Sugar Ray responded with a right to the body and a blistering left hook that caught Olson flush and sent him to the canvas for the 10 count. Robinson's fourth victory over Olson came at 2:51 of the fourth round.

"He made a mistake," Robinson said afterward. "He started another left hook to the body in the fourth round, but I beat him to the punch with my right to the body.

"I knew, too, that it was a good punch and that it set him up. The left hook to the chin, though, was the best punch, and I figured when he went down that he would not get up."

Olson was simply stunned. "I didn't see the punch coming," he said after the fight. "He just has the jinx on me." A lot of other fighters said the same after they lost to Robinson, one of the all-time masters of the sweet science.

91 College Track and Field: Brilliant Owens Dashes past USC
June 15, 1935

Forty thousand people came to see one man. Just three weeks before, Ohio State's Jesse Owens rewrote the record book in one hour, winning four events and setting six world records. Now he was on his way to the Los Angeles Memorial Coliseum to face the Goliath of collegiate track and field, the USC Trojans.

The newspapers were filled with continuous coverage of the 21-year-old Owens. He arrives; he meets local fans; he works out with his upcoming foes; he laughs with his teammates . . . and so on.

When Owens emerged on Saturday at the Coliseum, he was every bit as good as advertised. He zipped by USC's George Boone to win the 100-yard dash in 9.7 seconds, jumped 25-5 1/2 to win the long jump easily over USC's Al Olson (22-7 3/8), blistered two good USC sprinters in Foy Draper and Al Fitch while winning the 220-yard dash in 20.7, and won the 220-yard low hurdles easily in 23.1.

Noted track authority Bill Henry, writing in the *Los Angeles Times*, was just as impressed as the crowd: "Jesse Owens, Ohio State's great sophomore sprinter, won four first places from the greatest track team in the country, and he won them so easily that it was hard to believe what your eyes told you. It looked as though he had no limit."

But Owens was a brilliant talent on an otherwise good, but not outstanding, team. The Trojans, on the other hand, were loaded and had won two NCAA championships and finished second twice for Coach Dean Cromwell in the past five years. The dual meet scoring of the day counted only first-place finishes, and USC won the meet, 9-6.

Benny Benavidez was USC's hero, winning the two-mile run in 9:55.7 though falling on the sixth of eight laps and losing almost 40 yards. But his sprint caught up with Ohio State's Glenn Price, who had led most of the way, at the tape and kept USC's victory assured. If Price had won, the meet would have come down to the final event, the mile relay.

The Trojans were ready for an all-out effort, however, and Estel Johnson, Jim Cassin, Al Fitch, and John McCarthy set a new world record (later disallowed for lack of competition) of 3:12.4 in the relay. Their world-record effort was equaled by Trojan sophomores Phil Cope and Roy Staley, who dead-heated and tied the world record of 14.2 in the 120-yard high hurdles.

But it was Owens who was unforgettable. In Henry's words, "It's safe to say that the performance . . . was far more convincing than the records indicate. It was a very, very large afternoon."

Ice Hockey:
Kings' Unlikely Comeback Tops Bruins in Overtime
April 22, 1976

Going into its ninth year of existence, the Los Angeles Kings had only advanced past the first round of the Stanley Cup play-offs once. Even then, they didn't win a single second-round game in that 1969 series, losing four straight to the St. Louis Blues.

So after a second-place finish in the Norris Division behind Montreal in the regular season and a two-game sweep of the best-of-three opening play-off series against Atlanta, much was hoped for, but Boston stood in the way. The Bruins had tallied 113 points during the season, to the Kings' 85; moreover, Boston had a 4-1 record against Los Angeles—with a 19-9 advantage in goals scored—during the regular season.

So no surprises were registered as Boston racked up 4-0, 3-0, and 7-1 wins against the Kings, who did manage two close wins in games two (3-2 in overtime) and three (6-4). But trailing three games to two, and then 3-1 in the third period of game six at the Forum, things looked pretty bleak, especially with veteran Gerry Cheevers in goal for the Bruins.

But left winger Mike Corrigan scored his first play-off goal midway through the period, when he tipped a hot blast from the right side by Kings' center Marcel Dionne past Cheevers to close the gap to 3-2.

A capacity crowd of 16,005 screamed for one more goal to send the game into overtime, but Boston settled into a defensive posture and cleared the puck continuously from the Bruins zone. But the exuberance of the fans rubbed off on the home team. With 2:12 to play, Corrigan found himself, the puck, and Cheevers on the left side of the ice. The Boston goaltender tripped Corrigan, but as he went down, he managed to flick the puck toward the net; the shot ricocheted off Cheevers' stick and rolled into the goal! The siren sounded, the red light flashed, and bedlam rocked the Forum.

The Kings had two more chances to win the game in regulation time, but it ended at 3-3 and forced the second overtime of the series.

Facing elimination, the Kings were cautious, and both sides took few chances. But Kings center Butch Goring got a good shot from about 30 feet away late in the overtime that skipped past Cheevers and into the goal. Kings win!

The Forum crowd stood and cheered for a deafening six minutes as the Kings hoisted Goring for a victory ride around the ice. Even though Boston won game seven, 3-0, Goring's goal was the most-celebrated, marvelous moment in franchise history—until a miracle was born on the same ice six years later (see Moment 48).

Mike Corrigan of the Kings in a familiar spot during the 1976 Stanley Cup play-offs: scoring from in front of the net, this time against Boston's Gerry Cheevers.

93

Football:
Bo Knows Football
November 30, 1987

Bo Jackson takes off early and often against the Seattle Seahawks in 1987, including running by Seahawks linebacker Brian Bosworth (on the ground) on this sweep.

Al Davis, the managing partner of the Los Angeles Raiders, had done it again. Taking a chance on a talented player who might not even participate in professional football, the Raiders drafted Bo Jackson in the seventh round of the 1987 National Football League draft. Although Jackson was the 1985 Heisman Trophy winner in college at Auburn, he was much more a baseball player with the Kansas City Royals than a football player in the summer of 1987.

The rookie runner joined the Raiders well into the '87 season, after finishing in Kansas City. But as he and the Raiders headed to the Kingdome in Seattle for a Monday night game against the Seahawks, the Raiders were suffering through a seven-game losing streak.

Things didn't look much better as Jackson fumbled on the Raiders' first possession, which was quickly turned into a 7-0 Seahawks lead on a Dave Krieg-to-Daryl Turner pass of 19 yards. But Los Angeles responded under the cool direction of embattled quarterback Marc Wilson. In six plays, the game was tied as Wilson found tight end Todd Christensen for 21 yards, wide receiver Dokie Williams for 17, and then flanker James Lofton for 46 yards and the touchdown.

The Raider defense held Seattle to three plays and a punt, and Wilson took over again on the Raider 41-yard line. Jackson pushed through the Seahawks line for big gains of 15 and 13 yards, punishing tacklers as he went. Then Wilson found him all alone for a 14-yard touchdown pass to give Los Angeles a 14-7 lead early in the second quarter. For the struggling Raiders, this was looking too easy.

The Los Angeles defense again throttled Seattle, and the Seahawks downed a good punt on the Raiders' five-yard line. Two plays netted only four yards, but on third down, Jackson swept left looking for first-down yardage to the 15. But after safety Eugene Robinson unsuccessfully lunged at him, Jackson found a free path to the goal line, 91 yards away.

His sprinter's speed from his days on the Auburn track team cut in immediately, and no one was even close as Jackson zipped past the goal line, through the end zone, and halfway up the runway to the locker rooms. His teammates who tried to follow him down the sidelines and into the tunnel needed oxygen, while Bo jogged back. Raiders 21, Seattle 7.

"I saw the defender had the angle on me," he explained, "and I just threw my head back and ran for my life.

The Seahawks couldn't do much with Jackson, or the Raiders after that. The stunned Seattle team made mistakes on offense and defensive. Put simply, they couldn't stop Jackson. In the second half, his runs of 42 and 25 yards led to a third touchdown (two yards), two Matt Bahr field goals, and a 37-7 Raiders lead. It ended at 37-14 as Jackson gained 221 yards in all—a team record and the 13th-best performance in NFL history. Not bad for a rookie. But then, Bo *knows* football.

Horse Racing:
Revenge of the 'Biscuit
March 2, 1940

An unknown little horse, once an entrant in a $2,500 claiming race, came to Santa Anita in 1937 and lined up to compete in the Santa Anita Handicap against Fairy Hill, the favorite of the then-dominant Foxcatcher Farm. This unknown colt, owned by Charles Howard of San Francisco, startled observers by leading well into the stretch before being overtaken at the wire by Rosemont. The name of Seabiscuit was now spoken with respect.

In 1938, things were different. Seabiscuit had achieved national renown with victories in seven major events in the East and was promptly assigned top weight of 130 pounds for the Big 'Cap on March 5. Despite a poor start, George Woolf moved Seabiscuit from 14th to first on the backstraight and held the lead through the eighth pole, when Stagehand, a three-year-old carrying only 100 pounds, caught up to Seabiscuit down the final straight. The decision went for Stagehand by a nose in a new track record of 2:01 3/5 for the mile and a quarter. Howard said afterwards, "We'll be back and take another crack at it."

It wasn't going to be that easy. Seabiscuit, now a favorite of the Santa Anita faithful, suffered an injury in early 1939 and didn't return to the track for months. At the age of seven, and after a careful recuperation and training, Seabiscuit was racing again. But was he good enough to end his Big 'Cap jinx?

The hold the horse had on the public was evident by the enormous crowd of 68,526 that showed up to watch the sixth Santa Anita Handicap. Seabiscuit wore the top weight of 130 pounds, with Red Pollard up. Whichcee took the lead from the start, but unlike 1938, Seabiscuit was never more than 2 1/2 lengths from the lead. Pollard had Seabiscuit and Whichcee together at the eighth pole, and the crowd roared its approval as the 'Biscuit zoomed down the stretch to take a one-length victory over stablemate Kayak II and Whichcee. In what turned out to be his final race, Seabiscuit garnered his most elusive championship, with a new track record of 2:01 1/5 for the mile and a quarter.

Oscar Otis of the *Los Angeles Times* wrote of that day, "the cheering was from the heart—for the gallant old fellow is the kind of an animal that once you see him run, see him try, see that great heart of his nearly burst in an effort to get down to the wire, it stays in your heart for all time." Seabiscuit retired as the leading money winner of all time, but more importantly, he showed the emotion that could develop between a horse and the public.

Olympic Swimming:
Naber's Genuine ... Genuine Gold, That Is
July 24, 1976

"I am what you see I am," he said. "I'm not being a hypocrite. I'm emotional and sensitive, and I like to show it.

"I don't like to play the role of the clown, and I don't think I do. I just like to involve the crowd."

John Naber had the crowd on their feet in Montreal as the United States' men's swimming team began tearing their way through the rest of the world at the 1976 Olympic Games.

On the first day, he strode to the starting blocks for the qualifying heats of the 100-meter backstroke. Less than one minute later, the 6-6, 195-pound USC junior had not simply the fastest qualifying time, but a new world record of 56.19. One day later, he zipped through the two-lap final in another record of 55.49, well ahead of teammate Peter Rocca (56.34) and former world record holder Roland Matthes of the German Democratic Republic.

One hour later, Naber was back in the pool for the 200-meter freestyle, swimming against another Trojan teammate and world record holder Bruce Furniss. Naber led into the final lap; Furniss overtook him late, but he needed another world record to defeat Naber, 1:50.29 to 1:50.50.

No problem. Naber was smiling atop the victory stand again two days later as he tore through the third leg of the 4-by-200-meter relay to help the U.S. to another world record of 7:23.22, more than seven seconds better than the old world standard.

The next day? Another relay, with the world's best backstroker Naber leading off in the 4-by-100-meter relay en route to another world record of 3:42.22, which shaved more than five seconds off the existing world mark of 3:47.28.

After four races, winning three golds and a silver, Naber still wasn't finished. He dove into the pool two days later, on July 24, for the 200-meter backstroke, in which he was already the world record holder at 2:00.64. It didn't take him that long to finish; he became the first person to break the two-minute barrier at 1:59.19 and led a U.S. sweep with Rocca and Dan Harrigan taking the silver and bronze, respectively.

Five medals in five days, four of them gold. It's no wonder the mustachioed Naber wore a big, golden smile.

Unforgettable

Horse Racing:
The Shoe Fits . . . for the 1,000th Time
April 30, 1989

Willie Shoemaker may have worn Number 2 aboard Peace in winning his 1,000th stakes race, but he finished as the winningest jockey of all time.

In the eighth race at Hollywood Park on a lovely Sunday in April, some 27,330 fans watched a familiar sight come thundering down the track, heading for the wire. It was Bill Shoemaker, the winningest jockey in history, writing another headline.

In his final season of competitive riding, Shoemaker had a masterful ride on Peace, racing to the front, away from trouble, and holding on throughout. He fought off a determined challenge from the favorite, Steinlen, in the closing straight to win his sixth Premiere Handicap and become the first jockey ever to win 1,000 stakes races in his career. Shoemaker had won 8,796 overall, and 254 in races worth $100,000 or more.

"It's hard to imagine," said jockey Gary Stevens, who finished aboard Steinlen, one length behind the winner. "It's just phenomenal."

Eddie Delahoussaye, who finished third with Political Ambition, was similarly awed. "A thousand stakes!" he said afterward. "Man, that's a lot of races."

Shoemaker rode Peace in 1:33 flat for a new stakes record for the one mile; the win was extra sweet since the Premiere is HollyPark's oldest stakes race. Shoemaker first won it in 1951.

When he ended his riding career on February 3, 1990, Shoemaker was the standard by which all other jockeys would be measured. He had won 8,833 times and garnered more than $123 million in purses in a reign that began in 1949. He had won four Kentucky Derbys, twice in the Preakness Stakes, and five times in the Belmont Stakes.

In short, Shoemaker was a winner. Not surprisingly, he turned to training horses after his retirement, and . . . within months, he had his first of many winners to come.

97

Boxing:
De La Hoya Wins "Oscar" for Best Performance
March 5, 1994

Nineteen-year-old Oscar De La Hoya of East Los Angeles was nearing his goal. He had promised his dying mother two years earlier that he would return from the 1992 Olympic Games in Barcelona, Spain, with a gold medal. Now all that stood between him and his goal was the man who had defeated him in the first round of the 1991 World Boxing Championships: eventual world champion Marco Rudolph of Germany. In fact, Rudolph was the only opponent to defeat De La Hoya in his amateur career.

At the 1992 Games, the 132-pound (60kg) division was dominated by these two fighters. De La Hoya stomped three opponents by large margins, then outfought Korea's Hong Sung Sik 11-10 in the semifinals. Rudolph smashed two foes by 10-5 and 10-1 scores, then outpointed France's Julian Lorcy in the quarterfinals, 13-10, before being awarded a walkover in the semifinals.

But De La Hoya was much better. He was in control from the start, knocked Rudolph down once, and scored a smart 7-2 win to claim the only gold medal of the 1992 Olympic tournament for the United States. "I'm going to buy a lot of flowers and make a nice arrangement," he told Jon Saraceno of *USA Today*, "and set the medal down [on the grave] as if around her neck."

The honors De La Hoya brought to his family continued once he began fighting professionally, not long after his return from Barcelona. And one of his finest moments came on March 5, 1994, when he provided hometown boxing fans with a brilliant performance on "Oscar" night at the Grand Olympic Auditorium in downtown Los Angeles.

De La Hoya on his way to victory in Barcelona: in action (inset) and earning a decision over Korea's Hong Sung Sik in the semifinals (above).

The 70-year-old auditorium, named in honor of the 1932 Olympic Games, was refurbished and making its reopening with De La Hoya (11-0) as the feature attraction in a 12-round battle for the World Boxing Organization's junior lightweight (130 pounds) championship against the left-handed champion from Denmark, Jimmi Bredahl (16-0).

An exuberant crowd of 5,843 gathered in the arena and cheered De La Hoya's knockdowns in the first and second rounds. But Bredahl kept his composure and kept his distance, lengthening what might have been a short night for De La Hoya if he had been able to deliver more firepower at closer range.

But Bredahl's right eye was closed, and his face was so battered that the referee stopped the bout (TKO) after the 10th round. The match—and a world title—belonged to De La Hoya.

"It's a world title," he said later, of his second world championship—one amateur and one professional—in three years. "It means a lot."

Olympic Track and Field:
Houser's Golden Double at Paris
July 13, 1924

Clarence "Bud" Houser was a trim 6-2, 187-pound track-and-field champion. As a 20-year-old in 1921, he won his first national championship . . . in the shot put?

In events usually reserved for giants like 6-6, 286-pound Ralph Rose, who won six Olympic medals in the shot, discus, and hammer from 1904 to 1912, Houser was trimmer, but better.

Houser won a letter as a USC sophomore in 1924, but Ralph Hills won the national shot put title, and Thomas Lieb took the discus. Still, he qualified for the Olympic team in both the shot and discus, and on July 8 he joined 27 other competitors in the qualifying round of the shot.

At that time, each competitor received three trials in the qualifying round, with only the top three allowed to receive three additional tries. Houser's early mark of 49-2 1/4 was the best of the qualifying marks, and he led a U.S. sweep into the finals with teammates Glenn Hartranft (47-3) and Hills (48-0 1/2). Hartranft improved to 48-10 1/4 but couldn't challenge Houser, who took the gold.

Houser, Hartranft, Lieb, and Gus Pope entered the Stade Colombes five days later for the discus. Houser immediately took control with an Olympic record throw of 151-4, and easily outlasted Finland's Vilho Niittymaa (147-5) and Lieb (147-0) to win again. Only Robert Garrett (USA) had won both the shot and discus in the same Games previously, and that was in 1896. Not bad for a sophomore.

But Houser was only starting up. As a USC junior in 1925, he repeated his double in the shot and discus at the AAU national championships. As a senior in 1926, he doubled again, this time in the NCAA and AAU discus championships.

By 1928 the 27-year-old Houser had emerged as the world's finest discus thrower. Competing for the Los Angeles Athletic Club, he set a world record of 158-2 at Palo Alto on April 3, then won the national AAU championship and Final Olympic Trials at Cambridge, Massachusetts, on July 7, throwing 153-6 1/4.

So he was the favorite when he strode into the discus ring in Amsterdam on August 1. There were 34 competitors from 19 countries present, but Houser led the qualifying by breaking his own Olympic Record with a toss of 155-3, which held up for his third Olympic title.

Over time, Houser's achievements were often overlooked in the fever over Finland's Paavo Nurmi, who won nine gold medals and 12 in all from 1920 to 1928. But from Houser's time forward, no one has equaled his feat of winning both the shot put and discus in the same Games as he did in Paris. Magnifique!

99

Baseball:
Carew Gets 3,000th Hit, Joins Game's Heavenly Hitters

August 4, 1985

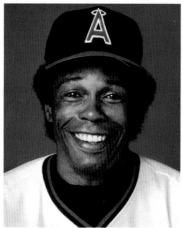

It was inevitable, but it was still fun. A giant crowd of 41,630 came to see history on a brilliant Sunday afternoon at Anaheim Stadium as the Angels defeated the Minnesota Twins, 6-5.

But the highlight was a simple single. First baseman Rod Carew had 2,999 hits coming into the game and needed only one more to reach a magical total of 3,000. In the more than a century of major-league baseball, only 16 other players had collected that many base hits. All of them are in the Hall of Fame.

Hitting against left-hander Frank Viola of the Twins, Carew, also a lefty, bounced out to the mound in the first inning. In the third, with the Angels down 1-0, shortstop Dick Schofield homered to tie the game, followed by a walk to designated hitter Brian Downing. Carew then came to the plate and, as he had so many times before, lined an opposite-field single over the head of third baseman Gary Gaetti for his historic hit. The Angels didn't score any more runs in the inning, and Carew finished the day at 1-for-5.

But the crowd rose to give the 39-year-old Carew a standing ovation to celebrate his permanent place among baseball's immortals. "When you get in the class with Ty Cobb and Rogers Hornsby and Pete Rose, it means a lot," said Carew afterward. "It's a very emotional thing, starting against the Twins, my first team, and getting the hit against them."

Carew was a sensation from the start of his career in Minnesota in 1967. In 12 seasons with the Twins, he collected 2,085 hits and won seven batting titles: in 1969 (.332), 1972 (.318), 1973 (.350), 1974 (.364), 1975 (.359), 1977 (.388), and 1978 (.333). Traded to the Angels before the 1979 season for four players, he immediately became a key in the Angels' first division championship in 1979 and hit over .300 in each of his first five seasons in Anaheim.

An elegant player with great vision and a seemingly effortless swing, Carew joined the 3,000 club in his 2,417th game and in his 19th major-league season.

"I was blessed with the ability to hit—with good eyesight, good hand-and-eye coordination," he said after the game. "When I first came up, the Twins expected me to hit .240 and play second base, but I knew I could do more than that." So much more that Carew, with his career total of 3,053 hits, would very soon join the game's greatest players in the Baseball Hall of Fame.

Baseball:
Bilko's 56th Ends an Era in Los Angeles
September 7, 1957

He was truly the "Toast of the Coast." Big Steve Bilko, the 6-1, 242-pound, slugging first baseman of the Los Angeles Angels, was again mauling Pacific Coast League pitching to the tune of more than 50 home runs a year.

He'd had an up-and-down career in the major leagues, mostly with the St. Louis Cardinals (his best year, 1953, included 21 homers and 84 runs batted in), but Bilko had done nothing but impress Southern Californians with his long smashes since being assigned to Los Angeles by the Chicago Cubs in 1955. He slammed 37 home runs in 1955, then 55 homers in 1956. He was named the Pacific Coast League's Most Valuable Player both years, and he came into this Saturday afternoon game against the Sacramento Solons with 55 homers as the season wore down to its close.

He was chasing the minor-league record of 60 home runs in a season, set in 1925 by Tony Lazzeri of Salt Lake City, who was later an outstanding second baseman with the New York Yankees. On this day, Bilko was opposed by Roger Bowman (5-10), while left-hander Tommy Lasorda, who also entered the game with a 5-10 record, threw for the Angels.

Lasorda gave up two runs in the first, but the Angels pounded Bowman for a run in the second and four in the third, then went to work on reliever Carl Greene. With the Angels and Lasorda in control, 6-2, Bilko led off the sixth inning.

Greene's first pitch was smashed over the right field fence, to the delight of the 3,724 fans at Wrigley Field, giving Bilko a team

The powerful swing of Steve Bilko is easy to appreciate in this photograph as he hits his 56th home run of the 1957 season for the Los Angeles Angels.

record for home runs in a season, one better than Gene Lillard's 1935 total of 55. Lasorda enjoyed the offensive support on the way to an 8-3 win.

Big Steve still had 13 games to go in the 160-game season to try and catch Lazzeri, but it was for naught. He finished the season with those 56 home runs, to accompany a .300 batting average and 140 runs batted in. But he and Los Angeles were in for many changes in the months ahead.

Walter O'Malley of the Brooklyn Dodgers purchased the Angels and Wrigley Field from the Chicago Cubs for $2 million in early 1957, and shortly after the season closed, the Dodgers announced they would be relocating to Los Angeles in 1958 (see Moment 10). It was time for major-league baseball in Los Angeles; the minor-league club that had been the Angels—which had won 14 PCL titles—was transferred to Spokane, Washington.

Bilko's time had come, too. He graduated to the major leagues again the following season with Cincinnati, and even played first base with the Los Angeles Dodgers in late 1958. But a few years later, his career was completed, as was the history of minor-league baseball in Los Angeles.

College Basketball Championship:
Ed O'Bannon Leads Bruins to Rout of Razorbacks
April 3, 1995

UCLA hadn't won a national basketball championship since John Wooden's retirement in 1975 (see Moment 4). Now they prepared to face defending national champion Arkansas (32-6) for the 1995 NCAA championship—without their key player.

Tyus Edney, the brilliant 5-10 point guard, had been the catalyst in UCLA's stretch run of 18 consecutive victories leading up to the championship game. It was Edney's coast-to-coast drive with 4.7 seconds remaining that had beaten Missouri 75-74 in the second round. It was Edney leading endless fast breaks that wore out Connecticut, 102-96, in the Western Regional final. And it was Edney's relentless drives to the basket for 21 points that made the difference in the hard-fought, 74-61 semifinal win over Oklahoma State and 7-0 center Bryant "Big Country" Reeves.

But an injury to his right wrist suffered in the Oklahoma State win had worsened, and Edney could not play. He couldn't even dribble the ball with his right hand, and after an early turnover, Bruin Coach Jim Harrick benched his senior star in favor of sophomore point-guard-in-waiting Cameron Dollar. It was now time for senior forward Ed O'Bannon, the national Player of the Year, to lead UCLA from the front court, rather than share the load with Edney.

The Bruins responded. "We wanted to make sure the whole world knew we were the best team in the country," said the 6-8 O'Bannon. "Simple as that."

O'Bannon, his 6-6 brother Charles, 7-0 center George Zidek, Dollar, and freshmen J.R. Henderson and Toby Bailey had the task of stopping all-American forward Corliss Williamson, guards Scotty Thurman and Corey Beck, and the rest of the Razorbacks.

Arkansas took a 12-5 lead, but the Bruins took charge under the calm direction of Dollar and wonderful interior passing. They led at halftime, 40-39. Could it last?

Ed O'Bannon slashed, drove, and flipped soft one-handers through the air to start the second half, and with support from Zidek's high-arching hook shots from the baseline and the above-the-basket heroics of Bailey—who slammed, jammed, tipped, and rebounded—the Bruins had a 55-45 lead with 15:30 to play.

When Arkansas cut the score to 67-63 with 5:22 to go, the 38,540 in Seattle's Kingdome could feel the rush of a second national championship trophy heading for Fayetteville. Somebody forgot to tell Ed O'Bannon.

"I was mad," he said later. "They had the momentum, they were fired up. But at that point, we came together, and we made sure we wouldn't fold. And we didn't."

Instead, they clubbed Arkansas with relentless rebounding (50-31 for the game) and good foul shooting (21-29), while also extending the lead back to 81-71 with 1:25 to go. It was over.

The final score was 89-78, and UCLA had its 11th national basketball championship. Harrick had won his first championship in his 16th year of major college coaching. Ed O'Bannon was named the Most Valuable Player of the Final Four for his 30-point, 17-rebound performance. Bailey added 26 points and nine rebounds, while Zidek contributed another 14 points.

"The guy is the best player in America, bar none," said a grinning Harrick of Ed-O. "He refused all year to let us lose. He always found a way to win."

It was a banner season for Ed and his 31-2 teammates. Just look inside Pauley Pavilion. Their banner is the one with "1995" on it.

Bruin coach Jim Harrick holds UCLA's first NCAA basketball championship trophy since 1975, earned with the help of final-game heroics by guard Cameron Dollar (inset top), center George Zidek (above), and Final Four Most Valuable Player Ed O'Bannon (opposite).

Profiles in Excellence

A look at the corporations, businesses, professional groups, and community service organizations that have made this book possible. Their stories—offering an informal chronicle of the local business community—are arranged according to the date they were established in the Los Angeles area.

American Airlines ■ Ameron, Inc. ■ ARB, Inc. ■ ARCO ■ Automobile Club of Southern California ■ Avery Dennison ■ Bal Seal Engineering Company, Inc. ■ Bank of America ■ Bright & Associates ■ California State University, Northridge ■ Cal-Surance Group Benefits, Inc. ■ California Angels ■ Compensation Resource Group ■ Daniel Freeman Hospitals, Inc. ■ Dole Food Company, Inc. ■ Dunn-Edwards Corporation ■ Eagle Delivery Systems, Inc. ■ First Interstate Bank ■ Great Western Forum ■ Hacienda Hotel ■ Hollywood Park, Inc. ■ International Business Machines Corporation ■ KNBC-TV ■ Los Angeles Athletic Club ■ Los Angeles Clippers ■ Los Angeles Dodgers ■ Los Angeles Turf Club ■ The Mighty Ducks ■ Mullin Consulting, Inc. ■ Nissan Motor Corporation U.S.A. ■ Ogden Entertainment Services ■ Pacific Bell ■ Parsons Brinckerhoff ■ Prime Sports ■ R. Rollo Associates ■ Ralphs Grocery Company ■ Southern California Committee for the Olympic Games ■ Southern California Edison Corporation ■ Steinberg and Moorad Law Offices ■ Transamerica Life Companies ■ United Airlines ■ Ventura Entertainment Group Ltd. ■ XTRA Sports 690 ■

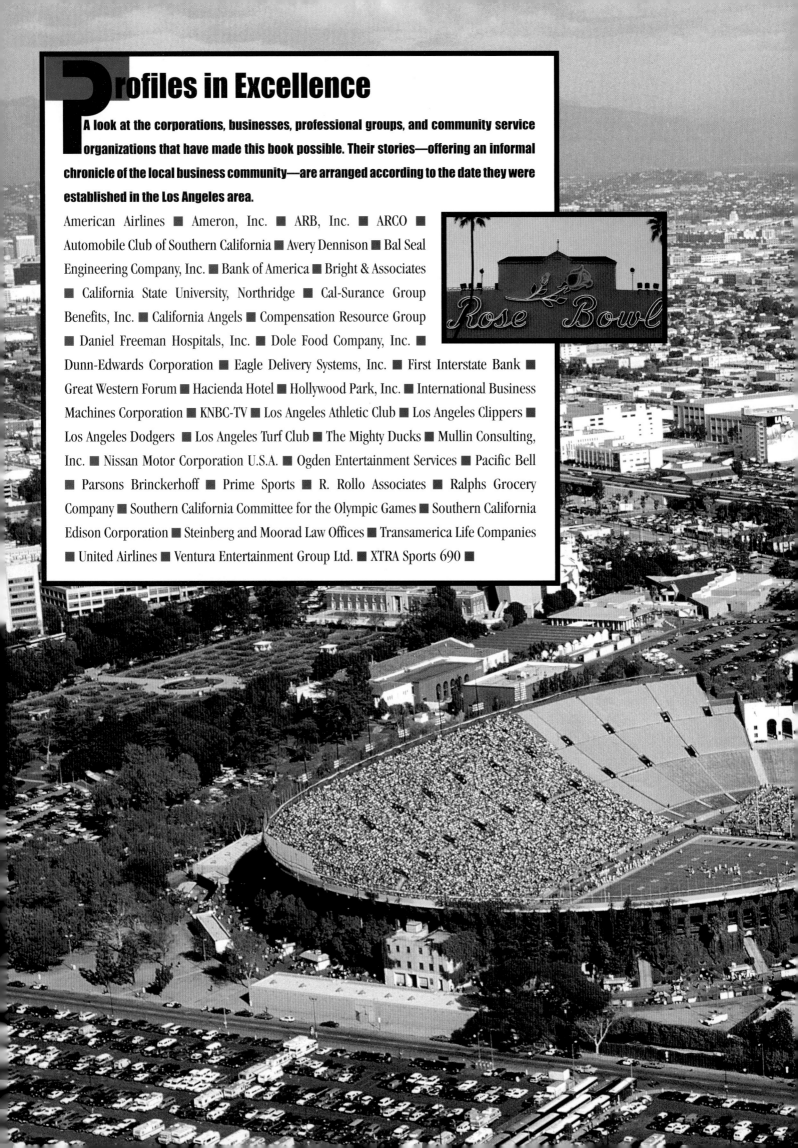

1873–1945

1873
Ralphs Grocery Company

1880
Los Angeles Athletic Club

1886
Southern California Edison
Corporation

1900
Automobile Club of Southern
California

1905
ARCO

1906
Pacific Bell

1906
Transamerica Life Companies

1907
Ameron, Inc.

1913
Bank of America

The following time line is presented in order to place in historical context the broad sweep of athletic achievements that have so enriched our area. Numbered items correspond to those of individual "moments" presented in the first section of this book.

916
International Business Machines Corporation

925
Dunn-Edwards Corporation

926
United Airlines

1928
First Interstate Bank

1929
ARB, Inc.

1930
American Airlines

1934
Los Angeles Turf Club

1935
Avery Dennison

1938
Hollywood Park, Inc.

1939
Southern California Committee for the Olympic Games

1944
XTRA Sports 690

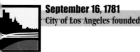

September 16, 1781
City of Los Angeles founded

September 8, 1880
Los Angeles Athletic Club founded

December 4, 1881
Los Angeles Times begins publication

Ralphs Grocery Company

When George Albert Ralphs opened his first grocery store in Los Angeles in 1873, there wer fewer people in the entire city (7,200) than there are Ralphs Grocery Company members toda (approximately 30,000 and growing). That's just one measure of how a small town grew int

Ralphs Grocery Company, founded by George A. Ralphs (far right), opened its first store at Sixth and Spring streets in Los Angeles (near right).

one of the nation's biggest metropolitan areas and how a neighborhood grocer founded one of the nation's most successful food retailing chains.

Not many supermarket companies have a history that can be traced for more than 120 years. Ralphs Grocery Company is one of the few. Ralphs' history is interesting and extraordinary. It is a classic American success story that bears telling and remembering. It is a story of overwhelming success based on a philosophy of commitment to quality, service, and innovation.

Values Fuel Growth

Enormously energetic and ambitious, George Ralphs founded his business with two philosophies in mind—to provide value-priced, top-quality products to cus-

tomers and to give them the customer-comes-first service they deserve. His first store was a neighborhood market at the corner of Sixth and Spring streets at what was then the edge of downtown Los Angeles.

As the city of Los Angeles grew, so did Ralphs Grocery Company, building its reputation for providing quality goods at competitive prices. Today, Ralphs is one of the western United States' leading supermarket companies, with more than 350 modern service-oriented stores serving cost- and quality-conscious consumers throughout California and the Midwest.

Ralphs has long been famous for its innovations. One of the first was a new approach to the traditional handling of fresh produce. To solicit business in the

early days, Ralphs provided lodging for farmers and stabling for their horses when they traveled to Los Angeles to sell their crops. This tactic attracted so many enthusiastic sellers that Ralphs was able to buy entire crops at one time. It also marked the beginning of two Ralphs Grocery traditions: farm fresh produce and volume buying with savings passed on to the customer.

By 1928 Ralphs had 10 stores—and another wild idea. By then, American families were driving their own automobiles. "A car in every garage" was the nation's dream, and Ralphs abandoned home delivery and instituted a cash-and-carry policy, self-service, and ample free parking.

Improvements Continue Today

◄ In the 1970s Ralphs continued adding new consumer-conscious benefits to its supermarket lineup, including unit pricing, freshness code dating, and no-frills generic products. The company pioneered another breakthrough in 1974, when it became the first supermarket chain west of the Mississippi River to equip its stores with laser scanning checkout systems. The new electronic checkout-stand scanners resulted in faster, more accurate pricing and more efficient customer service.

Until 1968 Ralphs was one of the few large supermarket companies that

Today's Ralphs supermarkets are designed to appeal to shoppers concerned about quality, nutrition, and price (below).

SMITH PHOTOGRAPHY

January 1, 1886
First Tournament of Roses Parade

November 14, 1888
USC plays first football game, wins 16-0 vs. Alliance AC

82 January 1, 1902
First Rose Bowl: Michigan 49; Stanford 0

remained entirely family-owned. Early that year Ralphs was acquired by Federated Department Stores (FDS) of Cincinnati and became an independent operating subsidiary of that corporation. The company changed hands again in 1988, when FDS was acquired by the Canadian-based Campeau Corporation.

In 1992 a holding company, now named Ralphs Supermarkets, Inc., was formed to purchase the outstanding shares of Ralphs common stock from Campeau. In June 1995 Ralphs Supermarkets, Inc. merged with Food 4 Less Supermarkets Inc., operator of approximately 260 supermarkets under the Alpha Beta, Food 4 Less, Boys, Viva, Cala, Bell, FoodsCo, and Falley's names in California and the Midwest, creating Ralphs Grocery Company, the largest supermarket company in Southern California. As a result of the merger, the new Ralphs Grocery Company is well positioned for the next generation of growth.

Today, Ralphs Grocery Company operates about 270 conventional-style Ralphs supermarkets and 70 warehouse-style Food 4 Less outlets. The company's supermarkets are designed for customers who are concerned about quality, nutrition, and price; have limited time; desire a wide selection of items; and prefer shopping at one location.

Efficiently designed to make shopping easy, today's typical Ralphs supermarket is 45,000 square feet and carries approximately 30,000 different items in such well-stocked departments as dry groceries, frozen foods, produce, meat, and dairy products, along with a wide assortment of general merchandise, and health and beauty aids. Most Ralphs conventional-style supermarkets also feature richly appointed bakeries, service delicatessens, and seafood departments with European-style service.

The company's Food 4 Less warehouse stores are massive 70,000- to 100,000-square-foot buildings designed to be low-priced alternatives to the typical conventional supermarket. All Ralphs stores are supported by an extensive net-

work of modern warehousing, distribution, and manufacturing facilities.

Ralphs also has a long and substantial tradition of community involvement. The supermarket company has made a corporate commitment to support programs and efforts to help improve the environment, education, and family and cultural life in the various communities it serves.

Additionally, Ralphs is a busy corporate player in the world of professional athletics. Since 1992 the company has sponsored the only Senior PGA Tour event held in the Los Angeles area— the Ralphs Senior Classic.

Ralphs Grocery Company has come a long way from its modest beginnings in 1873. And while the company is modern and dynamic, it still operates on the same sound principles upon which it was founded so many years ago—an unwavering commitment to customer service, quality products, and significant savings.

Ralphs' groceries feature freshly prepared entrées and hot foods from the Chef Express delicatessen (upper left) and some 300 varieties of fresh goods in the produce department (upper right).

Clockwise from top left: Ralphs' classic stores reflected the rich architecture of the Los Angeles area: Pasadena, 1939; Hollywood, 1929; Long Beach, 1931; and Wilshire & Hauser, 1929.

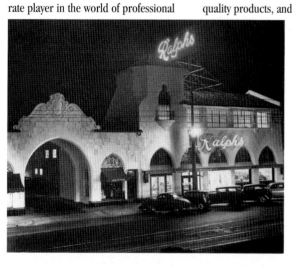

September 1903
Los Angeles Angels win first
Pacific Coast League title

January 10, 1910
First international air show held in the
United States, at Dominguez farm

November 5, 1911
First transcontinental flight (from New York)
lands in Los Angeles

The 100 Greatest Moments in Los Angeles Sports History   145

Southern California Edison Company

Southern California Edison Company, the second-largest electric utility in the United States, has been part of the Golden State for more than a century. Today, Edison serves more than 4.1 million residential, commercial, industrial, and agricultural customers in Central and Southern California.

SCEcorp is the parent corporation of Southern California Edison Company, founded in 1886, and two principal nonutility companies: Mission Energy Company and Mission First Financial. With headquarters in Rosemead, California, SCEcorp has assets of more than $22 billion.

Mission Energy is one of the nation's leading developers, owners, and operators of independent power facilities, a rapidly growing business. Based in Irvine, California, the company owns approximately 2,000 megawatts in 34 operating projects in domestic and foreign markets—enough power to serve more than 1.5 million people. Mission also has six projects in construction or the final stages of financing. In 1992 Mission Energy became the first independent power company to receive an investment-grade credit rating.

Mission First Financial, SCEcorp's capital and financial services arm, is a leading provider of capital and financial services to the energy sector. One of the country's most active corporate investors in high-quality affordable housing, Mission First Financial has more than 100 housing projects in operation or under construction.

Building Partnerships

SCEcorp builds value by making its enterprises as service-oriented and efficient as any in the world and by aggressively developing new markets. As the company readies itself for a competitive, deregulated future, partnering is a key to creating value in its businesses—partnering with customers to address their changing energy needs, with suppliers to make SCEcorp's operation more efficient and cost effective, with communities in Edison's service territory to make the region more competitive, and with other countries where there is a demand for the Mission companies' expertise.

"Partnership is a powerful notion," Edison Chairman John Bryson says. "We know our customers and the challenges they face. We will continue to help them, using our people and our experience. We're not an untested newcomer, seeking only the most lucrative of California's customers, ready to leave if the going gets tough. We have been here for more than a century. We are committed to California's future and we are here to stay."

Ready for Competition

Edison employees are transforming their company from an excellent, regulated utility into a tough, agile competitor. As Edison accelerates its readiness for the competitive marketplace of the future, it seeks to maintain the positive values of the regulated environment: stability, reliability, and energy efficiency, as well as a long-term investment horizon. At the same time, the company is sharply intensifying its focus on serving individual business and residential customers. For example, in the first half of 1995, Edison

Edison has been in California for more than a century, and both the company and its employees are committed to the Golden State's future (right).

Customers depend on Southern California Edison for specialized services that can help them be more competitive (below).

As Edison accelerates its readiness for the competitive marketplace of the future, it seeks to maintain stability, reliability, and energy efficiency, as well as a long-term investment horizon (right).

January 1, 1916
Second Tournament of Roses football game:
Washington State 14, Brown 0

October 3, 1919
First UCLA football game, a 74-0 loss
to Manual Arts High School

66 April 23, 1921
Charley Paddock sets four sprint world records
in one day

146

Unforgettable

introduced a broad set of initiatives designed to provide customers lower electricity prices, more pricing options, new service guarantees, and enhanced environmental quality.

"We are basing our marketing and business expansion plans on the foundation of what we have always done best. And, in partnership with our customers, we are learning to think in new ways," says Bryson.

Edison has set a goal to reduce "real" prices (adjusted for inflation) by 25 percent by the year 2000. Eligible business customers will have flexible pricing choices, including special economic development pricing that will help create and preserve jobs in Southern California. Customers will enjoy state-of-the-art electronic payment options, including pay-by-phone and direct payment. They will also see new billing options, including summary billing, computer billing, and diskette billing. Service guarantees mean that customers will receive a credit on their bill if Edison doesn't meet high-level performance standards.

Edison will expand shareholder funding of environmental quality initiatives, including energy efficiency investments and support for environmentally sound electric technologies. Environmental solutions have helped customers like Sunkist Growers and Knott's Berry Farm reduce overall energy consumption, improve productivity, and still meet Southern California's strict environmental standards.

For instance, Edison is developing a strong presence in the energy solutions market through ENVEST-SCE. Sales in that market could approach $100 million annually. In 1995 the United States Postal Service (USPS) signed an agreement with ENVEST for a 79-site energy efficiency modernization project of which the first eight sites are in Los Angeles and Orange counties. It is the largest energy efficiency partnership program ever entered into by USPS.

In the area of transportation solutions, Edison is addressing air quality problems in Los Angeles and the nation by supporting electric vehicle infrastructure and battery research. Edison also provides communications solutions, linking customers through its fiber-optic networks so they can monitor energy use and use it more productively.

Southern California Edison's entry in the 1994 Tournament of Roses Parade celebrates the utility's proud support of a great moment in Los Angeles sports history: the World Cup Soccer Championship.

Staying Power

Edison has been in California for more than a century and is committed to the Golden State's future. In fact, Edison's strategic plan calls for it to be a regional leader. That leadership can take many forms. Edison was one of many proud supporters who helped make the 1994 World Cup Soccer Championship a success.

The company recognizes that the vitality of the communities in its service territory is inextricably linked to the success of the company itself. Since 1992 Edison has helped nearly 250 companies remain or relocate in Southern California, representing more than 50,000 regional jobs.

Edison has come a long way since its founding in 1886. Likewise, the Mission companies have grown rapidly since their inception a century later. In a partnership with their customers, employees, shareholders, and the communities in its territories, SCEcorp and its businesses will continue to be leaders in product and service innovation and quality.

Southern California Edison Company, the second-largest electric utility in the United States, serves more than 4.1 million customers in central and southern California (left).

January 1, 1923
Rose Bowl site of USC's 14-3 win over Penn State

April 8, 1923
Los Angeles awarded Games of the X Olympiad at IOC meeting in Rome

October 6, 1923
Coliseum opens with USC's 23-7 win over Pomona

The 100 Greatest Moments in Los Angeles Sports History

147

The Los Angeles Athletic Club

The Los Angeles Athletic Club began in 1880 with 41 young men who wanted to create a place in Los Angeles for sports, health, and good fellowship. Their names read like a who's who of the city: Lankershim, Kerckhoff, Lancaster, and Decatur. Their pride in athletic prowess laid the foundation

The Los Angeles Athletic Club's superior facilities are recognized and used by many world-class athletes (far right). To date, more than 100 of its members have earned Olympic medals.

Olympic champion diver Pat McCormick (below left) displays her gold medals beside the club pool where she trained for the 1952 Olympic Games.

Sports celebrities (below right) gather for the presentation of the John R. Wooden Player of the Year Award, presented by the Los Angeles Athletic Club. From left: Marques Johnson, the first winner of the award; Coach Wooden; Michael Jordan, recipient of the award in 1984; Awards Chairman Duke Llewellyn; and Awards Emcee Tommy Hawkins.

for the club's future position in the world of amateur athletics.

In 1912 the club moved from rented quarters near the civic center to its newly constructed building—considered to be the finest training facility in the world—at Seventh and Olive streets in downtown Los Angeles. In addition to elegant restaurants, residential suites, and a fully equipped gymnasium, the club achieved an architectural first by building its swimming pool above the ground floor.

With the opening of its first-rate facility, the club entered an era of Olympic greatness, sponsoring and training Olympic athletes in many sports. To date, more than 100 of its members have earned Olympic medals. Deeper involvement with the Olympics began in 1932 when the club played an instrumental role in bringing the Olympic Games to Los Angeles for the first time. Half a century later, the club hosted meetings of the 1984 Los Angeles Olympic Committee, which included many of its members.

Making Athletic History

As a dominant force in amateur athletics, the club sponsored and coached national champions and national champion teams in a variety of sports, including swimming, fencing, boxing, water polo, gymnastics, basketball, handball, golf, tennis, and track and field. Club President Frank Garbutt helped to popularize the East Coast game of handball on the West

Coast by constructing handball courts at the club and introducing the game to members.

In the years following World War II, the club became an innovator in the fitness field, introducing the first indoor tartan-surfaced running track, the first glass-backed handball courts, and the internationally used Universal Gym for weight training. It was at the forefront of raising awareness about the importance of exercise to good health and developed programs to encourage

members—including women and children—to enjoy the benefits of physical activity.

In 1975 the Los Angeles Athletic Club created the John R. Wooden Awards, named for the legendary UCLA basketball coach. The annual awards recognize the outstanding collegiate basketball Player of the Year. Among the great players who have been honored are Larry Bird, David Robinson, and Michael Jordan.

Throughout its history, the club has participated in civic affairs, helping to bring professional sports teams such as the Dodgers, Rams, Raiders, Lakers, and Clippers to Los Angeles, and moving beyond the realm of sports to support youth and revitalization programs in the city. Today, the Los Angeles Athletic Club represents a rich blend of old and new. It reflects the achievements of the men and women who have brought it worldwide fame, while it offers new leaders in the athletic, business, political, and cultural arenas a unique haven for the pursuit of fitness and good fellowship.

98 July 13, 1924
Bud Houser's Olympic shot-discus double

August 5, 1925
Olympic Auditorium opens as Los Angeles' first major civic arena

January 16, 1926
Red Grange and Chicago Bears defeat Los Angeles Tigers in exhibition before 65,270

Automobile Club of Southern California

At the turn of the 20th century, Los Angeles car owners faced many challenges, including impassable roads, unreliable automobiles, and inconsistent traffic rules. In spite of the driving challenges, 10 men in Los Angeles recognized that the automobile would someday play a key

AUTOMOBILE CLUB OF SOUTHERN CALIFORNIA ARCHIVES ▲

role in the future and founded the Automobile Club of Southern California in December 1900. The club's aim was to promote safe, well-built, adequate roads; protect the rights and privileges of motorists; and provide travel services and social events for its members.

Among the Auto Club's social gatherings during the 1910s and 1920s were auto races. These races provided exciting sport for thousands of Los Angeles-area automotive enthusiasts and attracted racing greats such as Barney Oldfield and Eddie Rickenbacker. The races were also used to demonstrate the safety and reliability of cars, which in turn helped further the causes of more liberal speed laws and road construction.

In 1907, as road touring became more popular, the Auto Club first began posting direction signs for motorists. In the ensuing years, thousands of Auto Club direction and safety signs were erected on hundreds of Southern California roadways. The Club also produced maps and tour books recognized for their usefulness and accuracy. The Club eventually joined the American Automobile Association (AAA) so its membership could receive service anywhere across the nation.

As its membership increased, the Auto Club began adding offices throughout Southern California. Over the years, Auto Club staff became leaders of local

traffic safety committees, tourism bureaus, and chambers of commerce by providing Auto Club engineering and travel expertise.

Taking Aim at Traffic Problems

The Auto Club also offered its traffic engineering expertise to many Southern California cities—Los Angeles among them—to help address another growing concern: the increase in traffic congestion. In 1937 Auto Club traffic engineers studied the Los Angeles area and recommended a master plan that included a transit system and a network of elevated highways that resembled the freeways of today.

In 1974 the Auto Club helped found the city's first major carpooling effort, called "Commuter Computer," to assist in reducing vehicular congestion. Prior to the 1984 Olympics in Los Angeles, the Auto Club cosponsored transportation seminars that helped ensure free-flowing traffic during the course of the Games.

The organization's legacy of community involvement remains a continuous theme. Today the Auto Club works closely with individual cities as well as the state to improve driver and vehicle safety, reduce air pollution, and ensure adequate means of financing for area roads and various mass transit projects.

From car racing, sign posting, and mapmaking in the early days, Auto Club

member services today include a travel agency; auto, home, and boat insurance; vehicle pricing, purchasing, and financing; an Auto Club MasterCard; and travel planning computer software called IntelliTravel™. Services are provided through the Auto Club's 70 offices, a telephone service center, or the on-line computer service "Prodigy." The Auto Club also returns to its car racing roots as a 1995 sponsor of Danny Sullivan's PacWest IndyCar and participant in National Hot Rod Association career fairs for high school students.

Since 1900 the Auto Club has been an active, visible part of Southern California culture and today is the nation's largest AAA club, with more than 4 million members. As it rolls toward the 21st century, the Automobile Club of Southern California plans future growth by building on its rich history of community involvement and member service.

Clockwise from top left:
In 1907, as road touring became more popular, the Auto Club first began posting direction signs for motorists.

The Auto Club is a 1995 sponsor of Danny Sullivan's PacWest IndyCar.

In 1937 Auto Club traffic engineers studied the Los Angeles area and recommended a master plan that included a transit system and a network of elevated highways that resembled the freeways of today.

Since the 1920s, the Club has provided communities with crossing guard, alcohol education, and pedestrian and bicycle safety programs to help reduce traffic accidents.

AUTOMOBILE CLUB OF SOUTHERN CALIFORNIA ARCHIVES ▲

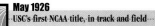
May 1926
USC's first NCAA title, in track and field

December 4, 1926
USC–Notre Dame series opens with
13-12 Irish win at Coliseum

January 1, 1927
First ever coast-to-coast radio broadcast
originates from Rose Bowl

ARCO

I n 1905 a former Iowa farmer and his partners founded a small oil refining and marketing business in Los Angeles that became, a decade later, Richfield Oil, the West Coast predecessor of ARCO, one of America's largest and most progressive petroleum companies. At the time, automobiles were only an occasional

ARCO's EC-1 Regular, the world's first reformulated gasoline, reduced emissions by 20 percent in older vehicles (near left).

The ARCO Jesse Owens Games opened track competition to millions of youngsters across the United States (far left).

sight on the nation's streets, but their rapid growth in popularity would shape both the community and the company. In a very real way, Los Angeles and ARCO grew up together, working in partnership to build a world-class city with economic and cultural opportunities for its growing population.

In the early days, Richfield's community involvement was tied to its marketing efforts. As America became more and more enamored of the motor car, daredevil drivers set forth on arduous jour-

The recently completed ARCO Training Center, located in Chula Vista, will serve young athletes for generations to come (below).

neys, and racetracks sprang up around the country. Richfield made its first foray into sports by sponsoring famous auto and marine racers in cars and boats powered by the company's gasoline with a 75 octane rating—then, an amazing figure.

From the Automobile to Track and Field and the Olympic Games

That modest beginning formed the basis of the company's community relations program, which, under the ARCO name, has become one of the finest in the country. One of the company's most rewarding programs was the ARCO Jesse Owens Games (AJOG), a track-and-field competition for youngsters nine to 14 years of age. Founded in 1964 in cooperation with its namesake, the legendary 1936 four-time Olympic champion, AJOG opened the world of sports to children. In its 30-year history, AJOG gave millions of young people the opportunity to compete in local, regional, and national track events, organized in partnership with local parks and recreation departments.

Now-famous track-and-field Olympic champions, such as Carl Lewis, Florence

Griffith Joyner, Evelyn Ashford, and others, got their starts with AJOG. They returned often to AJOG meets, serving as inspirational leaders for younger competitors. Carl Lewis, a four-time loser in his Jesse Owens regional competitions, provided visible testimony to the value of perseverance.

When Los Angeles was selected to host the 1984 Olympic Games, ARCO's support of the Jesse Owens Games made it a natural sponsor for track-and-field events. As part of its $9 million sponsorship, the company built practice tracks at six colleges and high schools in the Los Angeles area, and a state-of-the-art track at the Coliseum for the Olympic competition.

Today, ARCO has renewed its commitment to young people and athletics through its $15 million sponsorship of the ARCO Training Center in Chula Vista, California, the U.S. Olympic Committee's new warm-weather training facility. The recently completed core buildings provide housing, equipment, and training for young competitors in 14 sports. The center is also available to local schoolchildren and, in turn, center athletes are

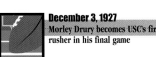
September 1927
First Pacific Southwest International Tennis Tournament at L.A. Tennis Club

December 3, 1927
Morley Drury becomes USC's first 1,000-yard rusher in his final game

December 1, 1928
USC wins first national football title at 9-0-1

company the top marketer of gasoline in the western United States. But ARCO's most important contribution came in 1987, when, once again, business and community needs combined to put the company at the forefront of revolutionary change in gasoline refining and marketing. The goal was cleaner air.

Although indigenous Native Americans referred to Southern California as "the valley of the smokes" more than two centuries ago, the problem of air pollution didn't really arise until the 1940s. Its source was eventually traced to automobiles, and for more than 40 years, Southern California struggled to reduce air pollution. Industry installed filters and scrubbers. Consumers gave up backyard incinerators. Cars acquired catalytic converters, and lead was removed from most gasolines. The improvement was significant, but not particularly visible. In desperation, air-quality officials were moving toward mandated replacements for gasoline with alternative fuels—primarily methanol—with conversion to electricity required by 2010.

ARCO considered the plan unworkable and turned its efforts to developing a better idea: a cleaner-burning gasoline. The result was EC-1 Regular, the world's first reformulated, cleaner-burning, emission control gasoline. EC-1 was designed for use in the dirtiest cars on the road—those manufactured before 1975, without catalytic converters—which were responsible for 30 percent of the area's vehicular pollution. EC-1 reduced emissions from such vehicles by 20 percent.

More importantly, EC-1 proved that the most efficient and cost-effective way to reduce vehicular pollution was in reformulating—not replacing—gasoline. In 1990 Congress concurred by including reformulated gasoline as an approved clean fuel in amendments to the Clean Air Act.

EC-1 was followed, one year later, by EC-Premium, which reduced emissions in high-performance cars. And in 1991 ARCO announced its formula for the "fuel of the future"—EC-X—the model for the reformulated gasoline that will be mandated for all California vehicles as of March 1996. When used statewide, the new fuel will reduce vehicle emissions by approximately one-third.

"Clean gasolines are a proud part of ARCO's long partnership with Southern California," says Bill Rusnack, president of ARCO Products Company, the corporation's refining and marketing division. "We are here for the long term, and we are committed to producing high-quality products that serve all Californians. It's a partnership we look to with pride."

It's also a partnership that has made ARCO an integral part of Los Angeles' growth since the turn of the century. With yet another century in its sights, the company is poised to continue its participation in the city's great moments.

Built in 1972 the ARCO towers were among the first high-rises constructed in downtown Los Angeles.

involved in local schools. Area teachers receive training in fitness and nutrition, and community groups use the facilities for organized athletic events.

At the Environmental Forefront

Concern for the public—its customers and neighbors—is an integral part of ARCO's business philosophy. Its customer-friendly, low-cost gasolines, and a.m./p.m. convenience stores helped make the

One of ARCO's most important environmental contributions was its research and development leading to new gasolines for cleaner air.

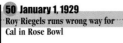

50 January 1, 1929
Roy Riegels runs wrong way for
Cal in Rose Bowl

September 1929
Hollywood Stars win first Pacific Coast League
title in play-off vs. Mission

January 1, 1931
USC wins national football championship at 10-1
with 21-12 Rose Bowl win over Tulane

Pacific Bell

Faster, higher, and stronger. Not only are these three attributes keys to an athlete's endurance and achievement, but they are also a method by which Pacific Bell has become a leader on the fast-moving information superhighway. ■ "Developing faster technology, setting higher goals, and main-

Pacific Bell had a history-making year in 1984—the year the company both adopted its new name and added the Summer Olympics to its long list of communications success stories.

taining a stronger presence in the business and residence marketplaces have been the goals of Pacific Bell since 1906," says Chuck Smith, vice president of Network Operations. "And as we are about to cross the threshold of the next century, these corporate objectives will not waiver. Our commitment remains in maintaining leadership in value, service, and technology."

From the press box and broadcast trucks to the electronic scoreboard and front office, Pacific Bell has provided technological, financial, and philanthropic support to countless athletic events and programs. The Super Bowl, the World Series, the Stanley Cup finals, the NBA championships, the Rose Bowl—name any sports showcase hosted in Los Angeles and Pacific Bell has probably been there. "Because athletic events are vital to the well-being of a region's economy and community spirit, Pacific Bell feels a responsibility to play an active role in the Los Angeles sports environment,"

says Gene Sherman, vice president of external affairs.

Traveling on the Information Superhighway

Pacific Bell's active involvement, however, is not limited to the world of sports. The company currently is involved in a $16 billion, seven-year upgrade to its core network infrastructure. By building an integrated telecommunications information and entertainment network, Pacific Bell will provide advanced voice, data, and video services to more than 5 million homes by the end of the decade.

The new network will also serve as a platform for a host of information providers and will offer telephone customers an alternative to the existing cable television monopoly. The integrated network is expected to spur the development of new interactive consumer services in education, entertainment, government, and health care, as well as to allow Pacific Bell to offer interactive

services customers want, including sports, movies, and television programming on demand.

"Control over what to watch and when to watch it will move away from others and to the customer, where it belongs," says Pacific Telesis Chairman and CEO Phil Quigley. "What Pacific Bell is doing through this innovative approach is moving California into the 21st century."

Pacific Bell and the Olympics

Until the 1984 Summer Olympics in Los Angeles, no single sports event had presented a greater challenge to Pacific Bell's involvement and expertise in telecommunications. Thousands of athletes, hundreds of press and electronic media representatives, and millions of spectators counted on Pacific Bell for a workable information and communications network. Without a reliable network, the Games of the XXIII Olympiad would have shuddered to a chaotic halt.

To ensure an Olympics that would

40 November 21, 1931
USC scores first win over Notre Dame, 16-14

January 2, 1932
USC defends national football title with 10-0-0 season and Rose Bowl win

8 July 30, 1932
Games of the X Olympiad held in Los Angeles

Unforgettable

The interlocking rings of the Olympic Games logo also symbolize Pacific Bell's connection to California, where a commitment to telecommunications, service, and quality has been interwoven for nearly 100 years.

pan from the ancient Appian Way to today's information superhighway, Pacific Bell installed the most sophisticated network ever devised in the history of sports. And because even the most advanced network would be useless without dedicated people to back it up, Pacific Bell employees assumed the immense tasks of taking business and residence orders specifically for the Games, installing thousands of miles of cable at various Olympic sites, devising revolutionary methods of transmitting data and voice, developing efficient ways to oversee the smooth operation of the network, and providing enough new lines to serve a good-sized city.

In these and thousands of other ways, Pacific Bell made the 1984 Summer Olympic Games a magnificent example of communications technology, and did so on what was undoubtedly the world's most visible stage. More than a decade later—six decades since the company participated in L.A.'s first Summer Olympics in 1932—stories are still being shared about the enormous feat that was accomplished. The memories are many, including one in particular.

The 1984 Olympic Opening Ceremonies were just minutes old. A group of Pacific Bell workers gathered around television sets in the Olympic Maintenance Test Center in Buena Park, the mini-phone company established to handle circuitry for the Games. For months they had labored for this moment.

Suddenly, ABC Television lost its picture. Simultaneously, red lights turned the center's alarm boards into Christmas trees. Was Pacific Bell's extensive telecommunications network having a problem? The world was watching.

In the succeeding, anxiety-filled moments, the problem was quickly traced to a widespread power failure, triggered when a metallic balloon, released as part of the festivities, drifted into nearby electrical lines. Both picture and power were soon restored and Pacific Bell was exonerated as hearts began beating again. The false alarm would be as close to a major problem as Pacific Bell would come during the two-week Olympiad.

Throughout the Olympic fortnight, the center's staff waited for trouble calls—calls that largely never came. Of about 8,000 circuits and many miles of cable installed for the Games, there were just 25 trouble reports. The scarcity of problems was attributed to everyone at Pacific Bell, from technicians to managers, as well as to advance planning, excellent communications, and a keen desire to do the job correctly.

Indeed, the Olympic flame that burned over Los Angeles during the 1984 Games was an enduring reminder that competition, carried out with integrity, has the power to ignite the passion for excellence in those who participate both on and off the athletic field.

The Los Angeles Memorial Coliseum—equipped with Pacific Bell technology and service—has hosted two Olympiads, Dodgers baseball, and Rams, Raiders, UCLA, and USC football, among other events and organizations.

60 August 4, 1932
Babe Didriksen stars in 1932 Olympic games

June 22, 1934
First NCAA track championship held outside of Chicago; USC wins title at Coliseum

December 25, 1934
Santa Anita opens on Christmas Day

Transamerica Life Companies

When the Olympic Games came to Los Angeles in the summer of 1984, Transamerica Life Companies (TLC) was there. With its substantial involvement as a major sponsor and as the "official insurer of the '84 Games," TLC acknowledged the importance of international

Special lighting accentuates the landmark pyramid-shaped San Francisco headquarters of Transamerica Corporation, parent company of Transamerica Life Companies (right).

The Transamerica Center, TLC's headquarters, is located in downtown Los Angeles near the site of both the 1932 and 1984 Olympic track-and-field events (below).

Karl K. Kennedy was the visionary entrepreneur who founded Occidental Life—Transamerica's predecessor—in 1906 (below right).

sporting events. The company developed a life, health, and accident insurance package that covered athletes, coaches, trainers, and Olympic staff members while they were in Los Angeles for the Games. Hundreds of civic-minded TLC employees volunteered many hours to help staff the Games and to assist in cleanup efforts at the conclusion of the events.

But it was more than volunteerism that brought TLC and the Olympics together. The same values that inspire an Olympic champion are evident in TLC's business philosophy—commitment, teamwork, and self-motivated achievement. Just as these qualities lead an athlete or a team to ultimate victory on the

field, so too have they helped Transamerica Life Companies become a premier provider of financial security products and services.

An Insurance Company for the West

At the turn of the century, public confidence in eastern companies had weakened because of perceived industry abuses. An entrepreneur named Karl Kennedy saw his chance to capitalize on his western roots. In 1906 he put together a group of farsighted investors and founded one of California's first insurance companies—Occidental Life Insurance Company—TLC's predecessor firm.

The fledgling company adopted an emblem that stressed its frontier roots—"A Star in the West"—and launched an aggressive advertising campaign trumpeting the benefits of keeping the region's dollars close to home. Wherever the company expanded, its reputation for innovation and creativity boosted both acceptance and sales. In 1930 Transamerica Corporation acquired Occidental Life, and by 1953 the company had sold $1 billion worth of insurance. In 1977 the organization celebrated its first $1 billion month. The name Transamerica Life Companies was introduced in 1984.

In 1994 TLC's annual earnings reached a new benchmark of more than $250 million. Today, thanks to the pioneering foresight that shaped its early growth, TLC continues setting company sales records

A dominant presence in the life insurance industry for nearly 90 years, Transamerica Life Companies, headquartered in downtown Los Angeles, comprises seven companies with combined assets of $29 billion and annual revenues totaling more than $3 billion.

TLC offers financial security products that protect families, help people prepare for retirement, and provide business owners with a more secure future. Its products are distributed through a network of branches, general agents, and brokers, as well as through mass marketing. TLC's parent company, San Francisco-based Transamerica Corporation, is ranked by *Fortune* magazine as one of the nation's 500 largest companies.

The largest and oldest of the Transamerica Life Companies—Transamerica Occidental Life—is one of the top 10 life insurers in North America in terms of life insurance in force. A leader in the industry when it comes to breaking new ground, Transamerica Occidental was a pioneer in preferential rates for nonsmokers, the first life insurer to offer

87 February 23, 1935
Azucar wins first Santa Anita Handicap

91 June 15, 1935
Jesse Owens and Ohio State face USC
in dual track meet

May 29, 1937
Heavenly Twins: Earle Meadows and Bill Sefton
clear world record 14-11 in pole vault in
Coliseum

standard underwriting to Asians, the first major company to support AIDS research with significant contributions, and the first major U.S. life insurer to offer universal life coverage.

TLC continually strives to provide the best possible service to customers. Accordingly, the first principle of its business philosophy underscores its commitment to its customers.

TLC and the 1994 World Cup

As a corporate citizen, TLC continues to play an active role in Southern California through in-kind and corporate contributions to many organizations, such as those assisting the homeless and people with AIDS. TLC employees have long recognized the value of giving back to their communities through substantial donations and volunteer assistance in support of numerous nonprofit and civic agencies.

Former TLC Chairman and CEO David Carpenter was a member of the World Cup USA '94 bid committee, which was instrumental in bringing eight soccer games to Los Angeles/ Pasadena, including the prestigious finals. As a regional spon-

▶ LONG PHOTOGRAPHY

sor of the quadrennial sporting event, TLC and its employees caught World Cup fever. TLC saw an opportunity to offer its employees a chance to participate in this extraordinary event through several volunteer programs. For example, tidying up the city of Los Angeles for its worldwide visitors, Transamerica volunteers went to work on a Saturday designated as "Clean Up Graffiti Day." In addition, the company decorated its buildings, cleaned sidewalks, and hung banners along city streets. The combined efforts of TLC's vol-

unteers contributed positively to the success of the World Cup.

The company saw the World Cup as an opportunity to better reach out to new markets within the Hispanic community. TLC designed World Cup-related incentive programs for its agents around the country to help stimulate sales in their respective communities.

TLC also helped bring the World Cup experience to Los Angeles' inner-city youths through its support of the Gaining Opportunities to Achieve Lifetime Success (GOALS) program. GOALS integrated the World Cup and soccer into the teaching of math, social studies, language, science, and physical education.

As TLC celebrates its 90th anniversary year in 1996, it is well on its way to achieving its vision—to be recognized as the premier provider of financial security products and services.

Clockwise from upper left: Transamerica Life Companies sponsored the World Youth Pavilion at Soccerfest, a World Cup indoor fair held in Los Angeles.

TLC's Alice Smith displays a selection of the company's Olympic souvenirs from the 1984 Olympics.

As a partner with San Pedro Street Elementary School, TLC—with help from employee Carol Bromberg and mascot Striker—worked with inner-city youths through the GOALS program.

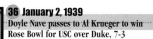

36 January 2, 1939
Doyle Nave passes to Al Krueger to win
Rose Bowl for USC over Duke, 7-3

April 17, 1939
Joe Louis defends his heavyweight title, KOs
Jack Roper in one round at Wrigley Field

94 March 2, 1940
Seabiscuit wins the Big 'Cap at Santa Anita

Ameron, Inc.

Founded in 1907, Ameron, Inc. is a multinational manufacturer of highly engineered products for the building, construction, and industrial markets. The company operates businesses in 15 countries in North America, Latin America, Europe, and Asia. ■ Traded on the New York Stock Exchange, Ameron is a leading producer of high-performance coatings; fiberglass, concrete, and steel pipe systems; and other specialized construction products.

Protective Coatings Group

Ameron has been a leader in the field of industrial and marine corrosion protection for more than 50 years, developing and marketing a broad line of protective coatings, finishes, flooring materials, and surfacings for steel and concrete, commercial and industrial equipment, and manufactured goods.

Ameron's products—which include virtually every major type of protective coating—are used extensively throughout the world in such industries as oil and gas production, refining, petrochemical production and processing, marine, pulp and paper, infrastructure maintenance, railroad, fossil and nuclear power, general manufacturing, and municipal water and waste treatment.

Specializing in advanced-technology products capable of delivering the high levels of protection demanded by the marketplace, Ameron has also earned an international reputation as an innovative, ecologically concerned company with products that meet or surpass the most stringent environmental and worker safety requirements.

Fiberglass Pipe Group

Ameron offers the world's most comprehensive line of fiberglass pipe products for the chemical/industrial market, the oil field, service station fuel handling, and offshore and marine applications. Ameron fiberglass pipe represents a cost-effective alternative to corrosion-prone metallic piping and nonreinforced thermoplastics.

Ameron's domestic manufacturing plants are in Burkburnett, Texas, and Spartanburg, South Carolina. Operations in the Netherlands serve industrial, government, military, marine, offshore, and oil field markets in Europe, Africa, and much of the Middle East with high-pressure piping systems as large as 40 inches in diameter. Serving the Asia-Pacific region, Ameron's business in Singapore produces filament-wound fiberglass fittings and reciprocally wound pipe in diameters from two through 36 inches. An affiliate—Bondstrand, Ltd.—manufactures fiberglass pipe products in Saudi Arabia.

Ameron sells fiberglass pipe and fittings both through its direct sales force

Clockwise from above:
Ameron's Pole Products Division manufactures concrete lighting poles in a variety of traditional and modern designs, as well as a complete line of steel traffic and lighting poles.

The Devil's Canyon water project, completed in 1994 as part of the California Aqueduct, included 4,500 linear feet of large-diameter Ameron reinforced concrete cylinder pipe.

Ameron's Amerlock and Amershield protective coatings were used on the domes, walkways, and interiors at the new W.M. Keck Observatory located on the 13,796-foot summit of Mauna Kea, a dormant volcano on the island of Hawaii.

May 24, 1941
First Coliseum Relays organized in Los Angeles

January 1, 1943
UCLA's first ever Rose Bowl appearance ends in 9-0 loss to Georgia

73 June 12, 1943
Dean Cromwell's Trojans win NCAA track title with just four entrants

156   **Unforgettable**

and through oil field supply houses, industrial stocking distributors, and sales representatives in the United States and more than 20 other countries.

Concrete and Steel Pipe Group

Ameron is known as a world leader in pipe technology and is a principal supplier of highly engineered concrete and steel pipe products in the western United States and Canada. Strategically located Ameron manufacturing facilities serve major population centers in California, Arizona, New Mexico, Oregon, Washington, Alaska, and Hawaii, as well as British Columbia and Alberta. American Pipe & Construction International, a wholly owned subsidiary, is the chief supplier of concrete and steel pipe products in Colombia, South America.

Gifford-Hill-American, Inc., an affiliated company, supplies concrete pipe to the south central United States from four manufacturing plants in Texas. Another affiliate, Ameron Saudi Arabia, Ltd., operates four concrete pipe manufacturing plants in the Kingdom of Saudi Arabia.

Designed to satisfy a broad range of performance requirements, Ameron concrete and steel pipe products provide low-maintenance, long-term conveyance for either potable water or wastewater. Typical services include high-pressure and low-pressure water transmission and distribution lines, inverted siphons in aqueducts, sewer force mains, cooling water systems for power plants, sewer outfalls, storm drains, culverts, liners for tunnels, and penstocks in hydroelectric generating stations.

Construction and Allied Products Group

Ameron's HC&D division in Hawaii manufactures and markets ready-mix concrete, crushed and sized basaltic aggregates, dune sand, cultured stone veneer, concrete pipe, and box culverts. These products are sold primarily to the construction industry and consumer markets on the islands of Oahu and Maui, with some sales on the other Hawaiian islands. HC&D is the largest supplier of ready-mix concrete and concrete pipe products in Hawaii.

Oahu-based production facilities include basaltic rock mining, crushing and sizing facilities, and a manufactured sand plant at Kapaa Quarry; a concrete pipe plant on the western side of the island; and ready-mix concrete batch plants at Kapaa Quarry, Sand Island, and Barbers Point. Facilities on Maui consist of quarrying and associated operations, including a ready-mix concrete plant near Kahului and two other batch plants at outlying locations.

Ameron's Pole Products Division supplies concrete and steel lighting and traffic poles to customers throughout the United States. The company operates two manufacturing facilities in California, as well as plants in Washington and Oklahoma.

The street and highway segment of the lighting and traffic pole business is primarily a specification market in which performance standards are established by public and government agencies. Ameron also offers many types of lighting poles for airports, parks, sports facilities, parking lots, and residential and commercial developments.

An Ameron Bondstrand caisson pipe (top left), specifically engineered to protect drilling strings and product lines on off-shore platforms, is being installed on a new platform headed for the North Sea, one of the most severe marine environments on earth.

More than 50,000 cubic yards of Ameron ready-mix concrete (bottom left) were poured during the construction of the beautiful new Ihilani Hotel and Resort on the western end of Oahu.

January 12, 1946
Owner Dan Reeves moves Cleveland Rams to Los Angeles

March 21, 1946
UCLA's Kenny Washington becomes first African-American to play in the NFL

68 December 3, 1946
Glenn Davis wins Heisman Trophy for Army

Bank Of America

Bank of America has been contributing to the growth and quality of life in California since 1904 when A.P. Giannini opened a small bank in San Francisco to meet the financial needs of the working class and small businesses. Since then, Bank of America has grown into one of the world's premie

financial institutions, meeting the needs of individuals, businesses, and corporate clients worldwide. With assets of approximately $215 billion, it is now the second-largest bank holding company in the United States, a consumer banking powerhouse operating approximately 2,000 retail branches and a 5,500-ATM network in 10 western states.

In addition to checking and savings accounts, Bank of America provides its individual clients a wide range of financial products and services; consumer and residential real estate loans; credit cards; investment services such as stocks, bonds, annuities, and mutual funds; trust services; and insurance.

For commercial businesses, corporations, financial institutions, and government agencies, Bank of America is a leading provider of credit and deposit services; payments and cash management services; risk management, capital markets, and advisory services; and other financial services such as leasing and venture capital. Internationally, Bank of America operates branches and representative offices in 37 countries.

Making California History

Bank of America was the first bank in the nation to create a statewide system of branches to gather small deposits into larger sums and move them around the state where they could be put to work building communities. Other bankers scoffed, then tried desperately to stop it, but the idea prevailed. Bank of America

Sports have been a part of Bank of America's heritage for decades, including its early years as the Bank of Italy when it sponsored basketball teams from the bank's San Francisco and Fresno branches.

The Women's Banking Department in Los Angeles in 1923—a division run by and for women—made Bank of America a pioneer in developing banking services for women.

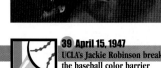

thus played a major role in helping free California farmers from the stranglehold of eastern banks and higher interest rates.

During the depths of the Great Depression, the bank launched a major "Back to Good Times" campaign to help break the prevailing mood of self-defeat by buying local bond issues to finance projects that put people to work. Since 1916 the bank has participated in notes and bond sales in Los Angeles County totaling more than $13 billion to help pay for schools, parks, libraries, hospitals, and many other public facilities.

Nowhere has Bank of America had a greater impact than in Southern California, which continues to be one of the bank's most important markets. A Los Angeles office, opened in 1913, was the bank's first branch in Southern California. Today, the bank serves all segments of the market, including small and medium-sized businesses, global corporations, individual customers, and government agencies at city, county, and state levels.

Bank of America has particular expertise in serving specialized needs in Southern California in the areas of high technology, agriculture, tourism, media, and entertainment. From its earliest years the bank led the way in developing the movie industry—helping United Artists, Columbia, and Twentieth Century get started—and financing independent pro-

ducers such as Cecil B. DeMille, Sam Goldwyn, David O. Selznick, and Frank Capra. It was Bank of America, in 1936, that helped a young cartoonist named Walt Disney by financing a project others called crazy—a feature-length animated film called *Snow White and the Seven Dwarfs*.

Bank of America and the Dodgers

Bank of America is also a player in the Los Angeles sports community, from contributions to youth sporting programs to support of professional sports franchises The bank's involvement with Major League Baseball in Los Angeles, for exam ple, began with now-retired Executive Vice President Harry Bardt.

Bardt was former senior administrative officer of the bank's Southern Division in the late 1930s. Through an acquaintance at United Artists—where he sat on the board of directors—Bardt was introduced to Walter O'Malley, head of the then-Brooklyn Dodgers, in 1939. Eighteen years later, when the Dodgers announced their move to the West Coast, Bank of America was part of a three-bank syndicate willing to finance a new stadium. When the other two banks with drew from the stadium negotiations, Bank of America offered to finance the entire project. O'Malley accepted on terms calling for a payback of $1 millior a year for 12 years, but the Dodgers paic it all in seven years. In 1967 Bardt was

39 April 15, 1947
UCLA's Jackie Robinson breaks the baseball color barrier

76 September 14, 1947
Jack Kramer wins second U.S. Nationals in a row

46 January 5, 1948
Ben Hogan wins second L.A. Open, looks ahead to 1948 U.S. Open at Riviera

Now–all together ! ON TO GOOD TIMES

GOOD TIMES

UNEMPLOYMENT

CALIFORNIA

BANK of AMERICA

amed to the board of directors of the Dodgers' organization.

O'Malley, who died in 1979, was succeeded in 1970 as head of the club by his son, Peter. The younger O'Malley brought the story full circle by joining Bank of America's board of directors in 1976. Two years later he joined the board of Bank of America Corporation, but stepped down from both posts in 1986 to devote more time to the Dodgers' organization.

Bank of America also supports the community through an extensive philanthropic program that provided more than $27 million in contributions to nonprofit organizations in Los Angeles County between 1981 and 1993. Many of those contributions went to school- and community-based youth sports programs. Notes and bonds that Bank of America has participated in to finance the growth of parks and recreation in Los Angeles total $13.5 million.

Bank of America is also active in support of job creation, home ownership, and multifamily housing development in low-income neighborhoods throughout Los Angeles. In 1994 it provided more than $5 billion in low-income loans and investments throughout the western United States, and it has earned a federal Community Reinvestment Act rating of "outstanding" from the Office of the Comptroller of the Currency.

After more than 80 years of supporting the Los Angeles community, Bank of America looks forward to many more decades of serving the largest and most dynamic market in California.

Bank of America launched a campaign during the Great Depression to help boost morale in California and provide credit to foster job growth (above).

Bank of America founder A.P. Giannini (left) sits in the dugout during a recreational baseball game between the Los Angeles and San Francisco banking offices in the 1940s.

May 1948
Rod Dedeaux's USC baseball team wins first title

May 21, 1948
Coliseum Relays draws biggest-ever attendance: 59,661

June 12, 1948
Hogan wins L.A. Open at Riviera Country Club with record score of 276

IBM

When IBM first established its Los Angeles office in 1916, the city was well on its way to becoming a world-class metropolitan center. For the next 80 years, the company watched the landscape of Los Angeles change from quiet shaded avenues, sun-drenched fields, and

IBM's Southern California activities are headquartered in the IBM Tower in downtown Los Angeles (right).

Since 1986 the employee group has coached Special Olympics participants (below) with computer games on 15 IBM personal computers.

fragrant citrus groves into the energetic, diverse, and ever-expanding metropolis it is today.

IBM has grown in much the same way since then, and has progressed from the punched card and electric typewriter business to its current role as a major force in the stored program computer industry and related services. Southern California today remains an important trading location for the global information systems giant, with more than 1,000 employees and $1 billion in annual revenues.

IBM develops, manufactures, and sells advanced information processing products, including computers and microelectronic technology, software, networking systems, and information technology-related services. Founded in 1911, the company employs 220,000 people in more than 140 countries with a total of $64 billion in annual revenues.

Committed to Los Angeles

"IBM has been a major corporate presence in the Los Angeles area for more than 80 years," says James W. Steele, general manager of IBM in Southern California. "Over the years, we've made key contributions to the community where our customers and employees live and work, including fast-action response to local disasters, enthusiastic sponsorship of the Olympic Games, job training programs, education reform, and an ongoing partnership with many local organizations."

IBM was well established in Los Angeles when the city proudly hosted the summer Olympic Games in 1932 and 1984. A key sponsor of the 1984 Olympics, IBM provided equipment and personnel to assist in all phases of the games. More than 400 IBM technicians worked on-site throughout all 40 Olympic venues—at the spectacular L.A. Coliseum opening ceremonies, swimming competitions at UCLA, basketball at the Sports Arena, and the marathon run into the heart of the city. IBM has served as the official information technology sponsor for the Olympic Games since 1992 and has a contract with the International Olympic Committee to serve in that role through the 2000 Olympic Games in Sydney, Australia.

Forty IBM volunteers also team up with student athletes between scheduled sports events at the annual California Special Olympics finals at UCLA. Since 1986, the employee group has coached Special Olympics participants with computer games on 15 IBM personal computers.

With a long-standing interest in Southern California sports activities and events, IBM is a charter member of the Los Angeles Sports Council. For many

56 September 5, 1949
Pancho Gonzales wins second
U.S. Nationals in a row

December 18, 1949
Eagles edge Rams, 14-0, to win
NFL title in Philadelphia

March 4, 1950
Noor upsets Triple Crown winner Citation
in the Santa Anita Handicap

Bank of America Foundation. This south central Los Angeles community program received such positive reviews that the company expanded the training program throughout the United States. Seeds first sown in Los Angeles have borne fruit in many other states. More than 65,000 students have graduated from the IBM programs with a placement rate exceeding 80 percent.

After the 1994 Los Angeles earthquake, the company donated $75,000 to the Red Cross Earthquake Fund, INFO LINE, United Way Disaster Fund, and the Mayor's Disaster Fund. IBM also donated equipment valued at $445,000 to other local organizations working to heal the community. And following the civil disturbance in 1992, IBM made a solid five-year commitment to the RLA (Rebuild Los Angeles) project. The devastated communities in the city received $31 million in equipment, services, and training from IBM, including an IBM-developed minority business program, 10 new job training center partnerships, and two learning center partnerships.

Although the IBM influence is felt worldwide, the company stays closely involved with the communities where it does business. IBM in Southern California is as strong today as it has ever been. Its partnerships with the business, civic, and sports organizations within the Los Angeles area are a source of great pride to the company, and will continue into the future.

Clockwise from below:
With more than 400 IBM technicians on-site throughout all 40 Olympic venues, IBM was a key sponsor of the 1984 Olympics.

IBM's behind-the-scenes technology kept the Olympic Games running smoothly.

Prince Charles visits the Foshay Learning Center in south central Los Angeles. IBM was a major donor of computers to the center.

...ears, the company has lent its support to ...ell-known sports organizations like the ...rofessional Golf Association, National ...asketball Association, and Major League ...aseball. Likewise, IBM executives and ...anagers continue to serve on the ...oards and committees of many other ...cal organizations.

IBM's commitment to the community ...s also evident in its focus on education. ...n the early 1990s, IBM invested equip...ent, software, and courseware in a ...ultimillion-dollar partnership with the ...alifornia Department of Education and ...alifornia State University system to ...efine teacher training, technology-sup...orted curriculum materials, electronic ...nformation exchange among educators, ...nd enhanced technology-based voca...onal training.

And the IBM-supported New Ameri-can Schools program at the Foshay Learning Center has sparked student creativity through the use of multimedia personal computers donated by IBM. Other IBM investments in K-12 education have been through such organizations as L.A. Educational Partnership, LEARN, Junior Achievement, Workforce LA, and local museums.

Disaster Relief for Los Angeles
Being a vital part of the community also means lending a hand in emergencies, and IBM's reaction to crises in Los Angeles has been swift and generous. After the 1965 Watts riots, for example, IBM launched the Los Angeles Urban League Data Processing Training Center to provide job training for the economically disadvantaged, in partnership with the Los Angeles Urban League and the

May 1950
UCLA wins first ever NCAA title, in tennis

December 24, 1950
Lou Groza's kick gives Browns a 30-28 win over Rams for NFL title

January 14, 1951
First NFL Pro Bowl held at Coliseum: Americans 28, Nationals 27

United Airlines

Since its first open-cockpit biplane soared into the sky in 1926 to deliver mail, United Airlines pioneering efforts have helped to expand commercial aviation and refine airline service. For the more than 75,000 United employees worldwide, "Fly the Friendly Skies" has been more than just a well

United is the largest passenger and cargo airline in the United States, offering more than 2,200 departures a day systemwide. Its wings span 143 destinations serving 30 countries on five continents.

Leon Cuddeback (below left) piloted the first flight of Varney Air Lines, United's predecessor, in 1926.

United's original eight stewardesses (below right), shown here in 1930, served passengers on a 12-seat Boeing 80A aircraft traveling between San Francisco and Chicago.

known slogan. For close to seven decades, it's been a commitment to providing excellent service to the millions of passengers who fly United annually.

Never have those friendly skies covered so much of the globe.

United today is the largest passenger and cargo airline in the United States, and one of the biggest in the world, offering more than 2,200 departures a day systemwide. Its wings span 143 destinations serving 30 countries on five continents. The airline and its fleet of some

548 aircraft transport an average of 203,000 passengers daily.

Connecting Points across the Globe

The carrier's domestic route system is built on its three hubs–Chicago's O'Hare International Airport, Denver International Airport, and San Francisco International Airport–which provide efficient access to United's global network. The airline's extensive domestic service offers daily nonstop departures

to more than 100 markets in the United States.

More than 26,000 United employees live and work in California, making the firm one of the state's major employers. As California's leading air carrier and a long-time operator in the "California Corridor," the company in 1994 introduced Shuttle by United, a low-cost, high frequency service between Los Angeles and San Francisco. With nearly 400 daily flights, the shuttle also serves some 14 other western market segments involving

July 14, 1951
Citation wins Santa Anita Gold Cup, is first with more than $1 million in career earnings

20 December 23, 1951
Rams win first NFL title in Los Angeles, 24-17, vs. Browns

79 August 1, 1952
Sammy Lee completes Olympic diving double

hoenix; Las Vegas; San Diego,
acramento, Oakland, and Burbank,
alifornia; Seattle; and Portland, Oregon.
huttle by United adds pleasure and con-
enience to short-haul air travel by offer-
ıg a variety of features, such as low fares
very day, assigned seats at check-in,
eamless flight and baggage connections,
rst-class seating, and the traditional
riendly service United Airlines' cus-
omers have come to expect.

Los Angeles is the fourth-busiest city
or United on its worldwide system.
pproximately 170 flights depart daily out
f the airline's 18-gate terminal at Los
ngeles International Airport (LAX),
ransporting between 15,000 and 20,000
assengers each day to all points on the
lobe.

Presently, United accounts for rough-
/ 22 percent of the market share at LAX,
tore than any other airline. Estimates
aken in 1994 indicate that United
irlines boarded an astonishing 5.5 mil-
on passengers at LAX alone. United's
ramatic growth in the Los Angeles mar-
et is matched by its rapid growth in
nternational markets.

Now the largest majority employee-
wned company in the world, United
egan its first scheduled service outside
orth America in 1983 with nonstop ser-
ice to Tokyo. Since then, United has
rown from this single overseas flight to
ecome the largest U.S. carrier across the
acific, transporting nearly 9 million trav-
lers on 70,000 international flights each
ear. United operates hubs in London and
okyo, as well as major connecting com-
lexes in Mexico City and Paris.

"In 1986 we acquired Pan Am's
acific Division, and that's when United
eally expanded significantly as an inter-
ational carrier," says United's Director
f Public Affairs Alan B. Wayne.

History of Innovation

nited Airlines has a rich history, tracing
s roots to the historic flight on April 6,
926, when a 90-horsepower Swallow
iplane took off from an open field in
asco, Washington, to deliver mail. Since
10se early days, the airline has built a
istory of innovation and leadership that

has contributed to customer convenience,
comfort, and safety.

In 1930 United introduced the
world's first flight attendant service. Six
years later, the first in-flight meal was
served up from its flight kitchen facility in
Oakland. The airline also introduced the
first nonstop coast-to-coast commercial
flights, the first automatic baggage-conveyor system, the first radar-equipped
fleet, the first fully automatic all-weather
landing system, and the first nationwide
automated reservations system. In 1990
United became the first commercial carrier to use satellite communications.

Today's trailblazing, however, comes
in many different forms. United's aircraft
maintenance facility in San Francisco is
the largest of its kind, and the company
also operates an industry-leading flight
training center in Denver.

A Vital Part of the
Los Angeles Community

United takes great pride in its extensive
operations in the Los Angeles area and
its contributions to the local economy.
United's long-standing commitment to
the city is evidenced in its support of
institutions like the California Museum
of Science and Industry in Exposition
Park, which is dedicated to the history of
air and space flight. The company is also
actively involved in the Make-a-Wish

The University of Michigan football team
traveled on United's "Michigan Football
Special" charter DC3 in the late 1930s.

Foundation, the United Way, and various
other Los Angeles charities. United Airlines
is prominently affixed on the sports scene,
as well. Over the years, the airline has carried virtually every professional sports
team, as well as sports teams of most of
the major colleges, and today is the official
airline of the U.S. Olympic Team.

Since its inception, United Airlines
has continually striven to be a leader in
the airline industry. Innovation, a constant commitment to high-quality service,
an unfailing dedication to safety, and a
growing global route system are the hall-
marks of United service. More than just
flying the friendly skies, United Airlines is
uniting the world.

United's commitment to
customer service brought
about many industry firsts,
including flight attendant
service, in-flight meals,
nonstop coast-to-coast
commercial flights, an automatic baggage-conveyor
system, and a nationwide
automated reservations
system. In 1990 United
became the first commer-
cial carrier to use satellite
communications.

88 September 21, 1952
Florence Chadwick swims to Catalina Island

65 May 8, 1954
Parry O'Brien breaks
60-foot barrier in shot put

31 November 20, 1954
UCLA goes 9-0, wins national football title

First Interstate Bank

The story of First Interstate Bank is a richly detailed one of growth, opportunity, challenge, and change. Yet its success over the years has been driven by a simple concept: constant devotion to banking convenience and community involvement. ■ Today's First Interstate Bank, headquartered in Los Angeles,

serves over 5 million retail and business customers through more than 1,100 domestic offices and 33 international offices in 17 countries. With regional headquarters in Phoenix, Los Angeles, Houston, and Portland, Oregon, First Interstate operates 18 banks in 13 contiguous western states.

Progressive Leadership

Banking visionary A.P. Giannini took the first tentative steps toward creating a national banking system when he formed Transamerica Banking Co. in 1928. The first bank to eventually become a First Interstate Bank was acquired by Transamerica in Oregon in 1930. Over the next few decades, Transamerica continued to expand its territory, evolving by 1981 to become First Interstate Bancorp. By the 1980s First Interstate owned banks in states throughout the West.

By the time recent chairman Edward M. Carson retired in May 1995, First Interstate had successfully grown into the nation's 14th-largest banking organization. Now under the leadership of Chairman and CEO William E.B. Siart and President William S. Randall, First Interstate is poised for its move into the next century.

First Interstate Bank, headquartered in Los Angeles, serves over 5 million retail and business customers through more than 1,100 domestic offices and 33 international offices in 17 countries.

Chairman and CEO William E.B. Siart (on right) and President William S. Randall (on left) have prepared First Interstate Bank for the century ahead.

Community Pride

"We believe in actively supporting the communities we serve." That statement, drawn from the bank's mission statement captures the spirit that drives First Interstate's 27,000 employees to become involved in the communities where they live and work. The bank proudly supports a wide variety of programs that benefit the many communities in which it does business. As part of that support, the bank has been heavily involved in a broad array of sports programs throughout its history.

As a prime example, the First Interstate Bank in California worked with the Community Development

90 May 18, 1956
Sugar Ray Robinson clubs Bobo Olson in title rematch at Wrigley Field

84 June 29, 1956
Charles Dumas becomes first ever to clear 7-0, wins U.S. Olympic Trials at Coliseum

63 December 7, 1956
Pat McCormick completes Olympic diving double-double

With regional headquarters in Phoenix, Los Angeles, Houston, and Portland, Oregon, First Interstate operates 18 banks in 13 contiguous western states.

association in 1932 to help finance the Olympic Games when they were held in Los Angeles for the first time. Fifty-two years later the Games returned to the City of Angels and once again First Interstate Bank played an integral role, serving as the official bank of the 1984 Summer Olympics. During this exciting time, the bank formed the First Interstate Bank Athletic Foundation, which actively promoted youth sports programs in the various communities in which it served. Additionally, through its Olympic Job Opportunities Program the bank employed several aspiring Olympic athletes.

The Foundation purchased the Helm's Bakery sports memorabilia museum and moved it to a newly renovated historic home just outside downtown Los Angeles. At the conclusion of the 1984 Olympic Games, the Foundation donated its museum and memorabilia to the Los Angeles Organizing Committee-Amateur Athletic Foundation. It is at this museum that the 1984 Olympic flame continues to burn today. A decade later, First Interstate continued its support of the Olympics as a network sponsor of the 1994 Winter Olympics in Lillehammer, Norway.

Throughout its territory, First Inter-

state Bank is well known for its support of sporting events and youth programs. The bank has sponsored numerous college bowl games, ski tournaments, rodeo competitions, Indy car racing, marathons, triathlons, and 10K runs. The company has also supported a number of professional and collegiate teams throughout the West.

Managing Success

First Interstate Bank embraces the concept of teamwork and incorporates that principle not only in its sponsorship of sporting events, but in its corporate philosophy as well. Quality service differentiates First Interstate from its competitors. First Interstate knows that its continued success will depend to a large extent on its ability to provide superior value and exceptional service to its customers. The company constantly seeks innovative ways to deliver a diverse range of financial products and services.

The successful financial institutions of the 1990s will be those that, like First Interstate Bank, have the experience to navigate changes, the resources to capitalize on opportunities, and qualified employees who remain responsive to the ever-changing needs of its valued cus-

tomers and communities. Although the financial services marketplace in which the bank operates is a dynamic, competitive, and transitional environment, one thing stays constant: First Interstate Bank remains dedicated to banking convenience and community involvement.

By the time of his retirement in May 1995, former Chairman and CEO Edward M. Carson had guided First Interstate to its spot as the nation's 14th-largest banking organization.

71 December 14, 1956
Downey vs. Anaheim matchup climaxes
CIF grid play-offs in Coliseum

100 September 7, 1957
Steve Bilko hits his 56th homer for the Angels
of the Pacific Coast League

March 9, 1958
Silky Sullivan's come-from-behind run
wins Santa Anita Handicap

ARB, Inc.

ARB, Inc. is a multifaceted, international construction company with strong ties to the growth and diversity of Los Angeles. The company traces its history to 1929, when operations were conducted from a site in Paramount, California, that has been occupied by ARB or one of its predecessors

continuously for nearly seven decades.

One of the largest and most highly respected engineering and construction firms headquartered on the West Coast, ARB is currently ranked among the top 100 contractors in the United States, according to *Engineering News Record*. The company provides a wide range of construction, fabrication, maintenance, and replacement services to major public utilities, petrochemical and energy companies, and numerous other customers.

Increasing Services Mark the Years

The privately held company has maintained family and management ownership since its founding. Initially, ARB focused on building pipelines to transport crude oil and petrochemical products, including gasoline, diesel fuel, jet fuel, and other assorted chemical projects throughout the West. Many of those early pipelines completed prior to World War II are still operating today, transporting products from the fields in Kern and Santa Barbara counties and elsewhere into the Los Angeles basin.

Today, ARB also installs complete distribution systems for natural gas utilities, as well as transmission pipelines. ARB's expertise in the use of highly specialized, directional drilling equipment enables them to install pipelines cost-

ARB, Inc. constructed the Loker Hydrocarbon Research Facility for the University of Southern California.

effectively beneath bays, riverbeds, and other environmentally sensitive areas throughout the world.

In addition to new pipeline construction, the company is a leader in providing pipeline maintenance services. The pipeline and utility infrastructure in and around Los Angeles has been in service for many years. Replacement, repair, and rehabilitation to existing systems are a large part of ARB's day-to-day business. Whether the goal is to increase capacity or pressure, or to replace weak or leak-

ing sections of pipe, ARB has the experience and capability to make the repair.

Building for the Future

ARB has become a leading provider of mechanical/industrial construction to many large and small refineries and process-related companies with facilities throughout the western United States. Services in the industrial area include the installation of major engineering equipment, such as compressors, boilers, turbines and generators, piping systems

ARB builds facilities like this structural steel site for a new petrochemical plant.

10 April 18, 1958
Dodgers move to Los Angeles

August 18, 1958
Floyd Patterson defends heavyweight title over Roy Harris

September 5, 1958
Art Aragon's biggest purse earned in beating at hands of Carmen Basilio

166

Unforgettable

Among ARB's many projects was the installation of a natural gas transmission line in the California desert.

(above and below ground), instrumentation, and control buildings. ARB also provides structural steel fabrication and erection services to the commercial and industrial sectors. In connection with the construction of industrial facilities, ARB typically provides performance testing and start-up services.

At its fabrication facility in Bakersfield, California, ARB fabricates and assembles complex process modules. These include low-temperature process units that convert air into liquid oxygen, nitrogen, and argon, as well as electrostatic filtering systems that remove otherwise irretrievable impurities from petroleum products.

The company also provides maintenance services to cogeneration plants, refineries, and similar mechanical facilities. ARB's skilled maintenance personnel provide inspection, overhaul, and emergency repair for scheduled and unscheduled outages and shutdowns.

In addition to pipeline and industrial construction, ARB is an active general contractor, supplying an array of both preconstruction and construction services to a diverse group of clients, the majority of whom have significant operations and facilities within Southern California. Although the construction experience of the commercial building group includes almost every major building type, emphasis is placed upon the company's expertise regarding facilities within the health care,

entertainment, pharmaceutical, institutional, high-technology, and aerospace industries.

Recent ARB preconstruction and construction projects include a heart valve manufacturing facility, a state-of-the-art biopharmaceutical manufacturing suite, a satellite uplink facility for a new television system throughout Latin America, the fast-track reconstruction of a parking structure to replace one destroyed in the Northridge earthquake, and the seismic upgrading of a major medical center.

There are many other facets of ARB's business, which include not only civil construction services, but also the manufacture and installation of prestressed concrete piling, provision of cement mortar linings for domestic water pipelines, and installation of underground systems for power and telecommunications.

Putting Safety First

In all of its operating divisions, ARB is committed to safe working conditions and practices. This commitment to safety is initiated by senior management and is emphasized to each employee through ongoing training and review. The results of this emphasis are reflected through fewer injuries and fewer safety issues. The company's injury frequency rate has continued to decrease, and its current safety record is second to none. Safety will continue to be a key element of ARB's corporate goals.

ARB has continued to expand geographically. In addition to its headquarters in Southern California, the company has operations in regional offices in Bakersfield, Fontana, and Pittsburg, California; Tulsa, Oklahoma; an international office in Quito, Ecuador; and a joint venture operation in India.

The company's goal is to maintain its continued growth while still providing the highest-quality construction services to its clients, which ARB has done for more than 60 years. The ability of ARB to grow and to successfully provide these services to its customers is a result of the quality and dedication of its employees. Throughout its history, the company has grown and diversified its services while maintaining two basic tenets: quality and integrity.

ARB's highly skilled employees meet the company's challenges, from hanging telephone conduit (left) to constructing a pickling line for a steel manufacturer (below).

62 **January 11, 1959**
Ken Venturi's final-round 63 wins L.A. Open

29 **May 7, 1959**
Roy Campanella saluted in Coliseum exhibition vs. Yankees

July 8, 1959
Sports Arena opens with boxing: Jose Becerra knocks out Alphonse Hamili

American Airlines

O**n October 15, 1930, American Airlines began serving Los Angeles, only four years after the company's inaugural flight. Since those early days, American has grown into the nation's largest air carrier, currently operating the world's largest commercial aircraft fleet. Along with its**

In 1953 American Airlines pioneered non-stop transcontinental service from Los Angeles to New York with the DC-7.

American Eagle commuter service, the airline flies some 4,000 flights daily in more than 300 markets.

Over the years, Los Angeles and American together have chalked up a number of firsts. American Airlines introduced the first fully pressurized DC-6, which offered sleeper flights between Los Angeles and New York, in 1947. In 1953 American pioneered nonstop transcontinental service from Los Angeles to New York with the Douglas DC-7. In 1959 American became the first airline to offer coast-to-coast jet service from Los Angeles International Airport with the Boeing 707. American made history again in 1971 when it introduced the world's first scheduled DC-10 flight from Los Angeles to Chicago.

To the 4,250 Los Angeles-based employees of American Airlines and its regional affiliate, American Eagle, the expression "We Mean Business in Los Angeles" is more than just a slogan. It evokes a long-standing commitment to providing quality service to the millions of passengers who travel to and from Los Angeles each year.

Los Angeles is a key city in American's route network. The airline provides extensive service from Los Angeles to cities throughout the United States, Europe, and Latin America, as well as the most nonstop flights on transcontinental routes to the East Coast. The airline has been providing nonstop service from LAX to London's Heathrow Airport since 1991, and connecting service to San José, Costa Rica; Guatemala City, Guatemala; and San Salvador, El Salvador.

Award-winning Service

American Airlines has won numerous awards for both its domestic and international service. Publications such as *Air Transport World, Business Traveler International, Financial World*, and *Corporate Travel* magazines have ranked the airline as "best" in both business and leisure travel.

The National Institute for Aviation Research at Wichita State University and the Aviation Institute at the University of Nebraska at Omaha have consistently named American the best airline in the country. Their study is the most compre-

hensive measurement of airline quality, and takes into account customer service, on-time performance, and baggage handling.

Positioning itself as the preferred domestic airline of business travelers, American's system of integrated hubs makes flying with the airline particularly convenient for business travelers who need frequent flights and comfortable service.

American's Three-Class approach provides a particularly high level of service for premium-class, first-class, or business-class passengers. Known on domestic flights as "American Flagship Service," and on international flights as "International Flagship Service," Three-Class has something for every traveler.

The domestic premium-class service features leather and sheepskin seats and offers the kind of comfort normally limited to international flights. Business class offers passengers a peaceful, professional environment, making it an ideal place to work or simply to relax. First-class passengers have individual video units that extend from their chair console, allowing them to view their personal choice of in-flight movies from an extensive library.

August 3, 1959
Dodgers host All-Star Game II of 1959 at Coliseum as AL wins, 5-3

14 October 8, 1959
Dodgers win World Series vs. Chicago in six games

41 September 6, 1960
Rafer Johnson wins Olympic decathlon gold over friend C.K. Yang

mileage credit in a variety of other ways, including hotel stays, car rentals, credit card purchases, and telephone calls. Mileage credits may be redeemed for free airline tickets, upgrades, and other travel awards.

In 1939 American became the first airline to establish a lounge for its VIP customers. Known as the Admirals Club, these lounges have become synonymous with comfort and elegance at the world's major airports. For those travelers who choose to work, the clubs often provide office equipment, facsimile machines, personal computers, and photocopiers.

Community Involvement

American Airlines' commitment to the arts in Los Angeles is exemplified by its many past and present sponsorships, including the Los Angeles Philharmonic, the Museum of Television and Broadcasting Festival, the Grammy Awards, and the People's Choice Awards, to name a few. The company's involvement in local

Making Travel More Rewarding

Today, millions of passengers worldwide enjoy the benefits of American's AAdvantage travel awards program, which allows participants to earn mileage credit every time they fly on either American or American Eagle. AAdvantage was introduced in 1981 and was the first mileage reward program of its kind.

The AAdvantage program also gives participants the opportunity to earn

sports includes sponsorship of both the UCLA and USC football and basketball programs and the Los Angeles Marathon. American was the official airline of World Cup '94.

Closely associated with the motion picture and entertainment industry in Los Angeles since its infancy, the airline has worked diligently to generate movie, television, and music industry travel. Many in these industries commute regularly on American's popular transcontinental route from Los Angeles to New York.

The airline's involvement in the movies began in 1951 when Jane Powell starred as an American Airline flight attendant in *Three Guys Named Mike*. American has also been featured prominently in recent hit films such as *Home Alone*, *In the Line of Fire*, and *True Lies*.

American has a long-standing commitment to providing high-quality passenger service in Los Angeles and has pledged to continue this tradition for decades to come.

Clockwise from top left:
American has been the airline of choice for traveling celebrities all across the globe, including Gina Lollobrigida (1956), Jimmy Durante (1958), Senator John and Jacqueline Kennedy (1960), and Joan Fontaine and John Huston (1951).

 October 24, 1960
Lakers lose first home game in Los Angeles to New York, 111-100

85 November 15, 1960
Elgin Baylor scores NBA record 71 points against New York Knicks at Madison Square Garden

 April 11, 1961
Angels win franchise's first game, 7-2, at Baltimore

Dunn-Edwards Paint

Dunn-Edwards Paint is a family-owned business with a remarkable heritage. Dedicated exclusively to paint professionals, the company has established a large and loyal following. In fact, Dunn-Edwards paints are preferred by more painters, architects, and designers than any other paints in the Southwest.

Dunn-Edwards paints and coatings cover a variety of applications, including architectural, commercial, and industrial. In addition, the company offers fine wall-coverings and a wide range of related supplies and equipment designed to ensure excellent results.

Painting the Town

Founded in Los Angeles in 1925 by Frank "Buddy" Dunn, Dunn-Edwards has always focused on the professional painter as the heart of the business. This philosophy was fully embraced by Art Edwards, a partner and eventual sole owner of the company. Based on his experience as a painting contractor, Art understood that reliable paint and dependable service would be paramount to professionals. During World War II, a

new factory and increased demand for paint helped establish Dunn-Edwards as a major supplier in Southern California. Shortly after the war ended, the company launched a store expansion program to better meet the growing needs of a booming Southwest market. This growth is now guided by Art's three sons, who have led the company since their father's death in 1988. The company now has nearly 70 company-owned stores throughout the western United States.

Through its corporate offices and research facility in Los Angeles, Dunn-Edwards maintains strict control over every aspect of its business. Using the finest raw materials, the latest technology, and state-of-the-art processes, the company produces millions of gallons of paint a year out of its Los Angeles, Phoenix, and Albuquerque factories. (The Albuquerque factory and stores are actually operated by Wellborn Paint, a fully owned subsidiary bought by Dunn-Edwards in 1986.)

In light of current concerns about the environment, customers are pleased to learn that Dunn-Edwards paints have not contained any lead or mercury for many years. In a continuing effort, a huge amount of research is dedicated to producing the safest quality products available.

A Strong Commitment to the Community

Dunn-Edwards is actively involved in a wide range of community projects. On a local level, the company has been involved in numerous neighborhood cleanup and graffiti abatement programs. On a larger scale, the company has established its highly acclaimed Unity in the Community painter training program. The program was established following the 1992 riots in Los Angeles during which several Dunn-Edwards stores were damaged. This experience created a greater desire for more hands-on community involvement. The program provides inner-city residents a free, seven-week course on the basics of painting, wallpapering, and running a business. The classes are taught by Dunn-Edwards employees and local contractors, who donate their time and talent. Upon graduation, students are placed with local painting contractors to apply their newly acquired skills.

Recently, Dunn-Edwards became a major sponsor of the Habitat for Humanity project—a program whereby people and companies donate time and material to build homes in urban redevelopment areas. The homes are then sold on special terms to those who otherwise find it extremely difficult, if not impossible, to buy a first home.

Dunn-Edwards relies heavily on its clear mission and strong sense of purpose to meet the changing needs of the professional paint industry. This commitment has earned the company an excellent reputation for premium products and personal service. With a firm foundation, Dunn-Edwards Paint is certainly poised for continued success.

Regardless of the surface, Dunn-Edwards interior and exterior paints have proved effective in a wide range of climates (above).

Dunn-Edwards produces millions of gallons of paint a year out of its Los Angeles, Phoenix, and Albuquerque factories (right).

Using the finest raw materials, the latest technology, and state-of-the-art processes, Dunn-Edwards maintains strict quality control over its products (below).

April 10, 1962
Dodger Stadium opens with Dodgers playing Reds

June 1962
Opening of the Long Beach Arena

July 4, 1962
Angels in first place on July 4 with 45-34 record

170

Unforgettable

Los Angeles Turf Club, Inc.

The spectacular view from Santa Anita Park's grandstand is unique among Thoroughbred racetracks (above).

Hosting such memorable race horses as Seabiscuit, Citation, and John Henry; world-class jockeys like Johnny Longden, Bill Shoemaker, and Laffit Pincay, Jr.; and famous stables, including Calumet Farm, Ogden Phipps, and Rex C. Ellsworth, the Los Angeles Turf Club's Santa Anita Park has played

a major role in the history of Thorough-bred racing in California, as well as in the United States.

While the sport of horse racing in California goes back well over a century, it was not until 1907 that E.J. "Lucky" Baldwin, a colorful entrepreneur, opened the original Santa Anita Park, a public, one-mile race track. With Baldwin's death two years later, racing at the original Santa Anita stopped, not to begin again until pari-mutuel betting was legalized in 1933 and the Los Angeles Turf Club purchased land near the original track in Arcadia to build a new Santa Anita Park.

A Rich History in Thoroughbred Racing

The Los Angeles Turf Club was founded by Dr. Charles H. Strub, a San Francisco dentist and minor-league baseball executive, and Hal Roach, the movie magnate. The founders persuaded investors to back construction of the $1 million track with a $100,000-purse race—the Santa Anita Handicap. Both the race and the building of the track were daring undertakings in the Great Depression, but history has proved that Strub and Roach made a wise investment.

Since racing at the new park began on Christmas Day 1934, "The Big 'Cap," now a $1 million race, has become the oldest continually run "hundred-grander," attracting many of the finest horses in the country. Azucar was the upset winner of the first Big 'Cap, setting a course for the race to become one of the sport's most sought-after prizes. It is such a competitive race that only one horse, John Henry, has ever won it twice. Seven Santa Anita Handicap winners have gone on to be chosen Horse of the Year later in the same season.

The Big 'Cap is just one noteworthy race held at Santa Anita Park. The $500,000 Santa Anita Derby is the most important stepping-stone in the West for Kentucky Derby hopefuls. In 1978 Affirmed won the Santa Anita Derby before going on to win the Kentucky Derby and, subsequently, the Triple Crown. Seven additional Santa Anita Derby winners have triumphed in the Kentucky Derby since 1952. Santa Anita's fame and prestige were extended in 1984 when the equestrian sports of the Olympic Games were held at the park.

A national leader in attendance and wagering for many years, Santa Anita's record single-day on-track crowd was 85,529 on Big 'Cap Day in 1985. Betting at Santa Anita Park and at its simulcast sites set a North American record of $36.2 million when racing's championship day, the Breeders' Cup, was hosted in 1993 by Oak Tree Racing Association, which annually leases the track for an autumn meeting.

Guided by the Strub family until 1993, Santa Anita Park has become a Los Angeles landmark. From its development during the Great Depression, the park has become a permanent fixture on the Thoroughbred racing circuit.

Santa Anita is complemented by the beautiful Kingsbury Memorial Fountain, an imposing central facade, and a series of friezes that depict a race in progress (below left).

A Los Angeles landmark since 1934, Santa Anita has drawn crowds of fans who enjoy outstanding racing against the stunning backdrop of the San Gabriel Mountains (below right).

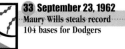 **33 September 23, 1962**
Maury Wills steals record
104 bases for Dodgers

 October 1962
Dodgers' Tommy Davis wins batting (.346)
and RBI (153) titles

 October 1962
Dodgers' Don Drysdale (25-9) wins
NL Cy Young award

Avery Dennison Corporation

Self-adhesive labels and postage stamps. Office labels for laser printers. Fastening tapes on disposable diapers. Automobile graphics. Apparel tags and fasteners. These are just a few of the hundreds of products serving consumer and industrial markets worldwide that are manufactured by Avery

Avery Dennison Corporation Chairman and CEO Charles D. Miller (right) has brought a strategic vision to the company's growing operations, providing the leadership to take the company into new ventures and markets.

Dennison Corporation, a leading producer of pressure-sensitive adhesives and materials, office products, and converted products.

Founded in Los Angeles in 1935 with the invention of the world's first self-adhesive price-marking labels, Avery Dennison established a new technology and a new industry that now serve major markets throughout the office products, retail, industrial tapes, durable goods, apparel, food, transportation, health care, and data processing industries. This focus on technological advancement has characterized the company throughout its 60-year history in developing new adhesives, new release coatings, high-speed label machinery, and many new manufacturing methods.

The company's emphasis on internal growth and strategic acquisitions, as well as its fundamental commitment to research and development, continues to expand the applications for self-adhesive technology into global markets.

Strategy Leads to Growth

From the mid-1970s, Chief Executive Officer Charles D. Miller has brought a strategic vision to Avery Dennison's grow-

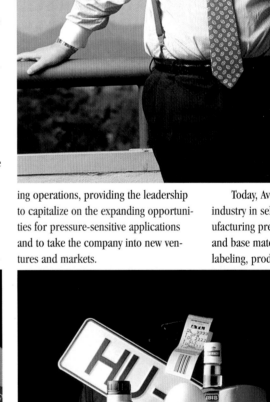

ing operations, providing the leadership to capitalize on the expanding opportunities for pressure-sensitive applications and to take the company into new ventures and markets.

Today, Avery Dennison leads the industry in self-adhesive technology, manufacturing pressure-sensitive adhesives and base materials for a wide range of labeling, product decoration, and infor-

Meeting the demands of changing office technology, Avery brand office products (near right) expand the capabilities of computer users with precisely engineered self-adhesive labels for the fast-growing laser and ink-jet printer base.

Avery Dennison products play an essential role in labeling everyday products (far right) from pharmaceuticals and detergents to automobiles and luggage.

34 January 1, 1963
USC 42, Wisconsin 37 in the wildest
Rose Bowl of them all

16 October 6, 1963
Dodgers sweep Yankees in World Series

October 1963
Dodgers' Tommy Davis wins
second straight batting title (.326)

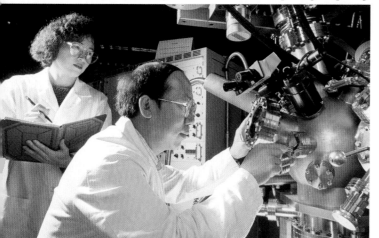

nation management applications. The company is a major supplier to the global office products market and produces labels, tags, printing, and fastening devices; self-adhesive postage stamps; and specialty products for other key markets worldwide.

Avery Dennison Corporation is organized into three core business sectors: pressure-sensitive adhesives and materials, office products, and converted products.

The corporation's pressure-sensitive adhesives and materials businesses are major suppliers to the computer and variable-information printing and packaging markets. Fasson-brand pressure-sensitive coated papers, films, and foils are sold to label printers, converters, and merchant distributors around the world. High-performance self-adhesive and extruded films are used in the transportation, home-building, and packaging industries. Self-adhesive tapes, medical-grade adhesives, and a variety of non-mechanical fastening systems are used in the electronics, aerospace, health care, and disposable diaper industries.

The company's office products businesses serve major superstores, mass-market outlets, and traditional stationers in North America and Europe, and have a rapidly expanding global presence. Its well-known consumer brands include Avery brand office labels, indexes, binders, and software, and MARKS-A-LOT and HI-LITER markers.

New products and technological advances in the company's converted products businesses, which manufacture labels, tags, printing and fastening devices, and other specialty products, further support Avery Dennison's expansion into key markets worldwide. The company is also a major supplier of self-adhesive postage stamps to the U.S. Postal Service and international postal agencies.

The Avery Dennison Corporate Center, headquarters for the company's worldwide operations, is located in Pasadena, California. In 1994 Avery Dennison ranked number 393 on the Fortune 500 list of the largest U.S. industrial and service companies. Sales in 1994 reached $2.9 billion. The company has approximately 15,400 employees in more than 200 manufacturing facilities and sales offices in 27 countries around the world.

New product innovation and expansion into new geographic markets are key elements in the company's future growth. Avery Dennison can support virtually any industry in any market around the world. The company has a significant base of growing businesses and the organizational infrastructure, market leadership, competitive advantages, and technological strengths to capitalize fully on emerging opportunities.

The Avery Dennison Corporate Center, located in Pasadena, is the headquarters for the executive and support staff of the company's worldwide operations.

Avery Dennison's office products—including sheet protectors, index dividers, report covers, binders, and markers—are market leaders backed by the power of the Avery brand name.

The Avery Research Center in Pasadena conducts fundamental research in new pressure-sensitive adhesive and coating technologies.

52 March 21, 1964
UCLA beats Duke for first NCAA basketball title

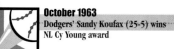
October 1963
Dodgers' Sandy Koufax (25-5) wins
NL Cy Young award

October 1964
Angels' Dean Chance becomes youngest
Cy Young winner ever (20-9)

Hollywood Park, Inc.

Since opening its doors in 1938, Hollywood Park in Inglewood has remained one of the preeminent Thoroughbred racetracks in the United States. The 340-acre facility includes not only dirt and turf racing ovals, but a lavish Las Vegas-style casino and a golf and sports center. A visit to Hollywood

"And they're off" has been the cry at Hollywood Park for more than 55 years (above).

The most unusual and ambitious phase of Hollywood Park's recent $100 million expansion project is the state-of-the-art Hollywood Park Casino (upper right).

Since 1938 Hollywood Park has been a fixture in Inglewood (lower right).

Hall of Fame jockey Bill Shoemaker, with 1980 Horse of the Year Spectacular Bid, captured a record 18 riding titles at Hollywood Park (below).

Park has become more than just "a day at the races."

Under the vision and leadership of Hollywood Park Chairman R.D. Hubbard, the facility in recent years has added numerous improvements. The most unusual and ambitious phase of Hollywood Park's $100 million expansion project is the state-of-the-art Hollywood Park Casino.

Expanding to Offer More

The 24-hour casino, the country's first live gaming casino built at a racetrack, opened in 1994. Built at a cost of $20 million, the casino features more than 150 live-action tables offering a variety of games from poker to Pan. It also offers the excitement of all pari-mutuel wagering conducted at Hollywood Park, including live and simulcast racing via satellite. In addition, the casino features luxury amenities including a gourmet restaurant, a 300-seat sports lounge, a 24-hour health club, and meeting space for up to 2,000 guests.

Refurbishment plans include the already completed Hollywood Park Golf and Sports Center, which opened in 1992. The 14-acre complex features a two-tiered driving range; a unique 18-hole natural grass putting course; 36 holes of miniature golf; and batting cages for baseball and softball.

Racing Clubhouse Offers Quality Amenities

Inside Hollywood Park's racing facility, the first floor of the clubhouse has been converted into an area designed for the serious horseplayer called the Players' Club. Earlier races are displayed on a bank of television sets, and handicappers may view previous days' races by request.

The North Park is an all-grass area the size of two football fields located at the north end of the grandstand. Concession stands, pari-mutuel windows, a playground—including a carousel—and

special entertainment for children are all available at the North Park.

Those wanting to get an up close look at the horses can visit the Garden Paddock, situated in the plaza area just outside the grandstand. Just prior to each race, fans can watch from a spacious balcony as the jockeys parade their respective horses around the walking ring before entering the track.

Contributing to the aesthetically pleasing scene at Hollywood Park are four large lakes, including two that are linked by a canal. The lakes hold 5 mil-

lion gallons of water and are encompassed by almost one mile of shoreline. All of these features make Hollywood Park—nicknamed the Track of the Lakes and Flowers—one of the most beautiful racetracks in the country.

Highlights at the Park

Over the years, many of racing's all-time greatest Thoroughbreds have graced the winner's circle at Hollywood Park, including the legendary John Henry, as well as Triple Crown winners Affirmed and Citation, who became racing's first mil-

49 November 28, 1964
USC comeback beats Notre Dame, 20-17, on pass from Craig Fertig to Rod Sherman

March 20, 1965
Bruins defend NCAA basketball title, beating Michigan 91-80

June 1965
Pauley Pavilion opens on the UCLA campus

▲ STIDHAM & ASSOC. ▼

on-dollar earner by winning the 1951 Hollywood Gold Cup in his final race. The Gold Cup is the highlight of the track's stakes program. Beginning with 1938 Horse of the Year Seabiscuit in the inaugural running, 11 Gold Cup winners have been honored as national champions.

One of Hollywood Park's most memorable days came on November 10, 1984, when a crowd of 64,625 turned out to watch the inaugural Breeders' Cup, which is considered the most exciting single day in Thoroughbred racing. Hollywood Park hosted the prestigious Breeders' Cup again in 1987 and is expected to host the event again in the near future.

Laffit Pincay, Jr., is Hollywood Park's all-time leading jockey, recording more than 2,600 wins. Hollywood Park was also the scene of the legendary Bill Shoemaker's 1,000th career stakes victory in 1990 aboard a horse named Peace.

Throughout its history, the park has

remained at the forefront of innovation. In 1971 Hollywood Park pioneered the now-commonplace exacta wagering. Two years later, the track helped establish a new weekend leisure pattern for thousands of Californians with the introduction of Sunday Thoroughbred racing.

In 1979 Hollywood Park introduced the concept of "early bird betting" to the racing world by which patrons can make wagers in the morning several hours before actual racing begins. The concept has since caught on nationwide and remains a successful innovation.

Since its inception in 1944, Hollywood Park Racing Charities, Inc. has allocated grants totaling more than $30 million to 87 nonprofit organizations throughout Southern California. Patrons of Hollywood Park, through their participation in charity racing days designated in the track's franchise from the state, have helped make the program a major success.

Hollywood Park currently is negotiating with the National Football League to construct a $200 million, 65,000-seat football stadium that would serve as a future home of one or more NFL teams and, possibly, college football's UCLA Bruins. The state-of-the-art facility, which

would be situated on the southwest portion of Hollywood Park's 340 acres, would stand directly across the street from the Great Western Forum, home to basketball's Los Angeles Lakers and hockey's Los Angeles Kings.

With the football stadium adjoining the basketball and ice hockey edifice, Hollywood Park—its historic racetrack refurbished and its luxurious casino in place—will become the cornerstone of the most extensive sports and entertainment complex in the world.

After winning the Triple Crown in 1978, Affirmed (above left) followed up by winning the Hollywood Gold Cup in 1979.

The legendary John Henry (above right) won the Hollywood Park Turf Club Handicap in 1980, 1981, and 1984, as well as the Hollywood Turf Cup in 1983.

Clockwise from near left:
Those wanting to get an up close look at the horses can visit the Garden Paddock, situated in the plaza area just outside the grandstand.

Visitors to Hollywood Park, seen here in 1938, have urged on some of Thoroughbred racing's greatest names.

Contributing to the aesthetically pleasing scene at Hollywood Park are four large lakes, including two that are linked by a canal.

Under the vision and leadership of Hollywood Park Chairman R.D. Hubbard, Hollywood Park in recent years has added numerous improvements.

7 September 9, 1965
Sandy Koufax pitches perfect game vs. Cubs

October 14, 1965
Dodgers win World Series in seven games vs. Twins

October 1965
Dodgers' Sandy Koufax (26-8) wins second NL Cy Young award

Southern California Committee for the Olympic Games

The 1932 Olympic Games in Los Angeles were immensely successful both aesthetically and financially. And although the 1936 Olympics were held in Berlin, by 1939 war was imminent in Europe and threatened to jeopardize the 1940 Games, scheduled for Helsinki. ■ With these events in Europe

William May Garland, longtime chairman of the SCCOG, brought the 1932 Olympic Games to Los Angeles and served as chairman of the 10th Olympic Committee (right).

John C. Argue, who chaired the bid for the 1984 Olympics, has been a driving force behind the SCCOG since his election as committee president in 1971 (below).

serving as a backdrop, United States Olympic Committee (USOC) President Avery Brundage contacted Paul Helms—head of the highly successful Helms Baking Company and a leading figure in the civic and sporting life of Los Angeles. Brundage thought that Los Angeles might be a suitable replacement host for the 1940 Olympics, and suggested to Helms that the city create a committee to bid for the Games. Thus, the Southern California Committee for the Olympic Games (SCCOG) was founded in 1939.

The SCCOG's bid to make Los Angeles the late replacement for the 1940 Olympics was unsuccessful, because the advent of World War II forced the cancellation of

the 1940 Games. Undeterred, the SCCOG refocused to support the Olympic movement in Southern California with hopes of someday returning the Games to Los Angeles. While this effort was under way, the SCCOG organized one of the most successful annual athletic competitions ever held in Southern California—the Coliseum Relays, which first took place in 1941 and continued for years.

Keeping the Faith through Adversity

Returning the Olympic Games to Los Angeles proved difficult. Under the leadership of committee presidents William

May Garland, Helms, Jack Garland, Bill Henry, and Lee Combs, the SCCOG tried every four years to convince the USOC to permit Los Angeles to bid for another Olympics. Each time, however, the USOC instead chose Detroit and each time the United States' bid failed.

Finally, the SCCOG's efforts paid off when Los Angeles was chosen by the USOC as the United States' bid city for the 1976 Olympics. However, the International Olympic Committee (IOC)—ironically, under the chairmanship of Brundage—selected Montreal over Los Angeles and Moscow. The IOC's decision was extremely disappointing to Bid

 35 November 20, 1965
Gary Beban leads Bruins to a come-from-behind, 20-16 win over USC

 November 23, 1965
Tailback Mike Garrett wins
USC's first Heisman Trophy

 26 January 1, 1966
Titanic Rose Bowl upset as Bruins
outlast Michigan State, 14-12

chairman Jim Kilroy, Los Angeles Mayor Sam Yorty, and the SCCOG's board. Many wondered whether Los Angeles would ever bid again.

Discouraged by defeat, a meeting was called in 1971 to dissolve the SCCOG. The only optimistic board member was attorney John C. Argue, and, in a surprise move, the board decided against disbanding the SCCOG and elected Argue its new president. Argue was already steeped in the Olympic tradition; his father, Cliff, had competed in the 1924 Paris Games, and both had been active with the SCCOG. Argue proved to be an energetic leader, intent on returning the Games to his hometown.

The effort to win the 1980 Games for Los Angeles again cleared the USOC's selection process, but the IOC instead chose Moscow. During the selection process, however, Argue and newly elected Mayor Tom Bradley each made a favorable, memorable impression on the IOC's leadership.

Despite the continuing aftershocks of the 1972 terrorist attack on the Israeli team in Munich and news of a $1 billion deficit in Montreal, Argue pushed for one more Los Angeles bid—for the 1984 Olympics. Thanks to strong leadership by Los Angeles City Council President John Ferraro, the Council in 1978 approved the bid by one vote. Los Angeles then defeated New York by four votes to become the USOC's bid city.

Argue then negotiated a series of contracts that placed financial and orga-

nizational responsibility in the hands of a previously unthinkable, all-private organizing committee; protected the city of Los Angeles from liability; and agreed to share surpluses with the USOC. In early 1979 the city's dream was realized. The 1984 Olympic Games were finalized, and in the words of IOC President Juan Antonio Samaranch, the Olympic movement was saved, and the course of Olympic history changed.

Savoring Success

The hard work of winning support at the local, national, and international level had been done by the SCCOG in collaboration with a cadre of business and civic leaders known as the Committee of Seven. They included Howard Allen of Southern California Edison, industrialist Justin Dart, labor leader Bill Robertson, Rod Rood of ARCO, film and television producer David L. Wolper, and attorney Paul Ziffren. Argue chaired both groups and was also named as founding chairman of the Los Angeles Olympic Organizing Committee (LAOOC), although he later stepped down in favor of Peter V. Ueberroth as president and Ziffren as chairman. Their efforts, combined with those of the staff led by General Manager Harry Usher and thousands of volunteers, made

the Games of the XXIII Olympiad a monumental success.

Despite having achieved its quest to bring the Games back to Los Angeles, the SCCOG's work was not finished. With Argue's personal guarantee, the SCCOG financed an update of *Bill Henry: An Approved History of the Olympic Games*, republished by his daughter, Pat Henry Yeomans. An excerpt from this book led directly to the Oscar-winning movie *Chariots of Fire*.

The SCCOG was also involved in saving the Helms Hall of Fame, which was facing disintegration. Peter and Ginny Ueberroth, First Interstate Bank, and members of the SCCOG were foremost in helping to save it, and the Hall has since become a substantial part of the Amateur Athletic Foundation of Los Angeles.

The success of the 1932 and 1984 Games in Los Angeles brought many honors to the SCCOG and its members. W.M. Garland and the SCCOG each were awarded the IOC's Olympic Cup. Jack Garland was key in bringing the 1960 Winter Games to Squaw Valley. Argue, Ueberroth, and Usher were bestowed the Olympic Order, the IOC's highest honor. Furthermore, four members of the SCCOG—W.M. Garland, Jack Garland, Anita DeFrantz, and Jim Easton—have served or are serving as members of the IOC. SCCOG members were also instrumental in establishing the Los Angeles Sports Council.

With Los Angeles as one of only three cities to have hosted the Olympic Games twice, the SCCOG today remains dedicated to bringing a third Olympics to Southern California.

Along the road that brought the Olympics back to Los Angeles, committee members remembered to have some fun. Enjoying a moment are (from left) John C. Argue, Howard P. Allen, Rodney W. Rood, David L. Wolper, and William R. Robertson.

Smiles were the result of the awarding of the 1984 Olympic Games to Los Angeles. SCCOG members (from left) included Anton Calleia, John C. Argue, Robert Selleck, Larry Houston, Ernie Van de Wegh, Supervisor and Mrs. Kenneth Hahn, Peggy Stevenson, City Council President John Ferraro, Jim and Hank Hardy, and Michael Portonova. Not pictured: John MacFaden, Don Sarno, Hank Rieger, Bill Schroeder, Pat McCormick, Parry O'Brien, Frank Dale, Fred Wada, Dr. Richard Perry, Duke Llewellyn, Dr. Norman Miller, Sam Bretzfield, Rene Henry, Bea Lavery, Jeanne D'Amico, Ray Remy, and Mayor Tom Bradley.

74 March 12, 1966
Johnny Longden wins final race aboard George Royal

April 19, 1966
Anaheim Stadium opens for first game:
White Sox 3, Angels 1

October 2, 1966
Dodgers win pennant in
final game vs. Phillies

XTRA Sports 690

For the latest in sports news and information, entertaining and compelling sports talk, or exciting play-by-play coverage of many of the region's most popular teams, radio listeners all across Southern California tune their dials to XTRA Sports 690. ■ Owned by Noble Broadcast Group, XTRA serves all of Southern California. As the flagship station for UCLA Bruins football and basketball, Los Angeles Kings hockey, and San Diego Chargers football, XTRA has become one of the premier all-sports radio stations in the United States. With its powerful broadcast signal, XTRA reaches sports fans as far north as Canada and as far south as Mexico.

A Talented Lineup

The primary reason for XTRA's success is its all-star lineup of talented air personalities. Steve Mason and John Ireland kick off the XTRA Sports weekday lineup from 5 to 9 a.m. with "The Big Show," a rather unconventional look at the world of sports from the fans' perspective. The coanchors rely on humorous insight coupled with a daily dose of bizarre audience participation that is sure to ease the morning commute.

"The Loose Cannons" with Chet Forte (former producer/director of "Monday Night Football" telecasts) and Steve Hartman (a Southern California native with an extensive knowledge of Los Angeles area sports) features spontaneous, opinionated, fact-filled, and never-predictable sports talk from 9 a.m. to noon.

The popular "Jim Rome Show" can be heard from noon to 4 p.m. His quick-thinking, in-your-face style brings energy and dry wit together in a cutting-edge show now syndicated on radio stations coast to coast.

Award-winning host Lee "Hacksaw" Hamilton, recognized as one of the top sports talk show hosts in the country, anchors the station's weekday afternoon slot from 4 to 8 p.m. Hamilton, who is also the voice of the San Diego Chargers, delivers a topical, in-depth analysis of sports not found elsewhere on the airwaves.

XTRA Sports also offers a wide variety of niche programming. "Let's Talk Hookup," a show about fishing; "Trackside with Roger Stein," which examines the world of horse racing; and "Talkin' Golf," aired in conjunction with the Southern California PGA, are just a few examples.

Coverage Goes the XTRA Mile

To complement its own programming, XTRA Sports is an affiliate of the ESPN Radio Network, and both the NBA and

With its powerful broadcast signal reaching sports fans as far north as Canada and as far south as Mexico, XTRA's Sports Pig has something to smile about.

SANDRA SMALL

XTRA Sports 690 keeps active in the community with fund-raisers, including this one featuring Tommy Lasorda (seated).

NCAA radio networks. In addition, the station regularly features an array of shows hosted by nationally acclaimed broadcasters such as Bob Costas, John Madden, and Pat O'Brien.

To provide more complete coverage for XTRA Sports listeners, the station oftentimes takes the show on the road, producing remote broadcasts from various sporting events and venues throughout Southern California, as well as the entire country. In recent years, XTRA has had a presence at such major events as the Indianapolis 500, the Kentucky Derby,

championship fights, the World Series, the Final Four, and NCAA bowl games. The station also broadcasts on-site from a host of PGA golf tournaments, including the Nissan Open in Los Angeles and the Buick Invitational in San Diego.

XTRA-AM originally signed on the airways back in 1944 as XEAC. After undergoing a series of name changes, the station became XTRA in 1961—the nation's first all-news station. During the 1970s, the station was known as "The Mighty 690" and featured contemporary hits radio before the popularity of the FM

band. The station later evolved into a golden oldies format and featured renowned disc jockey Wolfman Jack.

When XTRA switched to an all-sports format in 1990, people were questioning the viability of that decision. Despite the overwhelming success of the all-sports pioneer, WFAN in New York, many wondered whether this type of niche programming could work. XTRA has since proved those skeptics wrong. Tapping into the Los Angeles, Orange County, and San Diego markets, XTRA draws as many as 750,000 listeners any given week. Although women are increasingly tuning in, the station still reaches a predominantly male audience; approximately 85 percent of the listening audience are men.

Noble Broadcast, which in addition to XTRA owns and operates numerous other radio stations throughout the nation, is headed by Chairman John T. Lynch. The company flourishes under the leadership of its principals, who include Tom Jimenez, vice president of Noble Sports Marketing; Mike Glickenhaus, XTRA's executive vice president and general manager; Bill Arbenz, the Los Angeles station manager; and Howard Freedman, vice president of programming.

XTRA prides itself on its community involvement. Each year, the station organizes Operation Relief to help collect food, which is then donated to Southern California's needy during the Thanksgiving holiday. XTRA also supports Save Our Sports, a program designed to raise funds for high school athletics throughout the Southern California region.

XTRA has sales, marketing, and promotion departments in Los Angeles, San Diego, and Orange County, and five different studio locations, including major studio setups in San Diego and Los Angeles. XTRA Sports operates under 77,000 watts of power per day, allowing the station to effectively cover the entire Southland.

As "Southern California's Sports Leader," XTRA Sports 690 continues to provide its radio listeners the most innovative, entertaining, and compelling sports-oriented programming found anywhere on the dial.

Clockwise from top left:
"The Loose Cannons" with Chet Forte and Steve Hartman features spontaneous, opinionated, fact-filled, and never-predictable sports talk.

The popular "Jim Rome Show" features his quick-thinking, in-your-face style for a cutting-edge, nationally syndicated program.

Award-winning host Lee "Hacksaw" Hamilton delivers a topical, in-depth analysis of sports not found elsewhere on the airwaves.

March 25, 1967
Alcindor leads 30-0 Bruins to NCAA title
with 79-64 win over Dayton

July 11, 1967
First All-Star game at Anaheim Stadium
ends in 15 innings on Tony Perez homer:
NL 2, AL 1

July 12, 1967
Opening of Anaheim Arena, adjacent
to the Anaheim Convention Center

1946-1995

1949
KNBC-TV

1954
Daniel Freeman Hospitals

1958
Bal Seal Engineering Company, Inc.

1958
California State University, Northridge

1958
Hacienda Hotel

1958
Los Angeles Dodgers

1958
Ogden Entertainment Services

1960
Bright & Associates

October 13, 1967
Anaheim Amigos of the ABA open with loss
at Oakland Oaks, 134-129

October 14, 1967
Kings first game is a win over Philadelphia
at Long Beach Arena, 4-2

5 November 18, 1967
O.J. Simpson's touchdown gallop helps
No. 4 USC overcome No. 1 UCLA, 21-20

Unforgettable

1960	1975	1984	1987
Nissan Motor Corporation U.S.A.	Steinberg and Moorad Law Offices	Los Angeles Clippers	Ventura Entertainment Group Ltd.
1961	**1975**	**1985**	**1992**
California Angels	Parsons Brinckerhoff	Prime Sports	R. Rollo Associates
1967	**1978**	**1986**	**1993**
Great Western Forum	Compensation Resource Group	Cal-Surance Group Benefits, Inc.	The Mighty Ducks
1969	**1982**	**1986**	
Mullin Consulting, Inc.	Eagle Delivery Systems, Inc.	Dole Food Company, Inc.	

November 28, 1967
Quarterback Gary Beban wins
UCLA's first Heisman Trophy

53 December 9, 1967
Miracle finish allows Rams
to beat Green Bay, 27-24

December 30, 1967
Forum opens as Philadelphia
defeats the Kings, 2-0

KNBC-TV

With the most-watched news in Southern California and many of the most popular programs on television, KNBC Channel 4 is the leading television station in the communications capital of the country. It leads in an urban area containing the most concentrated and sophisticated industry-

KNBC-TV, California's leading television station, calls beautiful downtown Burbank home (right).

Two of the most widely recognized faces in the community are KNBC-TV anchors Paul Moyer and Colleen Williams (below).

related population in the world, as well as the nation's richest, most diverse consumer market.

In 1986 KNBC pioneered local, early-morning newscasts, now a programming staple from coast to coast, and it continues to lead the field. Each year the station wins many of the industry's most coveted awards—the Peabody, local and national Emmys, and Golden Mikes—for reporting stories sensitive to the community. Through extensive meetings with local leaders, an active speakers' bureau, cosponsorship of many programs like the Health Fair Expo and Toys for Tots, and programming that is consistently the most popular and most turned-to in Southern California, KNBC maintains a special relationship with the audience it serves and informs. It's a relationship that has been cultivated and nurtured for nearly 50 years, beginning with construction of the station transmitter on Mount Wilson in 1947.

Broadcasting Infancy

On January 16, 1949, the station went on the air. Television was in its infancy, Los Angeles was the fifth-largest city in the country (behind New York, Chicago, Philadelphia, and Detroit), and the East Coast was America's media center. Studio F, at NBC's Radio City in Hollywood, was transformed into the station's first television studio, and the originally christened KNBH was seen on approximately 80,000 television sets within range of its transmitter. That first 27,500-watt video signal reached over a 100-mile radius, with one viewer verifying reception from as far away as Fort Smith, Arkansas, a distance of 1,600 miles. By the end of the year, KNBH was carrying 117 hours of pro-

gramming with a total of 53 local advertisers running 65 commercial hours per month.

Like the Los Angeles area itself, the station experienced explosive growth and made great technological strides. As early as 1950, the station introduced the image orthicon and the mercury-vapor lamp, which improved kinescope reception quality by 50 percent and brought KNBH the first of its many major awards. Another award—the station's first national Emmy Award—soon followed when it transmitted the first commercial telecast of a sporting event, a Los Angeles Rams football game, broadcast by way of the Los Angeles/San Francisco Inter-City Microwave Relay. This telecast was an early indication of the station's extraordinary commitment to the finest, state-of-the-art sports coverage, a commitment that has been rewarded over the years with the market's largest, most loyal sports audience.

With its Tournament of Roses broadcast on January 1, 1951, KNBH once again established several broadcasting "firsts": the first television station to tie

in with a foreign-language radio station, effectively providing a second audio channel for Spanish; the first station with its own "sky-cam"—a converted B-25 carrying a Channel 4 cameraman who gave viewers a new appreciation for the huge throng gathered to watch the Rose Parade; and the first on-the-spot feed for large-screen projection at the Orpheum Theater in Los Angeles, where a second, standing-room-only crowd gathered to watch the festivities. January of '51 also marked the inauguration of KNBH's television newsreel operation. Local television's future was taking shape.

Months later, the station again made television history when a kinescope of General Douglas MacArthur's speech before Congress was seen by Southern Californians less than five hours after the general had given it in Washington, D.C. This marked the first time a telecast originating on the East Coast was seen on the West Coast on the same day. Soon, "Newspaper of the Air" and the "11 P.M. News" with Paul Pierce made their debuts. The "11 P.M. News" ran for five minutes each weeknight.

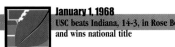
January 1, 1968
USC beats Indiana, 14-3, in Rose Bowl and wins national title

47 March 22, 1968
Alcindor's revenge: UCLA 101, Houston 69 in NCAA semifinals

27 June 8, 1968
Drysdale sets scoreless innings record at 58⅔

182

Unforgettable

At the time, KNBH was also the only station in the United States to carry a complete major college football schedule, in addition to such network telecasts as the major Eastern games, Gillette-sponsored boxing, the World Series, and horse racing from Caliente. News and sports were becoming a major part of the local broadcasting profile and Channel 4 was leading the way. It also led the way in technological innovations, becoming the first Los Angeles station to originate daily local programming in color.

Southern California's population flourished, and KNBH's popularity grew with it as the station helped define the capabilities and responsibilities of local television. Reflecting a firm commitment to the community it serves, the station—renamed KRCA in 1954 and then KNBC in 1962—produced many award-winning educational and public affairs programs and introduced to Los Angeles some of the area's most venerable and enduring television personalities, legendary pioneers in their own right. Dr. Frank Baxter, Ralph Edwards, Jack Latham, Chick Hearn, Jan Clayton, Jane Withers, and Ben Alexander were among the first, followed over the years by many of the most influential news personalities on the

air, including Tom Brokaw, Bryant Gumbel, Tom Snyder, and Pat Sajak.

For nearly five decades KNBC has continued to reflect the exciting, constantly changing character of Los Angeles,

becoming its eyes and ears—on the city and Southern California, across the country, and around the world. From floods, earthquakes, fires, and riots, to celebrations, dedications, and sporting events, the station and its employees have become the way the city sees itself and the world. As KNBC enters the brave new media world of the next century, the station continues the tradition of community involvement, technological innovation, and communications leadership that is its legacy.

KNBC's facilities continually upgrade to reflect the latest state-of-the-art broadcasting technology, which has changed considerably since the early days of television only decades ago (left and center left).

The year 1962 was monumental for the station. That was the year it moved to its Burbank lot and took on the name KNBC, to reflect its position as the West Coast flagship for the NBC network (below left).

KNBC—formerly known as KRCA—had its first home in Radio City in Hollywood (below right).

November 26, 1968
O.J. Simpson wins USC's second
Heisman Trophy by overwhelming margin

March 22, 1969
Alcindor, Bruins win third straight
NCAA title, beating Purdue 92-72

March 21, 1970
Sidney Wicks, Curtis Rowe, and UCLA overcome
taller Jacksonville, 80-69, for another NCAA title

Daniel Freeman Hospitals, Inc.

Daniel Freeman Hospitals has been meeting the health care needs of Southern California since 1954 through Daniel Freeman Memorial Hospital in Inglewood and Daniel Freeman Marina Hospital in Marina del Rey. The two facilities are part of a 14-hospital group of not-for-profit

Catholic medical centers nationwide, sponsored by the Sisters of St. Joseph of Carondelet.

With a combined total of 545 beds, both Daniel Freeman Hospitals provide a wide range of top-quality services to patients and their families. Although patients come from all over the world to benefit from the hospitals' comprehensive programs, services, staff, and equipment, Daniel Freeman's primary service is to its communities. In addition to offering such sophisticated care as open-heart surgery, the hospitals fill the community's everyday health care needs as well.

Top-Quality Special Services

The Daniel Freeman Heart Center has earned a reputation as one of the finest cardiac care programs in California. From prevention through rehabilitation, patients have the benefit of state-of-the-art equipment, services, procedures, and personnel. The Heart Center has some of Los Angeles' most highly experienced cardiologists in angioplasty and other procedures, as well as surgeons and specially trained cardiac care nurses, technicians, and therapists.

The Chest Pain Centers at both hospitals are accredited by the American Heart Association to provide life saving detection and intervention of heart attacks. The Fitness Center, located at Memorial, features lifestyle and exercise

programs for the prevention of heart disease and assists cardiac patients on the road to recovery.

The orthopedic units at both hospitals treat many sports-related injuries, as

well as patients with traumatic injuries. State-of-the-art technology and equipment are available for the complete analysis of athletic performance and the prevention of injuries. Daniel Freeman Hospitals also serves as the official health care provider for both the Los Angeles Clippers and the Los Angeles Ice Dogs. In fact, Daniel Freeman physicians can be seen during home games, ready to provide medical care on the spot if necessary.

Rehabilitation services at Daniel Freeman were started in the early 1960s to care for patients with strokes and neurological diseases. In 1976 a formal rehabilitation program, the first in the region, was initiated. Currently, the program serves patients with a variety of needs, including neurological, cardiac,

Clockwise from upper right:
The Daniel Freeman Hospitals Paramedic School is the largest in California.

The addition of Daniel Freeman Marina Hospital in 1980 brought the tradition of high-quality health care of the Sisters of St. Joseph of Carondelet to the Marina del Ray area.

The Sisters of St. Joseph of Carondelet have been helping ensure the good health of their neighbors since 1954.

45 April 29, 1970
Jerry West makes incredible 63-foot shot
vs. Knicks to force overtime

September 7, 1970
Ontario Motor Speedway opens
with Ontario 500

October 1, 1970
Alex Johnson becomes first Angel
to win batting title (.328)

184   **Unforgettable**

ulmonary, arthritis, cancer, and ortho-pedic disabilities requiring rehabilitation. The center also has first-rate facilities for physical therapy, occupational therapy, communication disorders, and clinical social services.

With more than 3,000 deliveries a year, Daniel Freeman Hospitals offers a full-service maternal and child health program for women and their families, from obstetrics through pediatrics. The hospitals also have a Level II neonatal intensive care unit, as well as a neonatologist and a perinatologist available 24 hours a day.

Daniel Freeman Marina Hospital's behavioral health services include a 30-bed unit for mental health services, a 20-bed unit for chemical dependency recovery, and the 10-bed adolescent mental health unit. Medical treatment and therapy are combined to strengthen individuals undergoing treatment, as well as their families. A chemical dependency recovery program, known as Exodus, offers the foundation for a lifetime recovery in a 12-step program.

The hospitals' emergency departments provide complete emergency care 24 hours a day, year-round. Other special-ty programs provided by Daniel Freeman include plastic surgery, the Nasal and Sinus Care Center, the Wound Care Center, and the Diabetes Care Center.

A Mission to Serve

Consistent with the mission of the Sisters of St. Joseph of Carondelet, part of the hospitals' strength is a commitment to the community. In 1992, through a unique public-private partnership with Los Angeles County, Great Beginnings for Black Babies, and the National Health Foundation, Daniel Freeman Hospitals established an outreach clinic providing early and consistent prenatal care. A satellite clinic opened in 1994 in the Hawthorne Plaza Mall.

In 1995 Daniel Freeman Hospitals and Charles R. Drew University joined forces to establish the Drew Family Care Center, which provides an ongoing training opportunity for family medicine resident physicians, many of whom will go on to practice in underserved communities. The physicians provide primary and preventive treatment for all ages.

A Leader in Community Health Care

Daniel Freeman Hospitals has evolved from humble beginnings to become a leading, community-based health care system. When the Sisters of St. Joseph of Carondelet agreed to build and operate a hospital in memory of Daniel Freeman, the founder of the city of Inglewood, they brought with them 300 years of leadership, compassion, innovation, and experience in caring for the sick.

The congregation was founded in 1650 in Le Puy, France. Breaking with the traditional cloistered life of nuns in that day, the new congregation went out daily from their houses to serve orphans, the poor, and those in prison. Soon they were asked to staff a hospice in Le Puy; their work in caring for the sick had begun.

Today, the 14 hospitals operated by the Sisters throughout the nation are organized into the Carondelet Health System. The organization assists member hospitals in strategic planning, purchasing, and insurance programs, allowing each hospital greater leverage in daily business operations.

But time, distance, and modern business acumen have not altered the Sisters' original mission or dimmed their devotion. Throughout the centuries and in each of the states, countries, and facilities they serve, the mission of the Sisters of St. Joseph remains constant: to provide quality services to those in need with excellence, compassion, and respect.

November 1970
UC Irvine wins first NCAA title, in water polo

March 27, 1971
Steve Patterson leads Bruins to fifth straight NCAA basketball title, over Villanova

18 January 7, 1972
Lakers streak to amazing 33 straight wins

The 100 Greatest Moments in Los Angeles Sports History   185

California State University, Northridge

An economic powerhouse—that's the San Fernando Valley in Los Angeles. Entertainment is the Valley's dominant industry, and aerospace, banking, insurance, and a host of small, expanding businesses—many of them high-tech firms—contribute to the area's diversified economic mix.

"We will create the kind of learning environment and campus community that will prepare our graduates for a lifetime of learning, ethical conduct, global sensitivity, and service," says President Blenda J. Wilson (below left, second from left).

Facilities such as the Delmar T. Oviatt Library provide Cal State Northridge students high-caliber learning (below right and opposite page).

Next page:
Dr. Steven Oppenheimer, a Fellow of the American Association of Advancement of Science, instructs students (left).

Northridge students experience the familiarity stemming from small classes that average fewer than 30 students (right).

For well-trained employees, the Valley has turned since 1958 to California State University, Northridge. Each of the area's major employers lists at least one Northridge graduate in its executive and management ranks.

That's one reason Cal State Northridge is everybody's business.

Northridge is the university of choice for the largest share of Valley residents who go on to college. It's among the largest trainers of teachers for Valley public and private schools. It also produces engineers, accountants, computer programmers, and nurses for Valley employers. Cal State Northridge ranks fifth in the nation, among universities of its type, in the number of graduates who go on for doctoral degrees in science and engineering.

Its graduates include Stephen Bollenback, CFO of the Walt Disney Company; Dirk Gates, president of Xircom; Dan Hahn, executive producer of "Aladdin" and "The Lion King"; Daniel S. Pena, Sr., chairman of Great Western Development Corp.; Edward Fruchtenbaum, president/COO of American Greetings; comedian Cheech Marin; Constance L. Jackson, president/founder of Permanent Patients, Ltd.; innovative educator Yvonne Chan; and many other Los Angeles notables.

"Most of the job growth in California in recent years, and most of the growth in the foreseeable future, will be in sectors that require higher education," notes Dr. Blenda J.Wilson, the university's third president.

A visible, dynamic public figure, Wilson caught the nation's attention with her response to the Northridge earthquake, which caused extensive damage to the university. Rather than close down the university, Wilson trucked in hundreds of temporary classrooms, mobilized emergency resources, and rallied faculty and students. As a result, the spring semester began only two weeks behind schedule and led to the largest graduation ceremonies in the university's history.

President Clinton visited the campus on the earthquake's one-year anniversary. He told the crowd of 10,000, "You are now the symbol of the ability of the people of this state to keep coming back after adversity upon adversity."

The San Fernando Valley, Los Angeles, and all California will continue to rely on Cal State Northridge for well-educated students who have learned through experience to rise to meet challenges and seize opportunities.

▲ PAUL TALLEY ▲

January 18, 1972
First All-Star game at the Forum: Jerry West is MVP as West defeats East, 112-110

March 25, 1972
UCLA's Bill Walton Gang finishes 30-0 season with NCAA title win over Florida State

15 May 7, 1972
Lakers win first NBA title in Los Angeles, defeat Knicks at Forum

 32 **December 2, 1972**
Anthony Davis: 6 touchdowns
vs. Notre Dame in 45-23 win

 51 **January 1, 1973**
Sam "Bam" Cunningham scores
four Rose Bowl touchdowns as
USC wins national title

 January 13, 1973
Dolphins complete perfect season with 14-7
Super Bowl win over Redskins at Coliseum

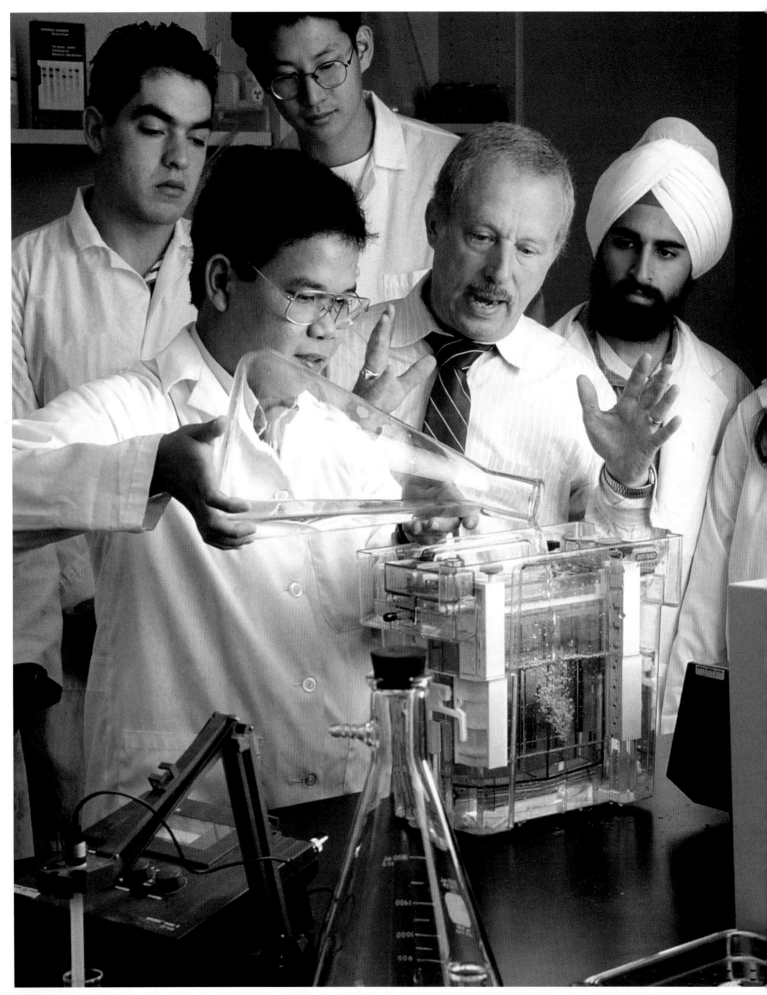

22 January 27, 1973
UCLA basketballers set all-time record with
61st win en route to 88-game win streak

38 March 26, 1973
UCLA's Bill Walton scores 44 vs.
Memphis State as Bruins win
seventh straight title

70 June 9, 1973
UCLA wins third straight NCAA track title

67 June 12, 1973
Amazing comeback powers USC to another
College World Series title under Dedeaux

October 9, 1974
Dodgers win pennant, defeat
Pirates in four NLCS games

October 1974
Dodgers' Steve Garvey wins
NL Most Valuable Player award

The 100 Greatest Moments in Los Angeles Sports History

189

Ogden Entertainment Services

Since Ogden Services began Los Angeles operations in 1958 with a tiny subsidiary called Ogden Confection Corporation, the company's presence in Southern California has been steadily increasing. From humble beginnings, the subsidiary—known today as Ogden Entertainment Services—has

experienced tremendous growth in the Los Angeles basin, paralleling the worldwide success of its parent corporation—the Fortune 500, New York-based Ogden Services. Under the leadership of CEO R. Richard Ablon, Ogden Services is now a $2.9 billion-a-year corporation, international in scope and service.

Whether the agenda calls for tea for two, a reception of 12, or an eight-course banquet for 20,000, Ogden caters to the specific needs of its diverse clientele—convention centers, arenas, stadiums, recreation and leisure facilities, private clubs, and universities.

Comprehensive Entertainment Services

One of the corporation's highly successful divisions remains Ogden Entertainment, which provides services to more large-scale entertainment and sports venues than any other company in the world. Known as a leader in comprehensive facility management and food and beverage operations, Ogden Entertainment offers a complete range of services.

One of the keys to the success of Ogden Entertainment is the continued growth of its food and beverage division. Ogden management recognizes the role of food and beverage service as a key ingredient for the crowd. The company

strives to maintain each event's own unique profile, personality, and constituency.

In addition to standard fare, Ogden provides customized menu items for its clients' facilities by including local and regional food and beverage favorites for which the fans have demonstrated a particular preference. This approach gives the food and beverage service a personalized, home court advantage. Ogden Entertainment provides food and beverage services to more than 140 facilities, covering a variety of entertainment and sports events. Facility management is provided at another 52 sites around the globe.

Southern California's Best

Annually, Ogden accounts sell close to 1 million gallons of soda, more than 300 gallons of beer, and enough hot dogs to stretch from San Diego to Los Angeles, a distance of 140 miles. In addition, Ogden Entertainment provides food and beverages at some of Southern California's most recognizable venues including Anaheim Stadium, Arrowhead Pond of Anaheim, Greek Theatre, Great Western Forum, Los Angeles Convention Center, Shrine Auditorium, and UCI-Bren Events Center.

The facility management arm of Ogden Entertainment also handles operations, management, and marketing of

Ogden Entertainment provides food and beverages at some of Southern California's most recognizable venues, including Anaheim Stadium (right).

Beautiful Arrowhead Pond of Anaheim, a multiuse, state-of-the-art facility, opened in June 1993 as one of the newest additions to the Ogden Entertainment empire (below).

◄ TOP SHOTS AERIAL PHOTO

92 April 22, 1976
Kings overcome Boston
in Stanley Cup play-offs

95 July 24, 1976
John Naber swims to four Olympic
gold medals in Montreal

January 18, 1977
First Super Bowl at Rose Bowl:
Oakland 32, Minnesota 14

192   Unforgettable

rrowhead Pond and the Forum. Each year, Ogden's Facility Management Division contracts generate $170 million in gross ticket sales to more than 5,600 events purchased by approximately 13 million people.

Ogden also prides itself on being at the forefront in the race to conserve the earth's resources by using environmentally safe, recyclable packaging for menu items. The corporation makes environmental awareness an easy-to-swallow concept by offering recycling opportunities at many of its facilities.

Ogden Entertainment's promotions division, Ogden Presents, gives the corporation a competitive advantage against other facility management companies by bringing world-class performers (including Paul McCartney, Madonna, David Copperfield, and the Bolshoi Ballet) and sold-out crowds to Ogden-managed facilities throughout the world. When it comes to the infrastructure of entertainment facilities, Ogden Entertainment is the world leader, providing more services to more venues than anyone else. Whether it's food and beverage or facility marketing and management, Ogden is known as the comprehensive service provider for all types of clients.

The Power of the Pond

Emblematic of Ogden's role in the management of major entertainment facilities was the June 1993 opening of one of the newest additions to the Ogden Entertainment empire, Arrowhead Pond of Anaheim. This multiuse, state-of-the-art facility will be operated by Ogden for 30 years. Within months of Arrowhead Pond's opening, the Walt Disney Company became the building's prime tenant with the debut of the NHL's Mighty Ducks of Anaheim. Ogden's dual management of the Pond and the Forum gives the company a potent one-two punch for promoters who are looking to double-play the Los Angeles market.

The arena is a model for the future of Ogden Entertainment and the rest of the facilities industry. Selected by the city of Anaheim, Ogden was asked to develop, design, and arrange financing for the $120 million project. Once the facility was scheduled to open, Ogden hired and trained a part-time staff of more than 1,100 employees to assist with event management. In operating this arena, the company's management services provide booking; marketing, public relations, and sales; crowd management; parking; and operations and financial administration. Ogden also maintains all of the food and beverage operations at the Pond, which includes 22 concession stands and 120 points of sale.

Arrowhead Pond is the largest and most prestigious sports and entertainment facility in Southern California. Superstars such as Barbra Streisand, Billy Joel, Rod Stewart, Barry Manilow, Whitney Houston, Kenny G, and George Strait have come to know the "power of the Pond" by performing to sellout crowds.

The building also hosts the home games of four professional sports franchises: the NHL's Mighty Ducks, the NBA's Los Angeles Clippers, the Continental Indoor Soccer League's Anaheim Splash, and Roller Hockey International's Anaheim Bullfrogs.

From a small candy-making shop in the 1950s to facilities management throughout Southern California and the United States, Ogden Entertainment's focus has been and always will be on providing customers the highest level of service and the best-quality products.

Ogden Entertainment counts the Los Angeles Convention Center (above) and the Greek Theatre (left) among its many venues.

GREEK THEATRE

 86 March 26, 1977
Unbeatable Trojans hailed as finest collegiate swimmers ever

October 8, 1977
Dodgers win pennant from Phillies in four NLCS games

 80 March 25, 1978
Ann Meyers leads Bruins to AIAW title in Pauley Pavilion

The 100 Greatest Moments in Los Angeles Sports History   193

Los Angeles Dodgers

Whether winning championships, developing star players nationally and internationally, o welcoming millions of fans to Dodger Stadium, the Dodgers organization is on the cutting edge. Twice the Dodgers have been recognized in editions of *The 100 Best Companies to Wor*

Clockwise from above:
Kirk Gibson's dramatic home run in Game One of the 1988 World Series was voted the greatest moment in Los Angeles sports history.

Jackie Robinson broke baseball's color line and became the Major League Rookie of the Year in 1947.

Beautiful Dodger Stadium—host to millions of fans—rests near the heart of downtown Los Angeles.

for in America. The 105-year-old baseball club is recognized worldwide for its colorful personalities, including 49 members of the National Baseball Hall of Fame in Cooperstown, New York.

Like a "Who's Who in Baseball" roll call, the names Jackie Robinson, Sandy Koufax, Duke Snider, Roy Campanella, Don Drysdale, Walter Alston, Pee Wee Reese, Leo Durocher, Zack Wheat, and Dazzy Vance are all Dodger Hall of Famers. Also enshrined in the Hall of Fame is longtime broadcaster Vin Scully, one of the most recognizable names in Dodger history.

A Team of Firsts

Dodger innovation may be measured by the numerous "firsts" that the organization has had since its early days in Brooklyn. The most important of these firsts was breaking baseball's color barrier in 1947, as Robinson signed a professional contract and became the first black to play in the majors. For social reasons, it was a risk Dodger President Branch Rickey felt he had to take.

Robinson, who grew up in Pasadena, California, and starred at UCLA, would not disappoint. He ignored the racial epithets and became Major League Baseball's Rookie of the Year. Two years later, Robinson won the National League MVP award. The societal impact of Robinson's achievement was acknowledged at a private dinner at Dodger pitcher Don Newcombe's house, when the Reverend Martin Luther King, Jr., said, "You will never know what you, Jackie and Roy (Campanella), did on the baseball field with the Dodgers to make it easier for me to do my job."

The Dodgers won their first World Series championship in 1955 in Brooklyn—the only one the team was to win until moving to Los Angeles in 1958. The team has since captured five World Series titles ('59, '63, '65, '81, and '88) and has won 21 National League pennants. The Dodgers have had 14 Rookies of the Year—twice as many as any other organization—including 1992 through 1994 recipients Eric Karros, Mike Piazza, and Raul Mondesi.

The Perfect Place to Play Ball

Dodger Stadium was privately built by Walter O'Malley in 1962, and it is world-renowned for its cleanliness, accessibility, and sheer beauty. The Dodgers have set numerous single-season attendance records in Los Angeles and have provided fans with many great moments and mem ories, including Koufax's 1965 perfect game and Kirk Gibson's electrifying hom run in Game One of the 1988 World Series.

Resting on 300 acres of beautifully landscaped grounds, including more tha 3,000 trees, Dodger Stadium was designed for baseball. Special events hav included Pope John Paul II celebrating Mass on September 16, 1987; Olympic Baseball's exhibition tournament in 198 and numerous concerts enjoyed by mor than 1 million fans, including 1994's "Encore: The Three Tenors," featuring Placido Domingo, Luciano Pavarotti, and José Carreras.

From Mexican star Fernando Valenzuela's incredible 1981 season, which started the "Fernandomania" era; to Chan Ho Park, the first Korean pitche in the majors; to Hideo Nomo, the first Japanese pitcher to make the big league from Japan's Pacific or Central Leagues, the Dodgers remain at the forefront and continue the development of America's national pastime.

April 1978
Pepperdine wins first
NCAA title, in volleyball

September 24, 1978
Dodgers first to reach 3 million
in home attendance: 3,347,845

October 7, 1978
Dodgers repeat pennant win vs.
Phillies in four NLCS games

Unforgettabl

Anyone who has rented a truck from Ryder, watched a television program on the Fox network, sipped a bottle of Miller beer, eaten Chinese food at the Wok Fast restaurant chain, or purchased eyeglasses from an EyeMasters store has likely seen the work of Bright & Associates.

LA SPORTS

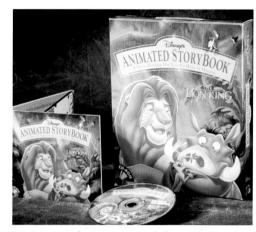

mandalay
ENTERTAINMENT

Headquartered in Venice, California, Bright & Associates is an international identity and design consulting firm founded in 1960 by Keith Bright, a leading figure in the design community for more than 30 years. Bright's combination of creative design with research and strategic marketing disciplines has been the cornerstone of the firm's success and has helped it grow to its current full-service staff of design and marketing professionals.

Serving a Varied Clientele

Bright & Associates has developed and implemented strategic design in many categories: brand and corporate identity, packaging, naming, signage, environmental, interactive, and collateral systems. Some of the industries covered have included telecommunications, financial services, food and beverage, travel and entertainment, personal care, pharmaceutical, retail, and sports.

Local clients include Walt Disney

Productions, UCLA, L.A. Gear, the New Los Angeles Marketing Partnership (a coalition of governmental, civic, and business organizations gathered together by Los Angeles Mayor Richard Riordan), KCET Store of Knowledge, Home Savings of America, Sony Pictures Entertainment, Blue Cross of California, and the Los Angeles Sports Council.

Working in the World of Sports

Bright & Associates created much of the design work featured at the 1984 Olympics in Los Angeles. The Los Angeles Olympic Organizing Committee selected the firm to design a coordinated series of pictograms for 23 events and to produce the post-Games reports, which totaled 1,500 pages and weighed 38 pounds! Since then, Bright & Associates has completed projects for yacht racing's America's Cup and soccer's World Cup.

The company has also carried out projects for clients across the country and around the globe,

including Miller Brewing Company, AT&T, Fox Broadcasting, Ortho Garden Products (Monsanto), Time Warner, Allergan Eye Care Products, and Hiram Walker & Sons (Beefeater Gin), to name just a few.

Bright & Associates has received more gold medals than most design firms have had clients. The company's work is on permanent display at the Smithsonian Institute and has appeared in *Communication Arts, Graphis, Idea, Industrial Design*, and *Print* magazines, as well as publications from other countries including Japan, Korea, Taiwan, and Australia.

"When you see a good design— whether it is on the side of a ship or a building, an annual report, an Olympic flag, or a book of matches, for that matter—you can feel it in your gut," says Bright. "People come to us because, with our discipline and our creativity, we can deliver that. Our design works. It hits the spot. It sells."

Clockwise from upper left:
Bright & Associates created identity for the Los Angeles Sports Council, CD-ROM packaging and logo design for Disney's *Lion King*, **identity for Mandalay (a financing and distribution company for television and movies), the "We" symbol for the New Los Angeles Marketing Partnership, the pictograms for the 1984 Olympics, and the symbol for Sony's Game Show Network.**

GAME SHOW NETWORK

Together we're the best. Los Angeles.

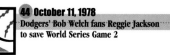 **44** October 11, 1978
Dodgers' Bob Welch fans Reggie Jackson
to save World Series Game 2

 October 20, 1978
Los Angeles formally awarded Games
of the XXIII Olympiad by the IOC

 January 1, 1979
USC shares national football title
with Alabama with 12-1 record

Nissan Motor Corporation U.S.A.

Since 1960, Nissan Motor Corporation U.S.A. has helped thousands of people and entertained millions more by supporting various community organizations and sporting events both in the Los Angeles area and across the nation. Such support has been a natural choice for a company that has emerged as a

leader in the U.S. marketplace with its collection of smart, exciting, value-oriented vehicles. Indeed, nothing is more exciting than inspiring and fulfilling dreams through athletic competition.

Nissan's U.S. presence and commitment are strong, as the company continues to increase its American design, engineering, and manufacturing capabilities. Approximately 65 percent of the vehicles sold by Nissan's U.S. Division are built in the United States, and the company directly employs 10,400 Americans among its U.S. offices and affiliate companies. Another 61,000 Americans are employed with the 1,250 Nissan and Infiniti dealers in the United States, and the company purchases billions of dollars worth of parts and materials from U.S. suppliers each year, who in turn generate thousands of jobs in their communities.

A Variety of Car Values

In recent years, Nissan Motor Corporation U.S.A.—the company's sales, marketing, and distribution operation— has achieved phenomenal success with an award-winning lineup of vehicles that includes the Maxima midsize luxury performance sedan, the affordable Altima luxury sedan, and the value-packed Sentra sedan. The Quest minivan; the sporty 300ZX, 240SX, and 200SX; the Pathfinder sport utility vehicle; and Nissan trucks complete the company's offerings. This array has earned the automaker the ranking as the nation's number two import brand, as well as

dramatically increased its U.S. sales.

Infiniti, the luxury car division of Nissan Motor Corporation U.S.A., offers a highly acclaimed collection of luxury performance cars that includes the Q45 luxury performance sedan, the J30 personal luxury sedan, the G20 luxury sports sedan, and the elegant I30 luxury sedan. With its unique commitment to the customer and its exacting attention to detail, Infiniti wins consistent recognition as an industry leader in customer satisfaction and product quality.

Today, Nissan Motor Corporation U.S.A. continues its tradition of excellence with a driving commitment to exceed customer expectations. Nissan believes it is time to expect even more from its vehicles, its services, and its community involvement, and perhaps nowhere are these expectations higher than in the world of sports.

The Thrill of Victory

Nissan Motor Corporation U.S.A. is a proud sponsor of many sports-related, community-based events in the Los Angeles area and nationwide.

In fact, Nissan is an official sponsor of the 1996 Olympic Games in Atlanta. The company's sponsorship will mean funding for the training of American athletes and for their travel to the Games.

The Nissan Open golf tournament, played each February at the Riviera Country Club in Pacific Palisades, California, is one of the company's most notable sports-related sponsorships.

Each year, proceeds from the tournament benefit more than 40 charitable and community service projects of the Los Angeles Junior Chamber of Commerce (LAJCC), the tournament's managing organization.

Nissan also is an annual sponsor of

Clockwise from top right:
The national headquarters of Nissan Motor Corporation U.S.A. is located in Gardena, California.

Young members of the Nissan-sponsored American Youth Soccer Organization (AYSO) get a kick out of a Nissan Quest minivan.

The elegant Infiniti I30 luxury sedan offers exceptional styling, performance, and value.

The award-winning Maxima midsize luxury performance sedan is the flagship of Nissan's three-sedan-model lineup.

LONG PHOTOGRAPHY

June 1979
Cal State Fullerton wins first NCAA title, in baseball

55 September 25, 1979
Baylor wins MVP award as Angels win first Western Division title

December 3, 1979
USC's Charles White wins school's third Heisman Trophy

The All Sport L.A. Watts Summer Games, another LAJCC-organized and -managed event. As the largest high school athletic competition in the nation, the games help each Southern California's ethnically diverse youth that hopes and dreams are the same regardless of race, creed, or national origin. Nissan supports the games with financial and volunteer efforts.

Nissan's Infiniti Division is the title sponsor and official vehicle of Los Angeles' most prestigious men's professional tennis event, the Infiniti Open. Held each summer at the UCLA Tennis Center, the tournament is considered to be the "road to the U.S. Open," the Grand Slam tennis event of which the division is the title sponsor. Infiniti is also the official vehicle and title sponsor of the U.S. Open Men's Singles Tennis Championship. In conjunction with these tournaments, the division has made a sizable donation to the Safe Passage Foundation, a nonprofit organization founded by the late tennis great Arthur Ashe to help introduce at-risk, inner-city youth to the game of tennis.

On a national level, Nissan is a major sponsor and participant with the Ameri-

can Youth Soccer Organization (AYSO), a nonprofit entity that promotes teamwork, learning, family, togetherness, and fun. Nissan provides AYSO with sponsorship of its soccer tournaments, the Quest for the Best good sportsmanship recognition program, and numerous Nissan vehicle purchase incentives for AYSO organizers and families.

Nissan also supports such sports as auto racing, through its internationally recognized motorsports program; skiing, through its presenting sponsorship of the annual Warren Miller ski film; and boat racing, through sponsorship of the International Jet Sports Boating Association's Bud Jet Sports tour.

Honoring Communities and Volunteers

Additionally, the company furthers its association with sports through a joint program with *Sports Illustrated* magazine. Titled "Hometown Heroes," this program features a monthly "spreadvertorial" in the magazine to recognize communities and volunteers who support successful youth sports programs.

Indeed, the variety and extent of Nissan's involvement with the sporting life

is far-reaching, illustrating that the company views its association with sports as an integral part of its business. After all, it has taken dedicated employees who are committed to excellence and who embody the very qualities that athletic competition fosters to achieve the company's current level of success. And if Nissan can help others develop the qualities necessary to realize their dreams and achieve a similar level of success, then this automaker has made a significant contribution to the nation's future.

Clockwise from top left:
Professional golfer Corey Pavin captures his second consecutive championship title of the Nissan Open, a PGA tournament sponsored by Nissan.

Andre Agassi demonstrates expert play at the U.S. Open Men's Singles Tennis Championship of which Infiniti is the presenting sponsor and official vehicle.

At-risk, inner-city youth learn both tennis and life skills at the Infiniti Safe Passage Foundation (SPF) tennis clinics.

23 January 20, 1980
Cinderella Rams battle Steelers in thrilling Super Bowl, finally losing 31-19

6 May 16, 1980
Lakers win title as Magic Johnson plays center in final win over 76ers

July 8, 1980
Dodgers host All-Star Game as NL wins, 4-2

The 100 Greatest Moments in Los Angeles Sports History   197

California Angels

Gene Autry and the California Angels, Disneyland and Mickey Mouse—it's impossible to measure their value for Anaheim, Orange County, Los Angeles, and all of Southern California. Together, the baseball franchise and the Magic Kingdom have turned Anaheim into a major-league city.

V.J. LOVERO

Reggie Jackson's 500th home run was just one highlight of his career with the Angels (near right).

Hall of Famer Rod Carew got hit number 3,000 with the Angels (far right).

Without a doubt, Disneyland and the California Angels inspired the county-wide building boom that changed an obscure network of lazy villages among the orange groves, bean fields, and strawberry patches into a thundering metropolis jammed with business parks, luxury hotels, and one of the world's busiest, most successful convention centers.

The Start of Something Big
The story of the Angels is a genuine Hollywood "once-upon-a-time" that dates back to December 1960 when Autry, the legendary singing cowboy superstar, attended the baseball winter meetings in St. Louis seeking a baseball broadcasting contract for his Los Angeles radio station, KMPC. Instead, Autry—the only person

ever to be honored with five different stars on the Hollywood Boulevard Walk of Fame for his contributions in radio, recording, film, television, and rodeo—returned home with his own ball club.

And so began the miracle. In less than four months, after starting from scratch, Autry and his partner, Bob Reynolds, signed a general manager, put together an entire front office, hired a field manager, ordered equipment, found a ballpark, set up a training camp in Palm Springs, opened general offices in Hollywood, filled a roster with players, and settled on a starting lineup in time for their first game on April 11, 1961. The Angels won the game 7-2 over the Orioles in Baltimore. The octogenarian Autry still calls that initial victory the most thrilling moment of his lifetime.

Managed by Bill Rigney, the Los Angeles Angels, as they were then known, finished their inaugural season with a 70-91 record. The club's .435 winning percentage still stands as the best of any

expansion team in Major League history. The Angels played at Wrigley Field in Los Angeles in 1961, but relocated to newly opened Dodger Stadium in 1962 where they remained through the 1965 season. The franchise moved south into brand-new Anaheim Stadium in 1966.

Many Memorable Moments
Some of the most historic moments in Angels history have included Nolan Ryan's four no-hitters and single-season record of 383 strikeouts; Reggie Jackson's 500th home run; Rod Carew's 3,000th hit; Don Sutton's 300th victory; and Mike Witt's perfect game. The stadium was also the site for both the 1967 and 1989 All-Star Games.

Other souvenirs for Angels fans are the team's American League West division championships (1979, 1982, and 1986); a Manager of the Year (Bill Rigney, 1962); a Cy Young Award winner (Dean Chance, 1964); a batting champion (Alex Johnson, 1970); a six-time All-Star shortstop (Jim Fregosi); an MVP (Don Baylor, 1979); and a Rookie of the Year (Tim Salmon, 1993).

The Angels' only elusive accomplishment is a World Series title. And when that time comes, you can be sure the singing cowboy will be whistling a happy tune.

V.J. LOVERO

Gene Autry (near right), the legendary "Singing Cowboy," attended the 1960 baseball winter meetings seeking a baseball broadcasting contract, but instead returned home with his own ball club.

Anaheim Stadium is home to the Angels (far right).

September 7, 1980
Rams open season in new Anaheim Stadium home with 41-20 loss to Detroit

October 5, 1980
Dodgers win three straight over Astros to tie for Western Division title

February 10, 1981
Kings host NHL All-Star game at the Forum

Great Western Forum

For nearly three decades, the Great Western Forum has reigned as one of the premier arenas in the world for both sporting and entertainment events. Built as a multipurpose facility in 1967, the GW Forum has since hosted more than 63 million spectators who have attended upwards

of 6,000 events.

In addition to its chief tenants—the National Basketball Association Lakers and the National Hockey League Kings—the landmark GW Forum, located in Inglewood, California, has featured world championship fights, concerts, the Harlem Globetrotters, track meets, ice shows, circuses, rodeos, roller hockey, indoor soccer, tennis matches, volleyball matches, and much more.

In 1979, in what was then the largest sports transaction in history, Dr. Jerry Buss purchased the GW Forum from Jack Kent Cooke—along with the Lakers and the Kings—for $67.5 million.

The Basketball Team of the '80s

Very few professional sports franchises can boast a history as rich as that of the Los Angeles Lakers. Since moving from Minneapolis in 1960, the Lakers have appeared in 18 NBA championship series, winning six titles. Their streak of 33 consecutive victories and an NBA-record 69 wins overall during the 1971-72 championship season is considered one of the most amazing accomplishments in team sports history.

During the 1980s, the "Showtime" Lakers captured five world championships and were voted professional sports' Franchise of the Decade by the Associated Press.

Some of basketball's greatest superstars have worn the Los Angeles Lakers uniform, including Jerry West, Elgin Baylor, Wilt Chamberlain, Kareem Abdul-Jabbar, Magic Johnson, and James Worthy.

A Showplace for Sports and Entertainment

NBA Championships aren't the only historic events to be staged at the Great Western Forum. In 1973 the largest live boxing gate ever on the West Coast was recorded when Muhammad Ali defeated Ken Norton in a split decision.

The first GW Forum concert paired

Tony Bennett and Duke Ellington in 1968, and hundreds of major outstanding acts have followed. In 1989 Neil Diamond played to a record-breaking 10 consecutive sold-out performances.

The GW Forum added another distinction in 1984 when it served as the venue for the men's and women's basketball competition during the Olympics.

Hockey Fever

Since joining the NHL in 1967, the Los Angeles Kings have successfully proved that hockey can be a hot commodity—even in sunny Southern California, where the team routinely plays before enthusiastic capacity crowds at the Forum. Many outstanding players have donned the Kings jersey over the years, including perennial all-stars Marcel Dionne, Rogie

Vachon, Dave Taylor, Luc Robitaille, and Wayne Gretzky, who is considered the game's greatest player ever.

During the 1992-93 season, hockey excitement reached an all-time high in Southern California as the Kings made a scintillating run at a championship, before losing to the Montreal Canadiens in the Stanley Cup Finals. Other memorable moments in franchise history include the "Miracle on Manchester"—a stunning come-from-behind victory against Edmonton in a 1982 playoff game—and Gretzky's eclipsing the NHL all-time goal-scoring record in 1994.

As it has for almost 30 years, the Great Western Forum will continue to provide top-notch sports and entertainment attractions for the millions of spectators who pass through its turnstiles.

▶ KEVIN MILLER/NBA

Home to the basketball Lakers and hockey's Kings, the Great Western Forum also serves as a venue for boxing events, record-breaking concerts, and Olympic championships (above).

Magic Johnson, one of basketball's all-time greatest players, heads for the hoop in the GW Forum (far left).

Hockey in Los Angeles has not been the same since the sport's goal-scoring record holder, Wayne Gretzky, took to the ice (near left).

▶ ANDREW D. BERNSTEIN/NBA

19 October 28, 1981
Fernando-mania leads to Dodgers' world title over Yankees

December 5, 1981
Tailback Marcus Allen wins USC's fourth Heisman Trophy

December 1981
USC wins first NCAA women's title, in volleyball

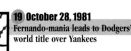

Mullin Consulting, Inc.

For more than 25 years, Mullin Consulting, Inc. and its predecessor firm, Management Compensation Group (MCG), have assisted a wide range of clients—from Fortune 500 companies to entrepreneurial organizations—in providing benefit programs for key executives. Founded by current Chairman and

Built in 1912, the Engine Company No. 28 Building (above), an architectural gem, had deteriorated to the brink of demolition by the early 1970s. Concerned citizens had it designated a historic landmark.

In 1983 Peter Mullin and several partners purchased the structure and began a five-year renovation, bringing the building back to life. The renovation was highly acclaimed, earning the Rose Award for preservation and beautification of Los Angeles' downtown district (upper and lower right).

A group of Mullin Consulting partners, principals, and associates stand outside Engine Company No. 28, home to Mullin's headquarters, a restaurant, and a non-profit theater alliance (below).

Chief Executive Officer Peter Mullin in 1969, the firm has been a pioneer in many areas of corporate benefits design and administration. Today, the company, with offices in Los Angeles, San Francisco, New York City, and Minneapolis, specializes in the creation, funding, implementation, securitization, and administration of nonqualified executive benefit programs for major corporations.

Serving a Changing Market

Since Mullin Consulting began serving corporate clients a quarter century ago, changes in retirement benefits regulations have radically altered the market. As ERISA and other legislation have reduced the benefits available from traditional, qualified retirement programs, Mullin Consulting has worked to provide supplemental, unregulated pension and deferred compensation plans.

The firm's founding partners were among the first to recognize the need for special benefits to retain and motivate employees. Over the years, this same management team has led Mullin Consulting through a fast-changing market environment; the firm's senior managers, who come from multidisciplinary backgrounds, average 15 years in the executive benefits industry. Today, along with 125 experienced associates, they serve 175 corporate clients and more than 18,000 executives, overseeing client assets of the more than $5 billion that fund Mullin programs.

Mullin Consulting is closely attuned to the insurance industry through M Financial Group, a network of experienced insurance providers, enabling the firm to access insurance carriers directly on the client's behalf. Through this link, Mullin Consulting develops investment-oriented, institutionally priced life insurance products. When compensation issues are involved, the firm works with its partner, Strategic Compensation Associates, formed in 1984, with offices

KURT MIYATAKE STUDIO

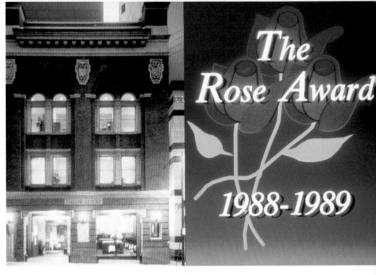

The Rose Award 1988-1989

48 April 10, 1982
Kings beat Edmonton, Gretzky in never-say-die play-off effort

June 8, 1982
Lakers win NBA title over Philadelphia, four games to two

June 1982
UCLA wins its first NCAA women's titles, in softball and in track and field

200

Unforgettable

Los Angeles, New York, London, and Mexico City.

Service to the Community

Since its founding, Mullin Consulting has taken a strong role in the greater Los Angeles community. Even the firm's headquarters, located in the historic Engine Company No. 28 Building, speaks to its commitment to its Los Angeles heritage. When the building, a national historic landmark, was constructed in 1912, it was the city's most expensive fire station ever, an architectural gem befitting the wealthy residential neighborhood that surrounded it. Some 60 years later, in 1972, the building had been reduced to a shell—used only for storage—and was teetering on the brink of demolition.

Fortunately, preservationists throughout the Southern California region recognized the architectural and historic significance of Engine Company No. 28 and worked to save it. In 1979 the building received national historic landmark designation. By late 1983 Mullin and several partners had purchased the building and agreed to restore it. Over the next five years, Engine Company No. 28 was brought back to life, a process involving numerous renovation obstacles, among them satisfying often conflicting requirements of the many federal, state, and local agencies governing all work done on historic landmarks. Balancing fire, safety, disability, and seismic codes with historic renovation specifications was a long and challenging process.

Today, the firehouse provides a beautiful and gracious setting for Mullin Consulting, as well as a restaurant (appropriately named Engine Company No. 28) and Theater L.A. (a nonprofit theater alliance). The renovation has been widely acclaimed. The partners have received back-to-back Rose Awards from the Downtown Breakfast Club in 1988 and 1989, a Los Angeles Conservancy Preservation Award in 1988 for "adaptive reuse entirely consistent with historic preservation standards," and the Los Angeles Business Council's Beautification Award in 1989.

Working with Special Athletes

In addition to its preservation efforts, Mullin Consulting has made a commitment to encouraging volunteerism among its partners and employees. The firm and its staff have been particularly supportive of California Special Olympics, an organization that helps physically challenged people participate in a wide variety of sports.

The company has backed Special Olympics through a combination of volunteerism and financial support. Over an eight-year period from 1986 to 1993, an average of 75 Mullin employees served as volunteers at the organization's Spirit of Friendship Awards Dinner, as well as the Summer and Winter Games. During that same period, the firm and its employees donated approximately $500,000 a year to California Special Olympics. Partners of the firm have served as board members and volunteer coaches for the Special Olympics program. In 1990 Mullin Consulting and its employees offered financial and volunteer support to a trip for 12 disabled athletes to climb Mount Kilimanjaro in Tanzania. The firm was honored at the Summer Games Breakfast of Champions as the "Outstanding Company" by California Special Olympics in 1994.

Mullin Consulting also provided support to physically challenged athletes participating in the Ride Across America, a bike trip from California to Florida in 1987. Most recently, the firm has offered sponsorship to the AXA World Ride, a globe-circling bike tour sponsored by World TEAM (The Exceptional Athlete Matters). The World Ride, which kicked off on March 17, 1995, runs through the United States, the United Kingdom, Europe, and Asia on a 12,549-mile trip.

Through its service to the community, strong management, innovative team of employees, and wealth of experience in the marketplace, Mullin Consulting has positioned itself as a unique financial services company for Los Angeles and beyond.

In 1990 Mullin Consulting, as part of its continuing support of the Special Olympics, helped 12 disabled athletes meet the challenge of climbing Mount Kilimanjaro. This climb, one of the most difficult in the world, was successfully completed despite a fierce snowstorm.

 October 2, 1982
Angels win second Western Division title

 January 18, 1983
Jim Thorpe reinstated; Olympic medals returned to his family at IOC meeting in Los Angeles

 January 24, 1983
Third Super Bowl at Rose Bowl: Washington 27, Miami 17

Steinberg & Moorad Law Offices

Widely recognized as the country's leading sports attorney, Leigh Steinberg has been practicing sports law for more than 20 years and has set the standard for excellence in athlete representation. In 1985 Jeffrey Moorad, who began his career as a litigation attorney, joined

forces with Steinberg, and today Steinberg & Moorad represents more than 100 athletes, including professional football, baseball, basketball, and hockey players.

The firm's client list reads like a who's who of the sports industry. On any given weekend, half of the NFL's starting quarterbacks might be Steinberg & Moorad clients. This esteemed group includes Steve Young, Troy Aikman, Warren Moon, and Drew Bledsoe. Other noteworthy clients include baseball stars Will Clark, Matt Williams, and Eric Karros, as well as basketball standout John Starks.

Steinberg & Moorad represents professional athletes who understand that with their visibility and financial reward comes a responsibility to serve as a positive role model. As part of their agreement with the firm, clients contribute both time and financial support to the community. Steinberg & Moorad insists that each contract include a clause requiring the player to give something back to his or her hometown, secondary school, university, or a national charity or foundation. As a result, the firm's clients have donated more than $30 million to various charities and scholarship funds nationwide.

Superior Legal Representation

Steinberg was born and raised in Los Angeles and attended the University of California, Berkeley, where he was student body president. He attended Boalt Hall School of Law at Berkeley, where he served as president of his senior class. His career began in 1975, when he negotiated a record-breaking $600,000 contract for his first client, quarterback Steve Bartkowski.

In 1984 Steinberg negotiated the largest contract ever recorded in professional football when Steve Young signed a $40 million deal with the now defunct USFL's Los Angeles Express. Years later Steinberg would break that record when he negotiated Super Bowl XXVII MVP Troy Aikman's current, seven-year, $50 million pact with the Dallas Cowboys. Steinberg & Moorad has represented the first pick in six of the last seven NFL drafts.

Steinberg believes strongly that sports franchises are critical to the heritage and overall economics of cities.

Therefore, he successfully helped lead the effort to keep Major League Baseball's San Francisco Giants from moving to Tampa/St. Petersburg, as well as the effort to keep the Oakland A's in Oakland.

An equal partner in the firm, Moorad brings an obsession for detailed research, a firm-but-fair negotiating technique, and a keen business mind to the practice. Moorad is a graduate of UCLA and a 198... graduate of the Villanova University School of Law.

Steinberg & Moorad maintains offices in Berkeley, California; Newport Beach, California; and Arlington, Texas. In all, contracts totaling more than $850 million have been negotiated by Steinberg & Moorad for its clients. As the nation's most prominent sports law firm, Steinberg & Moorad is clearly the leader in this competitive game.

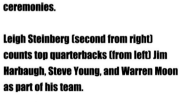

Clockwise from top right:
Leigh Steinberg (left) and Jeffrey Moorad represent the top names in sports.

Baseball players Kirt Manwaring (left) and Matt Williams (right) join Jeffrey Moorad (center) at the Gold Glove Award ceremonies.

Leigh Steinberg (second from right) counts top quarterbacks (from left) Jim Harbaugh, Steve Young, and Warren Moon as part of his team.

 March 6, 1983
L.A. Express opens play in USFL, beats New Jersey 20-15

 April 3, 1983
USC's Cheryl Miller and McGee sisters lead Trojans to first NCAA women's basketball title

 September 30, 1983
Dodgers win Western Division by three games with 91-71 mark

Parsons Brinckerhoff

very minute of the day, someone's life is made a little easier thanks to the engineering ingenuity of Parsons Brinckerhoff. Whether through the design of a subway, "diamond lane" roadway, tunnel, or airport, PB has been helping to facilitate mobility coast-to-coast for more than 100 years.

Founded in 1885, Parsons Brinckerhoff (PB) is internationally experienced in planning, design, and construction management. PB has a reputation for successfully completing many complex projects. Operating as an employee-owned firm, PB maintains more than 100 offices.

With its Los Angeles office open since 1975, PB also has area offices in Orange and San Bernardino. Staffed nationally by more than 4,800 professional, technical, management, and administrative personnel, PB's professionals are skilled in the disciplines needed for all phases of project development—planning; architectural design; financial feasibility; civil, electrical, mechanical, structural, and environmental engineering; and construction services.

The firm has traditionally been recognized for its transportation planning and design expertise on highways, bridges, airports, tunnels, and transit systems. Virtually every major metropolitan rail transit system in the nation, beginning with the New York subway in 1904, has benefited from the firm's design con-

DAVID SAILORS

tributions. PB has consistently earned a top ranking among transportation design firms for several years and is recognized by the industry as one of the foremost underground engineering firms in the United States.

Breaking New Ground

Parsons Brinckerhoff is currently involved in world-class infrastructure engineering and construction projects around the world, including Boston's $7.7 billion Central Artery/Tunnel; a $600 million Bergstrom Air Force Base conversion in Austin, Texas; the $1.2 billion Greater

Cairo Metro; and a $12 billion power plant in the People's Republic of China.

Over the past decade, Parsons Brinckerhoff has played a major role in designing Los Angeles' Metro Rail System—a 95-mile light- and heavy-rail transit network that is transforming the way area residents live and work. Approximately half of the 95 miles are in operation. Under PB's construction management, the Los Angeles-Long Beach Metro Blue Line was completed on time and within budget and now carries close to 45,000 riders daily. The backbone Red Line subway is being developed in three phases, the first of which recently transported its 10 millionth passenger. Subway progress has halted neither traffic nor the thousands of Los Angeles Marathon runners that have trod over temporary street decking, while directly underneath, construction of the subways continued. The start of revenue service on the Metro Green Line in midsummer 1995 provided another safe, convenient, and reliable transportation alternative for reducing Los Angeles' congested traffic.

With the 1994 naming of local Parsons Brinckerhoff executive Martin Rubin as chairman of the board, PB, for the first time in its history, went beyond its New York base of operations to fill its top position. Rubin, a PB veteran with four decades of service, has played an integral role in the company's most prominent transportation projects while assuming firmwide corporate responsibilities. He formerly served as president for domestic operations and presently remains as program director of Metro Rail's engineering management consultant team.

"The future for Parsons Brinckerhoff—both here in L.A. and worldwide— is a challenging and exciting one," says Rubin. "We are committed to continuing our standard of engineering excellence in providing technical solutions, in harmony with the environment, for better living."

With the 1994 naming of local Parsons Brinckerhoff executive Martin Rubin as chairman of the board, PB, for the first time in its history, went beyond its New York base of operations to fill its top position.

Los Angeles' Metro Rail System has as its backbone the Metro Red Line Subway, which recently transported its 10 millionth passenger.

78 April 1, 1984
Cheryl Miller, McGee twins lead USC
to second straight NCAA title

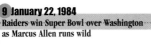

9 January 22, 1984
Raiders win Super Bowl over Washington
as Marcus Allen runs wild

57 April 5, 1984
Kareem Abdul-Jabbar sets all-time
NBA scoring record

Compensation Resource Group, Inc.

Compensation Resource Group, Inc. (CRG) is composed of professionals who believe that executives work best when they are motivated by their benefits and compensation, not when worried about them. Says Founder, President, and Chief Executive Officer William L. MacDonald, "When

you change compensation, you will change behavior."

On the basis of these convictions, MacDonald and his associates have built CRG into a national firm that provides executive benefits and compensation consulting to publicly held and large, private companies across the United States. Based in Pasadena, California, CRG has offices in 11 other cities.

One constant for CRG has been planned growth. From one office and seven employees in 1978, to 12 offices and approximately 90 professional employees in 1995, CRG has grown steadily and profitably.

CRG understands that in today's competitive business environment, attracting and retaining the best executives and directors is critical for success. And, having an effective executive benefits and compensation program has never been more important or more challenging. Corporations are faced with complex and ever-changing tax laws, discrimination against executives in regard to their benefit plans, and an acute shortage of qualified people. Additionally, traditional means of compensating executives are often ineffec-

CRG Chairman, President, and CEO William L. MacDonald (right) and Executive Vice President and Managing Director of CRG's Northwest Region Keith A. Tobias (left) help guide the firm today (far right).

Under the leadership of Executive Vice President and National Executive Compensation Practice Leader David M. Leach, CRG understands that executive compensation contributes to achieving a company's business strategy (right).

tive, and conventional techniques for creating and implementing compensation and benefits programs are obsolete.

To be successful, corporations require the skills and resources of pro-

fessionals with benefits and compensation experience and expertise.

CRG is at the forefront of working with clients to design, fund, implement, and administer executive compensation and nonqualified benefits programs.

"We help our clients recognize and understand their needs, identify appropriate objectives, and develop a plan of action to meet those objectives. Our long-term relationships assure ongoing administration of the plans as well. Our consultants work closely with clients to develop one cohesive program that is beneficial to both the company and the executives," says MacDonald.

Executive Benefits Practice

CRG's Executive Benefits Practice focuses on the design, funding, and implementation of nonqualified executive benefits plans. Utilizing a seven-step process, CRG suggests methods to deliver and administer executive benefits more effectively. These steps include discussing corporate objec-

69 May 5, 1984
Al Scates' Bruin dynasty leads to
NCAA titles and Olympic gold

May 15, 1984
Clippers announce move to
Los Angeles from San Diego

2 July 28, 1984
Games of the XXIII Olympiad
held in Los Angeles

204   **Unforgettable**

account team and management information services personnel who work with flexible software to administer various benefit and stock plans. CRG has also developed a unique system to measure the efficiency of benefits programs.

Executive Compensation Practice

CRG understands the vital importance that executive compensation contributes to achieving a company's business strategy. The company's National Executive Compensation Practice provides services encompassing the full range of compensation planning, development, and implementation including developing compensation strategies; defining the proper mix of annual and long-term compensation; designing annual and long-term incentive plans; analyzing employment contracts; and developing compensation programs for outside directors.

The CRG consulting team also considers the tax and accounting effects, as well as the cost and benefit trade-offs, of each compensation plan. The end result is a total compensation program that is strategically, economically, and culturally sound.

Aside from the corporate headquarters located in Pasadena, CRG has regional offices in Atlanta, Boston, Chicago, Cleveland, Denver, Houston, Las Vegas, Phoenix, San Francisco, Seattle, and Washington, D.C.

...ves and design issues; designing a prelim-...ary plan; designing funding and security ...lternatives; developing a final plan; ana-...zing and selecting a funding vehicle;

developing an implementation plan; and executing effective administration.

The firm's strong administration service provides clients with a dedicated

Clockwise from upper left:
CRG's Executive Benefits consultants include (from left) Senior Vice President Jennifer C. Sanders; Senior Vice President Craig E. Cayford; Executive Vice President Keith A. Tobias; Chairman, President, and CEO William L. MacDonald; and Vice President Sam Sheth.

In its Phoenix office, CRG turns to managing directors (from left) Senior Vice President Robert D. Wagner and Executive Vice President William V. Forrest.

Heading CRG's National Executive Compensation Practice are (from left) Senior Vice President Terrence Brown, Vice President Barbara L. Nitzkowski, Executive Vice President and National Practice Leader David M. Leach, and Vice President Donald L. Fisher.

58 August 3, 1984
Mary Lou Retton's perfect vault wins her the Olympic all-around title

89 August 5, 1984
Joan Benoit's front-running tactic steals first women's Olympic marathon

24 August 11, 1984
Carl Lewis duplicates Owens, wins four Olympic golds in Los Angeles

Eagle Delivery Systems

When Ray and Grace Maynard started Eagle Delivery Systems, they received only four tele[phone] calls on their first day of business. Today, Eagle Delivery is one of the premier on-cal[l] messenger services in Southern California, offering dependable, same-day service to all part[s]

of Los Angeles and Orange counties, the San Fernando Valley, and central California.

"It's amusing," says Ray Maynard. "People call us and say they must have something delivered in a couple of hours. That's normal for us. Try 30 minutes. That's a rush."

In the company's infancy, the Maynards purposely went after the "tough" clients, such as law firms with to-the-minute filing deadlines. With many years of prior experience in the delivery business, Ray Maynard knew when he began Eagle Delivery that the tougher, more demanding clients were often avoided by delivery services. Still, he accepted the challenge, finding great rewards when good service was given.

Eagle Delivery owners Ray and Grace Maynard operate one of the premier on-call messenger services in Southern California (right).

With speed of delivery and service as its watchwords, Eagle Delivery relies on Office Manager Rosemarie Egger and Dispatch Manager David Duenas to keep business going (below).

DON ELIZEY ◀

Timely and Efficient Delivery

Operating out of Los Angeles since 1982, Eagle Delivery's professional customer service representatives handle an average of 300 assignments a day, 24 hours a day. With satellite offices in the San Fernando Valley, Century City, and downtown Los Angeles, Eagle's entire operation is propelled by a multiuser computer system with custom-designed software written exclusively for the company.

Maynard created a unique and efficient dispatching system that has helped make Eagle an industry leader in both reliability and on-time deliveries. In high-density business districts, Eagle has messengers standing by in key office buildings to ensure quick response time. Its fleet of 25 couriers remain in constant two-way communication with dispatch headquarters, enabling them to monitor deliveries in progress.

Eagle provides premium quality service tailored to meet specific delivery requirements. The company offers three levels of same-day service: regular (delivery guaranteed under four hours), rush (under two hours), and Eagle (direct nonstop). Eagle also provides overnight, local-route courier service, as well as specialized same-day and overnight air courier deliveries to major cities throughout the United States.

Among Eagle's long-standing clients are the Los Angeles Dodgers, Nike, Speedo, and a variety of law firms, architectural firms, and financial institutions.

Although it is among the busiest delivery service companies in the area, Eagle still finds time to maintain an extensive training program for drivers and dispatchers. The company's method[s] are constantly being updated and stream[lined], with speed of delivery and service as the watchwords.

The company's ongoing success is testimony to Ray Maynard's early decisio[n] to strive for the demanding client and ha[s] helped establish Eagle Delivery Systems as the "Home of Personalized Service."

November 1, 1984
Clippers win L.A. home opener
over Knicks 107-105

November 10, 1984
First ever Breeders' Cup
held at Hollywood Park

61 **December 9, 1984**
Rams' Eric Dickerson runs for
single-season record of 2,105 yards

206

Unforgettabl[e]

T

he Los Angeles Clippers are more than just a basketball team. The organization takes a tremendous amount of pride in the community and touches thousands of lives throughout the Los Angeles area through its many innovative community-based projects. ■ The largest effort the

lippers are involved in is Neighborhood PRIDE, which encourages youngsters to ake "pride" in themselves and their ommunity. Cosponsored by ARCO, this rogram has resulted in the refurbishing f more than 60 inner-city basketball ourts and the hosting of over 50 instrucional basketball clinics. Several citywide asketball tournaments also have been onducted by the Los Angeles Department f Recreation and Parks.

The Clippers' highly successful Stay-n-School program urges junior high chool students to attend classes and mphasizes the importance of education.

The Clippers also sponsor the Late ight Hoops League designed to give t-risk adults a positive alternative to ang violence. This basketball league argets young adults from gang- and rug-impacted environments and llows them to play basketball three ights a week. After each game, the articipants are offered professional ne-to-one counseling. According to ocal police officers, crime in the area as significantly decreased as a direct esult of the program.

California Dreamin'

he origins of the Clippers franchise date ack to 1970 when the team was known

as the Buffalo Braves. Led by standouts Bob McAdoo, Jim McMillian, and Randy Smith, the club recorded a franchise-best 49 wins in 1975. Following the 1977-78 season, the team moved west to San Diego and changed its name to the Clippers.

Donald T. Sterling purchased the Clippers in 1981 and moved the team from San Diego to Los Angeles prior to the 1984-85 campaign. Sterling has achieved great success in his business endeavors, first as a lawyer and later in investments. Today, he is one of the largest real estate owners in California.

The Future Looks Promising

The man whose task it is to bring the Clippers to NBA prominence is Elgin Baylor, who joined the organization in 1986 as vice president of basketball operations.

One of the game's all-time great forwards, Baylor scored 23,149 career points in his 14 NBA seasons with the Lakers and was elected to the Basketball Hall of Fame in 1976. His 71 points against the Knicks in 1960 was at the time the highest single-game point total in league history.

Baylor's best move to date might have been the hiring of Bill Fitch as head coach in 1994. Fitch won an NBA championship as coach of the Boston Celtics in 1981, and has coached more games than anyone else in NBA history. Under the guiding influence of Fitch, the Clippers have quickly earned the reputation among NBA opponents as one the hardest-working teams in the league.

Combine the boundless energy of a talented core of young players, a highly experienced coach with a proven track record for success, and an organization steadfastly committed to winning, and the future of the Los Angeles Clippers looks extremely promising.

Clockwise from left:
Historic Los Angeles Memorial Sports Arena has been home to the Clippers since 1984.

A major community effort in which the Clippers are involved is Neighborhood PRIDE, which includes basketball camps like this one at Ernest Killum Recreational Center.

Hired by Elgin Baylor (on left) as Clippers head coach in 1994, Bill Fitch (on right) has coached more games than anyone else in NBA history.

11 June 9, 1985
Lakers finally beat Celtics for NBA title

99 August 4, 1985
Angels' Rod Carew gets
3,000th career hit

October 6, 1985
Dodgers win Western Division by 5½ games
with 95-67 record

Prime Sports

On October 19, 1985, the lives of sports fans throughout Southern California changed dramatically when a new cable sports network appeared on their television sets for the first time. Prime Sports, originally known as Prime Ticket Network, gave local viewers not only a choice, but a home team

network. No longer were their viewing options limited to weekend sports on the broadcast networks and occasional national games on ESPN. Southern California finally had its own sports network that televised games and events from local teams and colleges every night. Sports television, and many marriages, would never be the same.

Concentrating its coverage "in the shadow of our local stadiums," Prime Sports is dedicated to providing more live, local sports event programming than any other network or broadcast station in the market.

Clockwise from above:
Bill Daniels, cofounder of Prime Sports, was the driving force behind the network for its first nine years.

Prime Sports—the Home Team Network— presents local rivalries like the USC-UCLA football game among its roster of live sports telecasts.

Prime Sports' announcer roster includes legendary Los Angeles Laker play-by-play man Chick Hearn (left) and Stu Lantz (right).

Professional and College Sports Coverage

Prime Sports' marquee programming features the games of five professional sports teams—the NBA's Los Angeles Lakers; the NHL's Los Angeles Kings and Mighty Ducks of Anaheim; and MLB's California Angels and San Diego Padres. The network also televises college football, basketball, and other sports from USC, UCLA, other Pacific-10 Conference schools, San Diego State, and Pepperdine.

The Prime Sports programming menu includes practically every known

sport in the Western world from auto racing, to mountain biking, to international soccer, to Australian Rules football, as well as surfing, snowboarding, rugby, horse racing, and much, much more.

Produced in Century City, the Emmy-winning nightly sports news show "Press Box" is now seen live nightly across the nation. Hosted by an acclaimed team of anchors, the program features up-to-the-minute coverage of the day in sports with scores, highlights, features, and interviews.

Prime Sports also produces hours of taped sporting events and original sports

programming to help keep local sports fans in touch with the teams in their communities, cementing Prime Sports' position as the "home team network."

On-Air Talent Features Sports' Best

Virtually all events are televised live by an outstanding array of on-air talent, including some of the most recognized names in sportscasting. Lakers' legendary announcer Chick Hearn, Bob Miller on Kings' telecasts, and "The Voice of USC" Tom Kelly are just a few of the network's more famous voices.

Prime Sports has also given several sportscasters their first break in the business, including former UCLA and NBA star Bill Walton.

From Humble Beginnings and Into the Future

Prime Sports has reached the top, but its beginnings were humble. Founded by cable industry pioneer Bill Daniels and Lakers Owner Jerry Buss, the network began as a basic service distributed on handful of Southern California cable systems to only 680,000 subscribers. Today, Prime Sports has achieved almost 100 percent penetration in its coverage area, reaching 4.6 million customers via 175 cable systems across Southern California, Arizona, Nevada, and Hawaii

March 9, 1986
L.A. Marathon debuts with 10,787 entrants

37 October 11, 1986
Angels' emotion powers come-from-behind win over Boston in ALCS

November 1, 1986
Third Breeders' Cup held at Santa Anita Park

well as satellite, DBS, and wireless services.

The rapid growth of Prime Sports reflects the nationwide explosion in regional sports networks. When the network started in 1985, there were only three others in New York, Texas, and Washington, D.C. Today, more than 30 regional sports networks reach millions of viewers across the country.

Prime Sports now sets the pace among these regional players, but it was hard work and excellent leadership that carried the network to the top. In the beginning, Tony Acone, Prime Sports' first president, secured distribution on cable systems and increased the network's subscriber count, programming, and geographic reach.

Former ABC Network Television President John C. Severino and former ESPN President Roger L. Werner, Jr., have also served Prime Sports as president and chief executive officer over the years. During Werner's tenure, the network branched out by launching the nation's first Spanish-language sports network, Prime Deportiva, in 1993.

Prime Deportiva is now the nation's premier soccer network, with exclusive rights to more than 1,000 soccer matches from eight countries and eight prestigious soccer tournaments, including La Copa America and La Copa de Oro. The network has changed the way Latinos watch television, giving Latin viewers their sports in their own language.

In late 1994 Prime Sports began another chapter in its history when it was acquired by Liberty Sports, the sports programming arm of the world's largest cable operator, Tele-Communications, Inc. (TCI). Under the direction of President Ed Frazier, Liberty Sports owns or has interests in 14 regional sports networks across the country and is the world's largest distributor of sports programming, available to 54 million domestic homes and 53 million international homes.

Prime Sports General Manager Kitty Cohen has positioned the network for the future with a variety of new ventures, including an interactive test with one of its Southern California cable affiliates. Prime Sports also has begun to acquire sporting events rather than just televising them, as it looks to expand its presence in the sports world.

During the last decade, cable television has become a staple in the lives of Southern Californians. One of the biggest reasons is the emergence of Prime Sports. With its award-winning lineup and the support of its parent company, Prime Sports continues to be the leader among regional sports networks and to serve as Southern California's home team network.

Clockwise from top left: In 1994 Prime Sports was acquired by Liberty Sports under the leadership of President Ed Frazier.

Hockey great Wayne Gretzky plays for the Los Angeles Kings and for the city's Home Team Network—Prime Sports— as well.

"Press Box," the Emmy-winning national sports news program, provides scores, highlights, and interviews.

January 1987
Los Angeles Sports Council founded

January 26, 1987
Fourth Super Bowl at Rose Bowl:
Giants 39, Denver 20

June 14, 1987
Lakers win NBA title over Boston,
four games to two

Dole Food Company

A name recognized in many languages in almost every land, Dole Food Company is the world'[s] largest grower and supplier of fresh and packaged fruits, juices, vegetables, and nuts. In all, Dol[e] sells more than 170 different food products, is the industry's leading producer of canned and fres[h]

pineapple, and is the premier North American supplier of bananas, grapes, lettuce, celery, cauliflower, dried fruits, and nuts.

Nutrition, Taste, and Convenience

Today's consumer is looking for nutritious foods that fit a healthy, active lifestyle. Dole meets these needs with fresh, nutritious, and wholesome products that offer convenience and great taste with unsurpassed variety. With more than 70 fresh fruits and vegetables, and over 100 processed and packaged fruits, juices, and nuts, Dole is recognized by 98 percent of American consumers for high-quality, good-for-you food products.

To answer growing consumer demand for healthy, easy-to-prepare meals and snacks, Dole has introduced a complete line of convenient, value-added, precut vegetable and salad mixes. Dole is a leader in this industry, which has become the fastest-growing category in supermarkets.

Dole's multiproduct line is marketed not only in North America but throughout the world by the more than 100 Dole sales offices and brokers. Dole's products are sourced from the United States and more than 80 countries in Asia, Europe, and South and Central America. Dole is prominently situated in California's rich agricultural growing areas and along the western region of the country. Fresh vegetables are grown in California and Arizona; apples and pears are grown in Wenatchee, Washington—the heart of apple-growing country; and citrus is grown in both California and Florida. Fresh pineapple, which is shipped to supermarkets daily, is grown in Hawaii. In Thailand and the Philippines pineapple is grown for canning, juices, and other pineapple products. Dole's extensive banana plantations and additional farms for fresh fruits and vegetables are located in regions with some of the finest soils and climates throughout the world. Moving Dole's millions of cases of products around the world involves an extensive distribution system. Dole has the industry's most modern fleet of refrigerated container vessels to deliver its prod-

ucts, ensuring that the items delivered t[o] the neighborhood grocery store arrive i[n] peak condition.

More Than a Century of High-Quality Foods

The company was founded in Hawaii in 1851 and built its reputation on its com[-] mitment to "quality, and quality, and quality." These are the words of James Drummond Dole and are reflected in th[e] statement of principles upon which he founded and operated the company. Do[le] came to Hawaii—with an initial investment of $1,000, degrees in business an[d] horticulture, and a love of farming—to begin the world's first successful pineap[-] ple-growing and -canning operation, which was then called the Hawaiian Pineapple Company. Dole developed an[d] grew the pineapple business into Hawai[i's] second-largest industry. In achieving his goal of making pineapple available in every grocery store across the country, James Dole made the name "Hawaii" almost synonymous with "pineapple." Considered an exotic fruit, pineapple

 November 21, 1987
Fourth Breeders' Cup held at Hollywood Park

93 November 30, 1987
Bo (Jackson) knows running as
Raiders trounce Seahawks in Kingdome

 13 June 22, 1988
Lakers repeat NBA title by defeating Pistons in
seventh game

210   Unforgettab[le]

became the symbol of hospitality that is often depicted on fine furniture. When Mr. Dole began an innovative campaign of advertising with recipes in ladies' magazines, the popularity of the fruit grew and it was sought by households all over the nation.

The company later merged with Castle & Cooke to offer bananas and eventually almost every fresh fruit and vegetable grown in the world. The Dole brand name easily translated quality and nutrition to every fruit and vegetable the company grew and sold.

Today Dole Food Company's worldwide team of growers, packers, processors, shippers, and employees is committed to consistently providing safe, high-quality fruits, vegetables, and food products while protecting the environment in which its products are grown and processed. Jim Dole's dedication to quality is still the top priority. It is a commitment solidly backed by stringent quality control measures, state-of-the-art production and transportation technologies, continuous improvement through research and innovation, scientific pest management programs, and dedication to the safety of its workers, communities, and the environment.

Under the direction of Chairman and Chief Executive Officer David H. Murdock, Dole Food Company, Inc. conducts business in three primary operating areas: food production and distribution, real estate development, and resorts. The real estate division, Castle & Cooke Homes, Inc., is one of the largest developers and builders of single-family homes on the island of Oahu in Hawaii, and is one of the largest developers of residential real estate in Bakersfield, California. The company's resorts are located on Hawaii's island of Lana'i, which is 98 percent owned by Dole and is the last vestige of old Hawaii. The Lodge at Koele—nestled in the Norfolk pines— and the seaside Manele Bay Hotel are both recognized to be among the finest resorts in the world.

Committed to the Community

Dole is a major sponsor of the Shark Shootout, a golf tournament held annually at picturesque Sherwood Country Club, situated just a few miles from Dole's worldwide headquarters in Westlake Village, California. The event is hosted by PGA superstar Greg Norman and brings together a select field of 20 of golf's top professionals. Since it began in 1989, the tournament and its sponsors have helped raise more than $4 million for children's charities.

The company also participates in community-based events by donating funds and products to health-oriented programs. The goal of its charitable contribution program is to help effect positive change, particularly in the area of nutrition education for children as a way to prevent disease. Dole is also one of the largest donors to nationwide feeding programs for the needy.

For years, Dole has been a leader in nutrition education for children, working in collaboration with many of the nation's leading health authorities to teach students the value of healthy eating habits. The company created the first CD-ROM program designed especially to educate elementary grade students about the benefits of proper nutrition. Bobby Banana, Pamela Pineapple, Anthony Apple, and Juanita Watermelon come to life with individual personalities and voices through interactive multimedia and discovery learning in a way that excites children about nutrition.

These kinds of innovations and ideas, along with a relentless commitment to providing high-quality products, are the keys to success at Dole Food Company. Dole and its 46,000 employees are dedicated to this commitment. A strong worldwide team in more than 80 countries with experience and depth has taken pride in building Dole's brand and products to the premium position they enjoy today.

Clockwise from top:
The Lodge at Koele is one of the finest resorts in the world.

Dole Chairman and CEO David H. Murdock and PGA superstar Greg Norman attend the annual Shark Shootout held in Thousand Oaks, California.

The sun never sets on a Dole ship. The *Dole America* is one of the company's state-of-the-art refrigerated container ships, which ensure that products arrive at market in peak condition.

 25 August 9, 1988
Wayne Gretzky traded by Edmonton to Kings

 75 September 19, 1988
High schooler Janet Evans dominates swimming, wins gold in Seoul Olympics

 77 September 24, 1988
Jackie Joyner-Kersee sets untouchable heptathlon record of 7,291 in Seoul Games

100 Greatest Moments in Los Angeles Sports History   211

Cal-Surance Group Benefits, Inc.

For more than 20 years, companies have relied on the professionals of Cal-Surance Group Benefits, Inc. (CSGB) to deliver a full range of effective employee benefit programs with superior rates and service. As a leading regional independent insurance broker, Cal-Surance Group Benefits and its staff o

Cal-Surance's seven current senior-level executives sit on many industry advisory boards, enabling the company to remain on the leading technical edge of the industry (right).

Cal-Surance President and CEO Jim Hall received industry plaudits when he was called upon as a key spokesperson regarding statewide Proposition 186 and national health care reform (below).

DOWSING PHOTOGRAPHY STUDIOS

more than 30 dedicated professionals have proudly served the health insurance needs of their more than 250 clients.

From small start-up businesses to large, publicly owned corporations, Cal-Surance offers an experienced team of specialists and a customized level of service. "Our relationship with our clients is founded upon mutual understanding, trust, and professional, diligent service," says Jim Hall, company president.

Cal-Surance Group Benefits offers a full range of employee benefit programs including Group Life, Medical, Dental, Disability, Vision, Long-term Care, Employee Assistance Programs, and Wellness and Cafeteria Plans, among other services. These programs may be insured, self-insured, or partially self-insured based on the client's philosophy, financial objectives, and size.

CSGB corporate offices in Torrance, a suburb of Los Angeles, contain highly sophisticated computerized systems, providing Cal-Surance the accessibility and expertise to manage and service clients all across the United States, plus parts of Canada. The company can also assist clients with Property and Casualty coverages, Executive Benefits, and Retirement Plans through its working relationships with other independently owned companies, Cal-Surance Associates and Cal-Surance Benefit Plans, Inc.

CSGB clientele includes leading companies involved in such broad areas as banking, manufacturing, health care, professional groups, business and industry associations, communications, hospitality and food service, insurance companies, and local government units. While Cal-Surance Group Benefits, Inc.'s list of clients includes many New York Stock Exchange companies that are household names, the company serves employers of all sizes. Its Special Accounts unit works exclusively with companies employing 50 people or fewer.

Standing Apart from the Competition

In 1974 Jim Hall joined the original Cal-Surance Companies to manage the one-person Group Department. The department grew dramatically, and in 1986 Hall, along with John Mackerer and Jim Czesak, bought controlling interest o the Group Benefits Division from the par ent company, Cal-Surance Benefit Plans, Inc., ultimately creating Cal-Surance Group Benefits, Inc., as a separate legal entity in 1994. Subsequently, long-tenured Cal-Surance Group Benefits professionals Nancy Hoffman, Bob Volkel, and Andrew Skillen have become shareholders. In June 1994 Gary Delaney, a successful group insurance broker (who was also headquartered in Torrance), merged his practice into CSGB, Inc. to become the seventh shareholder.

Today, Cal-Surance Group Benefits, Inc. and its seven senior-level executives sit on many industry advisory boards, enabling Cal-Surance to remain on the leading technical edge of the industry. Cal-Surance is licensed with all major

17 September 28, 1988
Orel Hershiser surpasses Drysdale, pitches 59 scoreless innings

1 October 15, 1988
Kirk Gibson's pinch-hit home run wins World Series opener vs. Oakland

October 1988
Dodgers' Kirk Gibson wins NL MVP and Orel Hershiser wins NL Cy Young award

carriers, and its strong leverage and relationships within the insurance industry are used to deliver the most competitive rates and benefits for its clients.

What also distinguishes Cal-Surance from its competitors, says Hall, is the company's team concept. "We assign an account management team of two or three highly trained staff professionals to each client—an account director, an account executive, and an account manager or service representative. In service industries, the people make the difference. I think our team approach best meets the client's needs."

Cal-Surance's commitment to service is further demonstrated by the willingness of its professionals to travel to key locations to conduct open enrollment and management meetings. Such meetings

assure that employees have a complete understanding of all aspects of their benefit programs. Other unique services the company provides include assistance in government compliance and preparation of user-friendly benefit brochures (including Spanish translation if needed).

Local and National Presence

Originally, Cal-Surance Group Benefit's strategic planning called for having clients only within the greater Los Angeles area and within a one-hour flight from nearby Los Angeles International Airport—for example, the Phoenix, San Francisco, and San Diego areas. However, as a result of its extensive experience in effectively implementing managed care programs, Cal-Surance has gained a national reputation, and thus, a much wider clientele base.

"In terms of employee benefits, the West Coast has been more progressive than other parts of the country," says Czesak, who serves as senior vice president. "We have been through the education and transition issues of conversion to managed care, unlike most eastern and midwestern brokers."

Another area of specialization is the design and implementation of Flexible Benefit Programs. "During the uncertainty of national health care reform, most employers were taking a wait-and-see position regarding flexible benefits," says Mackerer, senior vice president and an expert in this area. "Now that it appears that uniform, government-run health care will not be implemented, employers' interest in this creative form of providing benefits has reemerged."

Hall received industry plaudits when he was called upon as a key spokesperson regarding statewide Proposition 186 and national health care reform. He spoke to various groups both locally and nationally to educate them about the complex issues.

Cal-Surance Group Benefits' revenue has grown for 20 consecutive years. The company has remained committed to giving its clients effective insurance solutions through technical excellence, innovation, experience, and service. Along the way, this team of dedicated insurance professionals has earned the confidence of scores of business owners and executives.

Using state-of-the-art computer systems, Cal-Surance account executives and service personnel deliver quality information, not just "data" (top left).

The account executives and account managers at Cal-Surance deliver a full range of effective employee benefit programs with superior rates and service (bottom left).

Cal-Surance Group Benefits and key members of its staff of dedicated professionals have proudly served the health insurance needs of their more than 250 clients (below).

▲ DOWSING PHOTOGRAPHY STUDIOS ▼

96 April 30, 1989
Willie Shoemaker wins 1,000th stakes race, at Hollywood Park

July 11, 1989
All-Star Game at Anaheim Stadium features Bo Jackson homer and 5-3 AL win

30 October 15, 1989
Kings' Wayne Gretzky sets all-time NHL scoring record

The 100 Greatest Moments in Los Angeles Sports History

213

The Ventura Entertainment Group, Ltd.

The Ventura Entertainment Group, Ltd. is a diversified broadcast and entertainment marketing/communications services company whose main business is providing marketing services to its corporate clientele. ■ With offices located in Los Angeles since 1987, Ventura is headquartered in

Ventura manages Procter & Gamble's motorsports racing activities—most notably, P&G's "Tide Car" sponsorship in NASCAR's Winston Cup Series.

Ventura Chairman and CEO Floyd W. Kephart has more than 30 years' experience in the world of business and finance.

Nashville, Tennessee. The firm also has offices in New York City and Charlotte, North Carolina. Ventura integrates marketing and media opportunities for corporations, destinations, products, television programming, broadcast properties, and out-of-home entertainment venues.

Ventura Chairman and CEO Floyd W. Kephart has more than 30 years' experience in the world of business and finance. He has been named to the board of several public companies and has served in various capacities in government, including working for the Kennedy administration and for the governor of Tennessee.

"I expect Ventura's growth to come from event sponsorship," says Kephart, a strong proponent of sports and event marketing. "Event sponsorship as an industry has grown more than 450 percent in the past 10 years—from $850 million in 1985 to $4 billion in 1995."

Combining talent, experience, and imagination, Ventura maximizes the commercial impact of sponsorships, promotions, programs, and media properties. Ventura manages the largest number of

corporate clients in the sports and marketing business. The firm's clients include national advertisers and many Fortune 500 companies, including General Motors, Coca-Cola, NFL Properties, Procter & Gamble, AT&T, Valvoline, CitGo, Volkswagen of America, and Vail, Colorado.

A Diverse Corporation

Ventura's diversity has led it into a variety of separate—yet related—industry segments. Three divisions form the core of the firm.

The largest of the three is the Corporate Services division, established to offer a complete range of production services and consulting capabilities to clients in the world of business and industry. Companies have long turned to Ventura for promotional assistance in everything from designing a few slides to producing extravagant events that introduce new products and marketing strategies to audiences ranging from the general public to the press, security analysts, shareholders, and employees.

"I anticipate that Ventura's growth in the emerging markets will come from

direct-response marketing of sports, entertainment, and educational products," says Kephart.

With this view in mind, Ventura has successfully completed its acquisition of Modern Talking Pictures, a company with a 58-year tradition of providing corporations and associations access to America's classrooms. In an era of limited resources, Ventura provides sponsors a direct channel through teachers to kids and their families by offering free supplemental teaching materials.

The segments within Corporate Services include Media Planning and Buying, Destination Marketing, Political Consulting and Campaign Management, Sponsorship Sales and Management, TV Production Sales and Syndication, Corporate Video Production and Educational Distribution, and Product Placement.

Through Ventura's TV Broadcasting Station Operations division, the company actively seeks to purchase television stations throughout the country. Ventura currently owns WHOA-TV in Montgomery, Alabama, and is acquiring WTWC-TV in Tallahassee, Florida.

 December 1989
Long Beach State wins first NCAA title, in women's volleyball

 59 November 17, 1990
Unstoppable offensive show ends at USC 45, UCLA 42 at Rose Bowl

 July 12, 1991
U.S. Olympic Festival held in Los Angeles

Ventura's Facilities and Design division provides planning and design consultation services to clients who are building or renovating corporate or television broadcast and production studios, theaters, arenas, conference centers, hotels, government facilities, or public buildings. What began as a lighting design firm has become a full-service production/communications provider to 14 national political conventions, Niagara Falls, Universal Studios, Epcot Center, and an unparalleled list of television shows, sporting events, and concert venues.

Business Climate

According to Kephart, the business climate for sports, entertainment, and lifestyle marketing is excellent. "Corporate sponsorship of events and marketing has almost tripled in the past five years, having grown from $1.5 billion in 1989 to $6 billion in 1995," he says.

Corporate America continues to support television programming and sporting venues regardless of how they are merchandised. However, the shift toward destination marketing—affiliating a product/brand with a destination that speaks to a common consumer—is one that Ventura has been instrumental in creating.

The company currently manages marketing objectives for clients who desire an affiliated lifestyle/image with the cities of Branson, Missouri, and Vail, Colorado.

Ventura's event management service—offered through its corporate division—develops, manages, and implements the corporate sponsorship of motorsports programs and major sports-related events. For example, the company manages Procter & Gamble's motorsports racing activities—most notably, P&G's "Tide Car" sponsorship in NASCAR's Winston Cup Series.

Looking Forward

Ventura Entertainment enjoys a unique perspective within the marketplace in offering its clients a creative, nontraditional marketing bridge connecting their product, brand, or service with a desired niche consumer.

The types of services Ventura provides will become increasingly important as the industry continues to seek ways to support its investments in cross-promotion efforts. Ventura has positioned itself to be the link between corporate America and the sports/entertainment industry. The firm plans to continue its pursuit of opportunities and strategic alliances that will contribute to its future growth and profitability.

Ventura Entertainment Group, Ltd.—a highly mobile and flexible company—excels in creating customized marketing services of the highest caliber.

Clockwise from above:
Whether managing the destination marketing of Vail, Colorado, identity products for NFL teams, or the dramatic, architectural lighting design of the Moulin Rouge at Universal Studios, Ventura Entertainment does it with style.

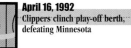
April 16, 1992
Clippers clinch play-off berth, defeating Minnesota

83 May 25, 1992
UCLA's Lisa Fernandez is too good as Bruins win another NCAA softball title

54 January 31, 1993
Community support for Super Bowl XXVII, at Rose Bowl, called "best ever"

The Mighty Ducks of Anaheim

Producers from Disney mixed hockey and Hollywood together a few years ago and came up with a smash hit called "The Mighty Ducks," a live-action comedy about a peewee hockey team and their misfit coach. The movie was so successful that it inspired Disney to enter the National Hockey

Led by Coach Ron Wilson (third from left), the Mighty Ducks tied a record for most wins by an NHL first-year club with 33 in their inaugural season.

League for real with the Mighty Ducks of Anaheim. Unlike the film version, however, this group of Ducks are anything but misfits. In fact, since joining the NHL in 1993, the Mighty Ducks have caused quite a stir both on and off the ice.

Led by Coach Ron Wilson, the Mighty Ducks tied the record for most wins by an NHL first-year club with 33 in their inaugural season. Their 19 road victories that season represent the record for the most ever by an expansion team. But bigger things are yet to come.

A Promising Future

Jack Ferreira, the team's vice president/general manager, and Pierre Gauthier, assistant general manager, together have assembled a nucleus of talented, young players who will continue to build the foundation for the Mighty Ducks of the future. Gifted prospects such as left wing Paul Kariya, defenseman Oleg Tverdovsky, and goaltender Guy Hebert solidify the future of a franchise committed to winning a Stanley Cup championship. Kariya, in particular, has the necessary skills to

become a bona fide NHL star, and he proved it by leading the team in scoring in his rookie season of 1995.

After earning a reputation as one of Hollywood's most versatile and creative executives, Michael D. Eisner joined The Walt Disney Company in September 1984 as chairman and chief executive officer. Eisner's strong belief in the future of hockey in Southern California and the importance of quality entertainment outside the home were factors in the company's decision to join the NHL. Disney's long-range plan is to make the Mighty Ducks of Anaheim a "legendary sports franchise" in the image of teams such as the Dallas Cowboys, Boston Celtics, and New York Yankees.

Combining entertainment with sports, Disney Sports Enterprises set out to create a total entertainment package for fans attending Mighty Ducks games at the Arrowhead Pond of Anaheim. It is a formula that has proved extremely successful. The Mighty Ducks have quickly become one of the league's hottest properties, playing to packed houses nightly their home arena, affectionately nicknamed "the Pond."

"We want to treat our guests and fans to the best entertainment in town,"

Celebrating a goal against the St. Louis Blues are (from left) Mike Sillinger, Milos Holan, and Bobby Dollas.

12 May 29, 1993
Kings defeat Toronto, reach Stanley Cup finals for first time ever

June 13, 1993
The Pond of Anaheim opens with Barry Manilow concert

72 August 28, 1993
Long Beach repeats as Little League champions

216   Unforgettabl

says Tony Tavares, president of Disney Sports Enterprises and the Mighty Ducks. "From the moment our guests walk in until the moment they leave, we want them to be 100 percent entertained."

Part of that entertainment includes Wild Wing, the enormously popular team mascot who roams the stands before and during the game, amusing fans with his zany antics. In addition, there are also the "Decoys," a group that performs dance routines on skates during intermissions; a 12-by-12-foot, full-color Jumbotron scoreboard; and a variety of interactive fan promotions to delight the crowd.

As fans flock to see the Mighty Ducks, they will be able to enjoy one of the most exciting teams in professional

hockey in one of the finest sports facilities in North America. Reflecting state-of-the-art design in both form and function, the Arrowhead Pond offers spectators a venue that is both beautiful to behold and perfect for viewing a hockey game. Conveniently located with easy access to five major freeways, the arena affords fans incredibly comfortable seating and some of the best sight lines and proximity to the action that can be found.

The Mighty Ducks of Anaheim have set new standards in sports marketing, and their merchandise is the leading seller in the NHL. Ducks merchandise is worn by people all across the United States, as well as all corners of the world. It has rapidly become one of the top souvenirs bought by tourists traveling in

Southern California and the United States. Purple, jade, silver, and white are the team colors. A catchy logo featuring a hockey mask shaped like a duck head provides the club with its own unique identity.

The Mighty Ducks in the Community

The Mighty Ducks believe strongly in continuing the Disney tradition of giving back to the community and providing opportunities for those less fortunate. Through a variety of events, player appearances, and other charitable activities, the Mighty Ducks have made a major commitment toward becoming an important asset in the community.

Disney's Growth Opportunities through Athletics, Learning, and Service (GOALS) Foundation is the primary recipient of the Mighty Ducks' community relations efforts. Established by The Walt Disney Company in 1994, the nonprofit program is devoted to removing barriers so that underprivileged children may freely enjoy organized sports, access quality education, and participate in community service projects. GOALS creates after-school and weekend programs that are structured around the team sport of hockey.

Whether on the ice or in the community, the Mighty Ducks of Anaheim continue to make a significant impact on the people of Southern California.

**Above, left to right:
Mighty Ducks—including Shaun Van Allen, Garry Valk, Valeri Karpov, and Paul Kariya—take to the ice.**

Denny Lambert talks with fans attending the Mighty Ducks' second annual FanFair to benefit Disney's GOALS Foundation (far left).

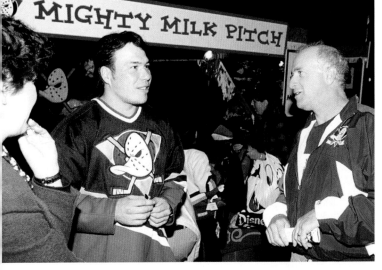

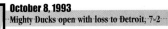

October 8, 1993
Mighty Ducks open with loss to Detroit, 7-2

November 6, 1993
10th Breeders' Cup held at Santa Anita Park

97 March 5, 1994
Oscar de la Hoya wins boxing match in Grand Olympic Auditorium

R. Rollo Associates

When business and industry tick down their list of resources these days, there's a new name in the lineup—the executive search firm. And more and more often, that specific name is likely to be R. Rollo Associates of Los Angeles, whose growing reputation in executive recruiting

reaches well beyond the traditional "headhunter" role of merely matching employee and employer.

The small, boutique consultancy, led by managing partners Robert S. Rollo and Peter W. Kelly, specializes in senior-level executive placement in top-tier corporations and institutions worldwide. Since its formation in September 1992, R. Rollo Associates has completed an extensive roster of significant assignments with some of the most respected names in business and industry today, including the largest transit project in North America; one of the nation's fastest-growing computer companies; one of the country's major financial services organizations; a worldwide integrated energy company; a premier investment management firm; and a world-class resort hotel company.

Staying Focused for Creative Solutions

A signature mixture of hands-on, personalized service and broad-based business understanding enables R. Rollo Associates to provide uniquely creative solutions to the challenges confronting today's employers. Breadth of industry experience, diversity of engagements, and an in-depth knowledge of the subtle nuances of senior-level placement have solidly positioned R. Rollo Associates—in just over three years—among the premier providers of executive search.

"Our early and continued success at advising the key decision makers of some of the most prestigious, well-managed companies in the world is the result of remaining small, focused, and very accessible to our clients," explains Rollo. "Staying lean and diligent allows us to intimately understand their priorities, objectives, and concerns. We join their team, and that relationship goes well beyond being handed a job description and delivering the right candidate. We

are regularly called upon to apply our expertise to a variety of current business issues, including executive compensation, organizational consulting, and board of directors composition."

Providing Clients with Personalized Attention

A mature industry and very much in demand, executive search firms today are well positioned to serve the unique needs of their diverse clients. And they're doing it faster and better—particularly small firms like R. Rollo Associates, which respond with welcome speed and familiarity.

"Bigger and better are no longer synonymous in the business of executive search, where timely, personalized attention is the true measure of success, both in the short term of the search and in the long-term, ongoing relationship between search firm and client," explains Kelly. "Gone are the days when an expansive network of far-flung offices

was required to deliver the most efficient and effective search. New technology and burgeoning information networks have allowed smaller executive search firms such as R. Rollo Associates to take on a broad range of engagements and seek out highly qualified candidates in both related and non-related industries. The successful completion of today's effective search is the result of the thorough, personalized attention of a seasoned, savvy, and experienced executive recruiter who understands the client's business culture and the requirements of the position."

This highly personal, consultive approach differentiates the R. Rollo Associates professional team as they play a critical advisory role in some of the most confidential, sensitive executive search assignments in business today. Joining forces with business and industry, R. Rollo Associates is helping to reshape the profile of today's executive.

Peter W. Kelly and Robert S. Rollo are the managing partners of R. Rollo Associates, a premier provider of executive search services worldwide.

21 June 22, 1994
USA beats Colombia for first
World Cup win since 1950

November 5, 1994
The Pyramid at Long Beach State opens

BONUS April 3, 1995
Bruins overcome injuries, Arkansas for
first NCAA basketball title in 20 years

218

Unforgettable!

Index of Sponsors

cknowledgments

Page

2-3	Photo © Bernstein Associates/Kevin Miller
4	Photo © Long Photography, Inc.
6	Photo © Long Photography, Inc.
8	Photo © Long Photography, Inc.
9	Photo © Long Photography, Inc.
14	1988 Dodger program courtesy Los Angeles Dodgers
15	Photo © Los Angeles Dodgers
	Memorabilia courtesy Los Angeles Dodgers
16	All photos © Long Photography, Inc.
18	Courtesy USC Sports Information Office
19	Photo courtesy USC Sports Information Office
	Newspaper © 1974 reprinted with permission from the
	Times Mirror Company
20	Courtesy UCLA Athletic Department
21	Photo © Long Photography, Inc.
22	Top photo AP wire photo; courtesy USC Sports Information Office
	Bottom photo courtesy UCLA Athletic Department
25	Photo © Wen Roberts/Photography Ink
26	Perfect game recording courtesy Los Angeles Dodgers
	Photo © Los Angeles Dodgers
27	Photo © Long Photography, Inc.
	Memorabilia courtesy Los Angeles Dodgers
28	Photo courtesy Amateur Athletic Foundation of Los Angeles
	Newspapers © 1932 reprinted with permission from the
	Times Mirror Company
29	Newspapers © 1932 reprinted with permission from the
	Times Mirror Company
30	Photo of Marcus Allen © John McDonough/NFL Photos
31	Trophy and trophy ceremony photos © Long Photography, Inc.
32	Photos © Los Angeles Dodgers
	Program cover courtesy Los Angeles Dodgers
33	April 28, 1958, Time Inc. Reprinted by permission; provided by Los Angeles Dodgers
34	Photos © Wen Roberts/Photography Ink
35	Program cover courtesy Los Angeles Kings
	Photo © Bernstein Associates/Andrew D. Bernstein
36	Photo © Wen Roberts/Photography Ink
37	Photo and memorabilia courtesy Los Angeles Dodgers
38	Photo © Long Photography, Inc.
39	Photo © Wen Roberts/Photography Ink
40	Courtesy Los Angeles Dodgers
41	Courtesy Los Angeles Dodgers
42	Photo © Wen Roberts/Photography Ink
43	Courtesy Los Angeles Dodgers
44	Photo © Vic Stein/NFL Photos
	Newspaper © 1951 reprinted with permission from the
	Times Mirror Company
45	Photo © Allsport USA/Shaun Botterill
46	Courtesy UCLA Athletic Department
47	Top photo © Vernon J. Biever
	Bottom photo © Long Photography, Inc.
48	Photo © Long Photography, Inc.
49	Photo © Long Photography, Inc.
50	Photo © Bernstein Associates/Andrew D. Bernstein
51	Top photo © Long Photography, Inc.
	Bottom photo courtesy UCLA Athletic Department
	Newspaper © 1966 reprinted with permission from the
	Times Mirror Company
52	Photo © Los Angeles Dodgers
53	Courtesy California Angels
54	Courtesy Los Angeles Dodgers
55	Courtesy Los Angeles Dodgers
56	Top photo © Bernstein Associates/Art Foxall
	Bottom photo © Bernstein Associates/Andrew D. Bernstein
57	Courtesy UCLA Athletic Department
58	Photos © Long Photography, Inc.
59	Photo at left © Long Photography, Inc.
	Photo at right © Los Angeles Dodgers
60	Photo of Pete Beathard courtesy USC Sports Information Office
	Photos of Ron VanderKelen and Willie Brown courtesy Pasadena Tournament of Roses Archives
61	Top photo © Long Photography, Inc.
	Bottom photo courtesy UCLA Athletic Department
62	Top photo courtesy USC Sports Information Office
	Bottom photo courtesy Pasadena Tournament of Roses Archives
	Newspaper © 1939 reprinted with permission from the
	Times Mirror Company
63	Courtesy Pasadena Tournament of Roses Archives
64	Photo courtesy Department of Special Collections, University Research Library, UCLA
	Program cover courtesy California Angels
65	Photo courtesy UCLA Athletic Department
	Newspaper © 1973 reprinted with permission from the
	Times Mirror Company
66	Photo courtesy UCLA Athletic Department
	First Day Cover courtesy Los Angeles Dodgers
67	Photo courtesy USC Sports Information Office
	Newspaper headline courtesy the *Los Angeles Evening Herald*; provided by Amateur Athletic Foundation of Los Angeles
68	Photo courtesy UCLA Athletic Department
	Newspaper © 1960 reprinted with permission from the
	Times Mirror Company
69	Courtesy Pasadena Tournament of Roses Archives
70	Cover photo Walter Iooss/*Sports Illustrated*; from the collection of Richard B. Perelman
	Photo © Vernon J. Biever
71	Photos © Los Angeles Dodgers
72	Photo © Long Photography, Inc.
73	Courtesy Amateur Athletic Foundation of Los Angeles
74	Cover photo Richard Clarkson & Associates/*Sports Illustrated*; from the collection of Richard B. Perelman
	Newspaper © 1968 reprinted with permission from the
	Times Mirror Company
75	Photo © Bernstein Associates/Andrew D. Bernstein
76	Top photo © Long Photography, Inc.
	Bottom photo courtesy USC Sports Information Office

Key to Cover Photo

1. 1988 NBA championship trophy, Los Angeles Lakers
2. Super Bowl XIV program, Los Angeles Rams vs. Pittsburgh Steelers
3. Long Beach Grand Prix inaugural program
4. Kareem Abdul-Jabbar's jersey, Los Angeles Lakers
5. 1927 and 1932 USC football programs
6. 1984 Los Angeles Raiders media guide
7. Los Angeles Raiders pennant
8. Super Bowl XVIII ring, Los Angeles Raiders
9. Super Bowl XIV guide, Los Angeles Rams
10. Super Bowl XIV badge, Los Angeles Rams
11. John Wooden Retirement Dinner program, 1975
12. UCLA Bruins basketball jersey
13. 1984 Olympic Games postcards
14. 1935 and 1941 football tickets, USC vs. UCLA
15. Circa 1949 tennis racket
16. Circa 1948 golf club
17. Photo, Hollywood Park race
18. Photo, Ben Hogan and Fielding Wallace, 1948
19. Hollywood Gold Cup trophy
20. Wayne Gretzky's helmet, Los Angeles Kings

21. Hockey puck, Los Angeles Kings
22. Jesse Owens' bronzed shoe, 1935
23. Photo, Jesse Owens
24. Photo, Carl Lewis, 1984 Olympic Games
25. Opening Ceremonies program, 1984 Olympic Games
26. Photo, Babe Didriksen, 1932 Olympic Games
27. 1984 Olympic Games tickets
28. Torch, 1984 Olympics torch relay
29. World Cup USA program, 1994
30. USC football jersey
31. USC football helmet
32. 1988 World Series trophy, Los Angeles Dodgers vs. Oakland Athletics
33. Autographed baseball, Sandy Koufax
34. Autographed baseball, Nolan Ryan
35. 1979 California Angels button
36. American League Western Division Championship button, California Angels
37. UCLA Rose Bowl pennant
38. Game-used bat, Kirk Gibson
39. Autographed bat, Rod Carew

MOMENTS IN
SPORTS
TOWERY
PUBLISHING, INC.

LA SPORTS

Los Angeles
Times